Jerseyana
The Underside
of New Jersey History

Library of Congress Cataloging-in-Publication Data

Second paperback printing, 1994

Mappen, Marc.
 Jerseyana : the underside of New Jersey history / Marc Mappen.
  p. cm.
 Collection of author's columns originally published in The New
York Times in 1984 and 1988–1992.
 Includes bibliographical references and index.
 ISBN 0–8135–1818–0 (cloth) — ISBN 0–8135–1819–9 (pbk.)
 1. New Jersey—History, Local—Anecdotes. I. Title.
F134.6.M36 1992
974.9—dc20   91–41139
                          CIP

British Cataloging-in-Publication information available

To Ellen

Contents

From Prehistory to 1799

Nineteenth Century

Twentieth Century

List

of Illustrations

Preface

This book is a collection of columns on New Jersey history that originally appeared in the New Jersey Weekly section of the *New York Times*.

A lot of local history is written with deep respect and piety for the past. Not so here. The essays in this book look at New Jersey history from the underside. The reader will find stories about crimes like the rubout of Dutch Schultz, lost causes like that of the Tories, corruption like the case of the treasurer of Jersey City who ran off with the municipal treasury, disasters like the explosion at the Black Tom terminal, and assorted grotesqueries like the fact that the man who discovered New Jersey was later devoured by cannibals.

My purpose is not just to sell copies of the book through cheap sensationalism (although that is certainly part of it), but to attract a wider interest in the rich and fascinating past of our state. Local history deserves a broader audience than just local historians. While trying to entertain the reader, I have also sought to observe the canons of the historical profession for sifting the evidence and building hypotheses. This is popular history, but I hope it is also good history.

I owe thanks to many people. First to Fletcher Roberts and Marlie Wasserman. Fletcher, the editor of the New Jersey Weekly section of the *Times*, took a chance on publishing a monthly column on history. Marlie, the Associate Director of Rutgers University Press, took a chance on publishing a collection of those columns. Thanks also to *Times* staffers Gloria Saffron and Ernesto Solis-Lugo who would patiently edit my copy, and would explain why I could not use the word "bastard" in a family newspaper, and to Marilyn Campbell, of Rutgers University Press, who let me put the word back in.

Dozens of people read my columns in advance, gave me tips, checked my facts, and encouraged me. In particular, I want to thank Annette Allen, Harriet Bloom, Robert Burnett, David Burns (who suggested the name Jerseyana), Amy Cohen, John Cooney, Tom Hodge, Carl and Ann Kessler, Edward Skipworth, Sandra Moss, and Stanley Trooskin.

Thanks also to the librarians at the Rutgers University Libraries, the Newark Public Library, and the New Jersey Historical Society.

I owe a debt to the historians of New Jersey whose work I have read and whose advice I have solicited in my research. The "Suggestions for Further Reading" section at the back of this book enables me to acknowledge them, something I could not do in the monthly column.

My wife, Ellen, read every single one of these columns with keen editorial and historical eye. My children, Benjamin and Rebecca, let me take time off from the obligations of fatherhood in the 1990s to pursue obscure corners of New Jersey history. To Ellen, Ben, and Becca, my love and gratitude.

From Prehistory
to 1799

Walam Olum. Say it three times: Walam Olum, Walam Olum, Walam Olum. It's a nice sound to roll around on your tongue. It's also the subject of a lively controversy about the origins of New Jersey's Indians.

At the heart of this controversy is one Constantine Samuel Rafinesque, who in 1836 published a book in Philadelphia with the modest title *The American Nations; Or Outlines of Their General History, An-*

)

The Walam Olum

cient and Modern, Including the Whole History of the Earth and Mankind in the Western Hemisphere; the Philosophy of American History; the Annals, Traditions, Civilizations, Languages, &c, of All the American Nations, Tribes, and States.

In his tome, Rafinesque stated that some years before he had received from a Doctor Ward an Indian document written in hieroglyphics on wood—the Walam Olum. Rafinesque said that Dr. Ward had obtained this curious document from an Indian settlement in the territory that is now Indiana in exchange for providing medical care. Walam Olum translates as the Red Score, or painted record. The Indians who gave it to Dr. Ward were Delawares, the tribe that had flourished in New Jersey before the arrival of Europeans.

From another, unnamed person, Rafinesque said he had obtained verses in the Delaware language that accompanied the hieroglyphics. Rafinesque then asserted that after years of study, he had managed to translate the verses into English, and he gave some examples.

Rafinesque died three years after the publication of his book. His notebooks, which contained copies of the picture writing along with the Delaware verses and his translation, passed through several hands. In 1885 an authority on the Indians, Dr. Daniel G. Brinton, used these notebooks to publish the complete verses, with a more accurate translation and commentary.

What does the Walam Olum say? In the wonderfully strange language of the Delaware Indians, the saga begins "Sayewi talli wemiguma wokgetaki," which is translated as "There at the edge of all the water where the land ends."

The story relates how Great Spirit created the earth, and how the Delaware people originated in a faraway land. They are invaded by an evil people, so they flee "across the frozen water," where they wander for many generations fighting hostile people until they enter a new, uninhabited land: the paradise of New Jersey.

Now if the Walam Olum is in fact a genuine recounting of Indian mythology, it is valuable indeed—one of the few written sources of Native American life dating from before the European discovery of America.

But is the Walam Olum a genuine Delaware creation myth? We have several good reasons to doubt its authenticity. First, there is the shaky nature of Rafinesque's story. Who was the mysterious Dr. Ward? Why would Indians be so quick to give him a priceless and irreplaceable piece of their heritage? Who was the anonymous person who supplied the verses?

Rafinesque himself was a curious character who had been bounced from the faculty of Transylvania College in Kentucky and who supported himself by selling patent medicines. He was regarded as a crank by the orthodox scientists of his day. The prehistory of the American Indians is a subject that has been rich in fakers and forgers, and perhaps Rafinesque was one.

What makes the whole thing truly suspicious is the fact that the original Walam Olum has vanished; all that survives are Rafinesque's notebooks.

Scholars have advanced other criticisms: the pictographs do not resemble other known examples of Delaware images, the legend is not known from any other historical source, and surviving Delawares never heard their parents speak of the saga. And the archaeological evidence suggests that the Delawares evolved from ancestors who had lived in the New Jersey area for thousands of years, and not from any outside migration.

All of this has led some anthropologists to regard the whole thing as a fake.

Supporters of the Walam Olum note that although Rafinesque was an eccentric, he had nothing to gain by fabricating the story. His account of the Walam Olum was only a tiny part of his tome on the Indians of North America.

What about the fact that the original Walam Olum is missing? Defenders have discovered that a Baltimore man named Brantz Mayer, who obtained Rafinesque's notebooks, also had in his possession during the mid-nineteenth century "pieces of birch bark with picture writing and hieroglyphics." Whatever became of Mr. Mayer's bark is unknown.

Maybe someone threw it out the way your mother threw out your collection of comic books and baseball cards.

Then there is some confirming evidence in the accounts of the early European travelers and missionaries who encountered the Delawares long before Rafinesque. Some of these accounts seem to echo elements of the Walam Olum, including reports of writing on bark and legends about a migration from the west.

The weight of the evidence seems to be that the Walam Olum is a genuine Indian artifact. But this leads to other questions. Does it actually date from the period before whites arrived in New Jersey? Is it a reliable account of the Delaware migration?

There are scholars who say that the myth recounted in the Walam Olum predates European contact and that it corresponds to what we know of the migration of paleolithic people from Asia to America across the Bering Strait.

These supporters try to link places mentioned in the Walam Olum to geographical landmarks. They say they are able to identify not only the Bering Strait (the "frozen water" of the saga), but also the Yukon, the Columbia, the Mississippi, and the Mackenzie rivers, the Great Plains and the Atlantic Seaboard. One scholar claims to have deduced from the Walam Olum that the Delawares crossed over the Bering Strait in A.D. 366, crossed the Mississippi around A.D. 1000, and arrived in New Jersey in A.D. 1396.

But it seems more likely that the Walam Olum is a relatively late production; that it comes from after the arrival of the Europeans, that tragic era when Indian culture disintegrated under the horrors brought by the whites: liquor, disease, and firearms. It may have been written as late as the nineteenth century, by which time the Delawares had long been driven out of New Jersey and were being pushed farther and farther west by white settlers.

It has been theorized that the Walam Olum was a sort of tragic last cry of the Delaware culture, written by an Indian who was vainly trying to recapture the vanished old ways and perhaps to summon a messiah who would save his people from the whites. The Indian who wrote it may have known something of the Christian Bible and its account of creation, battles, and migrations.

If that is the case then the Walam Olum should not be considered a literal account of the journey of the Delawares, but more of an amalgam of old, half-remembered stories mixed up with Christian, European influences. In that sense it is a nostalgic literary creation about a vanished time in the lost eden of New Jersey. The Walam Olum, then, is a sort of Indian *Gone With the Wind*.

Who among us is not fascinated by accounts of prehistoric humans? There is something intriguing in the mysterious origins of our species; in our distant ancestors' coming down from the trees, learning to walk upright, to make tools, and to speak.

This is the story of one curious branch of our family tree, an early form of *Homo sapiens* who, it was thought, lived right here in the Garden State. It was firmly believed that more than ten thousand years ago

Trenton

Man

primitive humans hunted woolly mammoths and saber-toothed tigers on a dark and forbidding Stone Age landscape that would one day hold such familiar sights as the Short Hills Mall and the Raritan Toll Plaza.

The concept of "prehistoric man" originated in nineteenth-century Europe when scientists began to discover in caves and remote valleys the bones of human beings mixed together with crude stone tools and the remains of extinct animals. Much of this was found under deep layers of earth, indicating that it was very old indeed.

To a society that believed that the world was created in 4004 B.C., these discoveries were disconcerting, and the devout tried to explain them away. For example, the peculiar human bones found in Neanderthal, Germany, it was argued, were not a primitive form of human life but simply the remains of a deformed idiot.

But as the work of geologists and biologists advanced, it became clear that the biblical chronology was simply wrong. By the time Darwin published his theory of evolution, it was possible to accept the idea that the human race had a very long prehistory, and that there had been a Stone Age before the invention of bronze and iron. This Stone Age was further divided into an early paleolithic age and a later neolithic age.

Now into our story comes Charles Conrad Abbott (1843–1919), who lived on his family farm, Three Beeches, just outside Trenton. Although Abbott had been trained as a physician, his true love was the study of nature, and from his rural home he authored books such as *Upland and Meadow, A Naturalist's Rambles about Home* and *The Birds about Us.*

He said of his native region, "Live six months on the Delaware meadows and the recollection of that experience will not fade away, even though you mount the shoulders of a saint and peep into paradise." (He wrote, obviously, before such landmarks as Hot Dog Johnny's arose on the Delaware Valley landscape.)

Abbott's farm was the site of an old Indian settlement, and he found countless arrowheads and other artifacts. In 1867 he made an interesting discovery. Digging beneath gravel on a bluff overlooking the Delaware he found stone implements much cruder and more weathered than the graceful Indian arrowheads, spearpoints, and other tools he was accustomed finding closer to the surface.

The gravel, he knew, had come from the melting of the glaciers; what lay below the gravel must thus predate that melting. Putting this together with what he had read about the new European science of prehistory, he concluded that a paleolithic race had existed in New Jersey during the Ice Age, somewhere from ten thousand to fifty thousand years ago.

Abbott sent examples of his stone tools to the leading French expert, Gabriel de Mortillet, who excitedly announced to the Society of Anthropology in Paris that these finds were very close to Stone Age implements being unearthed in Europe. "This makes it more probable that there was formerly a great bridge between America and Europe," de Mortillet said. In short, the same race of primitive humans that inhabited the Old World had also lived in the New.

Who were these primitive people and what had become of them? Judging by the crude nature of their implements, this race must have been at a cultural level well below the Indians; they evidently had not even discovered the bow and arrow. The prevailing scientific view was that in Europe, these primitive humans had become extinct.

But Abbott cautiously advanced a different hypothesis. In America, he speculated, they had not been extinguished. Instead, they had been pushed by the invading Indians into the cold and inhospitable northern regions, where their descendants became Eskimos.

Abbott went on to theorize that these early Eskimos had been in the New Jersey region as late as A.D. 1300—just before the arrival of Columbus. The Indians were relative latecomers, having arrived from somewhere in Asia. (Perhaps "from a submerged continent" in the Pacific, he suggested.)

Abbott published his findings and theories in several books, notably his 1881 *Primitive Industry,* and attracted some strong support. His Trenton farm was visited by the most eminent geologists, paleontologists, and anthropologists of Europe and America, and the discovery of glacial humans in the Delaware Valley was discussed at international symposiums.

Abbott was offered jobs at Harvard and the University of Pennsylvania. He accepted the latter and for a time was curator of the University of Pennsylvania's department of American Archaeology. His stone implements were displayed at Harvard's Peabody Museum, the American Museum of Natural History, the Smithsonian, and elsewhere. Other investigators began to dig in the area, and some supporting evidence was found, such as the fossil of an extinct animal under the streets of Trenton.

But there were skeptics, mainly centered at the Smithsonian Institution, who thought that Abbott was completely wrong. These critics argued that humans had arrived in North America a mere two thousand years ago, long after the glaciers.

Abbott was accused of sloppy archaeology; his critics charged that his paleolithic tools were actually "quarry blanks"—partially finished stone implements thrown away by Indian artisans—that had eroded into the glacial gravel. These implements appeared weathered simply because they were made of argillite, which did not hold up as well as other types of stone.

For years, this was one of the hottest debates in American archaeology and geology. By the time of Abbott's death in 1919, however, the Smithsonian view had prevailed. In the mid-1930s excavations at the Three Beeches site by a young woman archaeologist from the New Jersey State Museum, Dr. Dorothy Cross, seemed to settle the issue once and for all.

Dr. Cross confirmed that the earliest inhabitants of the farm site were Delaware Indians from the Middle Woodland period, which is now dated from 500 B.C. to A.D. 500. The Trenton gravel implements found by Abbott were, in fact, merely quarry blanks dating from that recent period.

And so the matter rested. The story of Trenton Man was a faint embarrassment to the city of Trenton and to supporters of Abbott. No doubt local wags made jokes to the effect that the only specimens of primitive human life to be found in the city were in state government.

But wait—the story takes another turn. In 1926, archaeologists discovered a group of fossilized bison in New Mexico; spearpoints found together with these remains indicated that these bison had been killed by human hunters around twelve thousand years ago. This date was subsequently confirmed by the discovery of similar spearpoints in other New

World locations and pushed back still further by the carbon-14 dating of archaeological sites.

Scientists now believe the Indians first arrived in North America over a land bridge from Siberia something like fifteen thousand to twenty-five thousand years ago while the glaciers were still here. These Indians spread over North and South America, and later separated into sub-groups such as the Delawares of New Jersey and the Eskimos of the Arctic.

So there were humans in New Jersey just about when Abbott thought they were, even though they were not Eskimos and not a branch of European paleolithic culture, and even though they had nothing to do with the tools he had discovered. As the archaeologist Herbert Kraft says, "Abbott was right, but for the wrong reasons."

Archaeologists tell us that New Jersey in the glacial age was far different from our time. The sea level was lower, so the coast stretched out fifty miles farther east into the Atlantic. The temperature was about 18 degrees cooler, and the landscape abounded in animals like the mammoth, mastodon, elk, walrus, and dire wolf. (I don't know what a dire wolf is either, but I don't think I would care to meet one.)

The first Indian inhabitants of New Jersey were not subhuman in any way. They were intelligent, fully formed *Homo sapiens* not beetle-browed Neanderthals or hunched-over cavemen. Given haircuts and dressed in business suits, these first Jerseyans could pass by on a busy Trenton street corner today without getting a second glance.

Whether they would want to be on a Trenton street corner is another matter entirely.

C hristopher Columbus discovered America, but he didn't discover New Jersey. That honor belongs to Giovanni da Verrazano who, in 1524, was the first European to see the land that would one day become our state.

(Okay, okay, so "discovered" is politically incorrect, since there were already a few million human beings living here when Columbus and Verrazano showed up. So let's say that Columbus and Verrazano were

The Man

Who Discovered

New Jersey

explorers who were the first to bring back word of what they had found to Europeans.)

Verrazano was one of the great men of his age, like Luther, who redefined religion; Copernicus, who redefined the shape of the solar system; and Michelangelo, who redefined the image of man. What Verrazano did was to redefine the map of the world.

There were no birth certificates and daily newspapers five centuries ago, so what little we know of Verrazano comes mostly from fragments, some of which were published long after his death. Historians have disagreed about where he was born, how he died, and whether he actually did what he claimed to have done. He is a mystery, a bit like the terra incognita he discovered.

According to tradition Verrazano was born around 1485 to a wealthy and cultured family in the beautiful and powerful Italian city of Florence. But historians have never found his name in the records of the Verrazano family of that city. An alternative explanation is that he was born in Lyons, France, which had a large colony of Florentine merchants and bankers, including a branch of the Verrazano clan.

He was certainly a sailor, and there is some evidence that as a young man he had traveled to Syria and Egypt. A "Jean Verasen" is said to have been on an expedition in 1508 to Newfoundland, and it may have been Verrazano.

By the 1520s, much of the South American continent had been charted by the successors to Columbus. But what lay between Florida and Newfoundland was still a blank space on the map. Seamen and traders hoped it was empty ocean that could provide the longed-for easy passage to Asia.

Verrazano persuaded François I, the king of France, to authorize an expedition to the New World, and a syndicate of moneymen in Lyons supplied funds for the voyage.

In January 1524, Verrazano and his crew left France in a lone ship, *La Dauphine*. They jumped off to the New World from the Madeira Islands, which in that age functioned as a sort of space station, a staging area for voyages into the unknown.

Surviving a violent storm, they reached the North American coast around March 1. They then sailed northward for the next four months, naming capes, mountains, islands, and harbors as they went along, giving them romantic names such as the Forest of Laurels, the Field of Cedars, and Arcadia.

Navigation was crude in that era, and Verrazano's estimates of latitude, longitude, and distance traveled were often far off the mark. As a result, there has been a great game in the centuries since then of trying to identify the places described by the explorer.

Where did he first reach land? Guesses have ranged as far south as Florida and as far north as the Carolinas. What was the island he discovered off the coast of New England? Some say Block Island, some say Martha's Vineyard.

As he sailed up the coast, he came in early April to a "very green and forested" land, which he named Lorraine. The sailor-historian Samuel Eliot Morison, who retraced Verrazano's voyage by air and sea, concluded that this was probably New Jersey. Verrazano saw a cape he named Bonvietto (Cape May?), a bay he called Vandoma (Delaware Bay?), and a small mountain he called Saint Polo (the Navesink Highlands?).

Then, probably on April 17, he found an attractive harbor that seemed to lead to a large lake. The explorer named this bay Angeloume, but because the wind turned unfavorable, he did not stay long. This was undoubtedly New York harbor.

From time to time on his voyage up the coast he landed to scout out the land. He was a keen observer of the Indians, noting their appearance and their customs. He had an eye for the ladies as well as the land; in the place he called Arcadia he came upon a young Indian woman he described as "molta belleza et d'alta statura" (very beautiful and tall). Her screams prevented him from taking her back to the ship, but he seized an eight-year-old boy who was with her and took him back to France, much like one might snare a parrot. (This sort of thing helps to explain why Indians today are not enthusiastic about celebrating Columbus and his fellow explorers.)

Verrazano continued his voyage north off the coast of New England and Canada, finally returning east to Europe. He arrived back in France in early July, more than six months after he had left. His trip was important; for the first time it established that there was an enormous North American continent.

The explorer did make one stupendous goof, however, which confused mapmakers and explorers for many years. Early on in his voyage he came to a narrow strip of land, on the other side of which was what seemed to be a vast expanse of ocean. He concluded that he was seeing an isthmus, like Panama, separating the Atlantic from the Pacific. Of course, he was dead wrong. Morison thinks that what Verrazano actually saw was the Outer Banks off the Carolinas.

In the nineteenth century, a number of historians called into question whether Verrazano ever made his famous voyage. They pointed to his bizarre statement about the isthmus and his general confusion about his exact position. These skeptical historians were also puzzled by the fact that no account of the voyage could be found in French archives, even though the expedition had been undertaken on the authority of the king. Some of these doubters were snooty, Anglophiliac New Yorkers who, it has been suggested, wanted to believe that the location of their great city had been discovered by the Englishman Henry Hudson, and not by the Italian Verrazano.

But early in the twentieth century, an Italian scholar discovered a remarkable manuscript in a family library in Rome. It is a handwritten description of the voyage, dated July 8, 1524—just about the time *La Dauphine* returned to France. In the margins of the manuscript are notes written in a different hand, with lively observations. For example, one of these notes describes how a group of Indians stuck out their buttocks to show their contempt of Verrazano.

The manuscript was evidently dictated to a scribe by Verrazano when he returned from the New World, with the marginal notes written by the explorer himself. It confirmed the reality of his voyage.

So Verrazano was rehabilitated, and in 1909, Italian Americans erected a monument dedicated to the explorer in Battery Park. Today the mighty bridge named after him spans the entrance to the harbor he explored.

But there is more to the mystery of Verrazano: his death. It seems that in a book published in Spain in the eighteenth century, Verrazano, referred to as Juan Florentine, became confused with Juan Florin, a notorious pirate who was hanged by the Spanish in 1527. The idea that Verrazano died in disgrace appealed to the same crowd of historians who questioned whether he had actually explored North America.

But the more reliable account, and one supported by several sources, gives a different end to the great explorer. It seems that while on an expedition to the Caribbean in 1528, he rowed from his ship to an island inhabited by a fierce tribe of Carib Indians. The natives seized the explorer and killed him. It is said that his brother watched helplessly from the boat while Verrazano was hacked to pieces and eaten.

Devoured by cannibals or hanged: either way it was an undignified end for the man who discovered New Jersey.

New York and New Jersey get annoyed with each other once in a while, like when some big Wall Street firm relocates to Jersey City, or when New York ups its taxes on New Jersey commuters. But it's unlikely that relations between our two states will ever get as nasty as they did back in 1679–1680, when the governor of New York had a Jersey governor arrested.

The governor of New York in those years was Sir Edmund Andros, a brusque British army major appointed to his post by the Duke of York.

Conquered

by New York

From his headquarters on Manhattan island, Andros cast covetous eyes across the Hudson at New Jersey.

New Jersey, at that time, was in a confused condition. It was owned by absentee English proprietors, who had divided the colony into two separate provinces, East Jersey and West Jersey, and who collected rent from the settlers. There was constant turmoil between the settlers and the proprietors over land rights.

In 1679, Andros announced that the proprietary governments were invalid and that both East and West Jersey were now under his authority. He issued orders that ships trading with New Jersey had to stop in New York City to pay customs duties, and he announced that he would build a fort at Sandy Hook to enforce his rule. Those who resisted, he declared, were traitors to the king and would be punished.

It was easy for Andros to take over West Jersey, which had a handful of inhabitants and no real government. But in the more populous East Jersey, Andros met with resistance from the governor, Philip Carteret, who was the representative of the absentee proprietors.

From his residence in Elizabethtown, Carteret warned Andros "not to molest me, . . . nor the People under my Charge." He declared that Jerseyans would resist "with our Lives and Fortunes, the People being resolved to live and dye with the Name of true Subjects and not Traytors." Agents of Andros found in Jersey, said Carteret, would be "proceeded against by Imprisonment, Tryal, Condemnation and Penalty, as his Majesty's Laws direct to Spies or Disturbers of the Publick Peace."

Andros turned up the heat. He sailed with a party of men from Manhattan to Elizabethtown. To avoid a battle, they left their muskets and pistols behind, and carried only their swords. Once ashore, Andros imperiously demanded that Carteret surrender to him, and he brushed aside Carteret's plea that they should submit their disagreement to the king. No doubt the old soldier Andros also used the occasion to take a look at the defenses Carteret had erected.

Once he was back in Manhattan, Andros issued an arrest warrant, on the grounds that Carteret was illegally exercising authority over the king's subjects. Carteret described what happened next:

> On the 30th day of April last, [Andros] sent a Party of Soldiers to fetch me away Dead or alive, so that in the Dead Time of the Night [they] broke open my Doors and most barbarously and inhumanly and violently hauled me out of my Bed . . . . I have not Words enough sufficiently to express the Cruelty of it; and Indeed I am so disabled by the Bruises and Hurts I then received that I fear I shall hardly be a perfect Man again.

He was dragged to Manhattan where he was thrown in jail.

There are a lot of complaints these days about white, Anglo-Saxon, Protestant culture. But we ought to remember that a fundamental part of that culture was a respect for law and individual liberty. Andros might have wanted to keep Carteret in prison, or maybe hang him, but English law compelled him to bring his rival before a jury in a Manhattan court of law.

That jury, to Andros's anger, stubbornly refused to convict Carteret of any crime, and he was able to go back to Elizabethtown a free man. But Andros was able to strip Carteret of his governorship. Sir Edmund had achieved his ambition of conquering New Jersey.

Running New Jersey was not as easy as Andros might have thought. The settlers of East Jersey simply transferred to Andros their old hostility against the proprietors. They demanded that he guarantee to them their rights as Englishmen, that they be given the right to make their own laws, and that elections to the Assembly be held once a year.

Andros fought back by dissolving the Assembly. A Jerseyan who declared that Sir Edmund was a "rogue and a traitor" was arrested.

To describe what happened next, we must shift the scene from the scraggly American colonies to the powerful world of the English royal court, and in particular to the major league intriguer James, the Duke of York.

The American colonies were part of James's realm. It was he who, years before, had turned New Jersey over to the proprietors. And when he later decided to eliminate the proprietors, it was he who put Andros up to the job.

But the New Jersey business was small potatoes. James's real ambition was to become the next king of England. He was known to be a Catholic, however, and he was opposed by the Protestant establishment of the realm. The Duke knew that he had to win allies from among the dissident Protestant sects, prominent among whom were the Quakers. Ah, but how to bring the Quakers to his side?

It just so happened that a group of wealthy and influential English Quakers had purchased proprietary shares in West Jersey. It was their intention to turn the colony into a haven in the New World for their fellow believers. The Quaker proprietors were complaining in London that the power grab by Andros was putting their title to the land in doubt and discouraging the emigrants from England.

To save face and to appease the Quakers, the Duke obtained a legal ruling confirming that New York had no authority over New Jersey. The Duke then issued orders restoring the rights of the proprietary governments of East and West Jersey. Andros was recalled to England, and Philip Carteret was restored to the governorship.

The Duke did eventually manage to win the throne, and he became King James II. He sent his old friend Andros back to America a few years later, this time as governor of the New England colonies. In that position, Andros tried to make New Jersey and New York part of his New England empire. But in 1688, the people of England threw out James II as a despot (this was the Glorious Revolution, as you may recall from your old Western Civ. course). When the news reached America, Andros was arrested in Boston and shipped back to England. New Jersey was saved once again from a hostile takeover.

These days the relations between New York and New Jersey are a lot more friendly, and surely the governor of the Empire State wouldn't think of invading the Garden State. But just to be on the safe side, maybe we should still keep an eye on our friends on the other side of the Hudson.

I n this era of rapid change in New Jersey, it's nice to know that some traditions endure over the centuries. We are speaking here of corruption and bribery, which are as much a part of the state scene as the Jersey tomato, and maybe a lot more vigorous.

Every year, New Jersey produces a good harvest, and newspaper readers are accustomed to reading about scandals in highway construction, school bus contracts, motor vehicle insurance, and the like.

The First Bribe

Connoisseurs of sleaze have been especially intrigued by the recent case of a state legislator who faked his own death in a boating accident in order to escape prosecution for a pension fund kickback scheme. He was arrested in the Islamic Republic of the Maldive Islands. While in jail he asked his girlfriend to obtain a local woman he could marry, hoping thereby to become a convert to Islam and to beat extradition. His attempt failed, and he was sent back to New Jersey, where he wound up in jail.

You may well be asking yourself how long this sort of thing has been going on in the Garden State. As identified by the writer Thomas Fleming, the first recorded bribe in New Jersey history took place in 1703. The recipient of this historic first palm greasing was one Edward Hyde, Lord Cornbury, who served as the first royal governor of New Jersey from 1703 to 1708. Cornbury was a scoundrel as bizarre as any in the history of New Jersey. His story has intrigue, a hint of kinky sex, and a couple of happy endings.

The son of an aristocratic family, Cornbury (1661–1723) was the quintessential vain, fawning, place-seeking nobleman, always pressed for cash and always on the lookout for the main chance. Quite early in life he realized that as a first cousin to the royal family, he would not find it necessary to depend on his own meager talent in order to advance his career.

Through royal patronage, he landed the plum job of governor of New York. When New Jersey asked for a royal governor, his first cousin, Queen Anne of England, added that office to Cornbury's duties. (The fact that the governorship of New Jersey was a sort of part-time job suggests that the colony was not exactly the jewel in the crown of the British Empire.)

Cornbury brought to this work the basic assumption that the colonies were cash cows that could be used for his personal benefit. New Jersey presented an interesting prospect for milking.

The colony consisted of a mere 10,000 people, settled in a few small towns in the midst of thousands of square miles of potentially good farmland. Those few inhabitants were locked in controversy, sometimes violent, with one another over who had the legal rights to the land—an issue confused by overlapping royal grants and charters, leases, inheritances, and Indian deeds.

To oversimplify matters so that we can get on with the story, one can speak of two opposing groups vying for the new governor's favor: the proprietary party (the landlords) and the anti-proprietary party (the tenants).

As soon as he had been named governor, Cornbury was visited in New York by the representative of the proprietors, who explained the colony's situation to his lordship, and slipped him £100 to help him realize the proper course of action. (This was the historic first bribe.) Another £100 was provided a few weeks later. The clarity and logic of this argument was so powerful that Cornbury threw his support to the proprietors.

In the subsequent election for the Assembly, voting was rigged in a manner that enabled the proprietors to win a majority. But there was soon a falling out over the amount of money the Assembly would grant for the governor's salary.

The anti-proprietary faction now saw an opportunity, and undertook a mighty fundraising campaign among its adherents. The money thus collected became known as the "blind tax" because nobody would admit for what it was destined. In fact, the money (which may have amounted to as much as £1,500) was delivered to a flunky of Cornbury's in New York.

In the next election, Cornbury used his muscle to give control of the Assembly to his new friends, the anti-proprietary group. The lawmakers, in gratitude, granted him an appropriation of £2,000 per year for two years to run the colony's government, of which Cornbury took the major share for his salary, and distributed most of the rest to a small group of cronies. To fund this appropriation, the Assembly approved a bitterly resented new tax.

This group of cronies came to be referred to as the Cornbury Ring, and included assorted men on the make, who found various ways to extract money from New York and New Jersey. Among other things, the ring managed to sell off huge tracts of Jersey land for its own profit.

Cornbury and his ring also undertook a personal vendetta against the Quakers of West Jersey. Cornbury turned on them not only because, as a High Anglican, he found their religion despicable, but also because in the shifting alliances of New Jersey politics they were linked with his political opponents, the proprietors. The governor used the fact that the Quakers' religion forbade them from taking oaths to deny them seats in the Assembly and to kick them off land-granting boards. He also approved a law that required all those who failed to serve in the militia to pay a stiff fine; this fell directly on the pacifist Quakers.

Added to Cornbury's crimes was a disconcerting personal habit: from time to time he appeared in public dressed up like a woman. Three explanations have been offered for this behavior. First, that he bore a certain resemblance to his royal cousin, Queen Anne, and by dressing up he was in a sense representing her in America. Second, that his basic problem was alcohol, and he dressed up only when drunk. Third, and most plausible, that he just got a kick out of it.

Whatever the reason, it does demonstrate that Cornbury was so contemptuous of Americans that he didn't try to hide his predilection.

After four years of misrule, Cornbury finally accumulated enough enemies among proprietors and anti-proprietors, Quakers and non-Quakers to give him trouble. When he approached the Assembly to ask for his customary support bill, the legislators instead documented a list of grievances. In May 1707, the Assembly called upon the governor to read him the list.

This was a shocking encounter for Cornbury. Instead of treating the governor with the deference due to a nobleman, the Speaker of the Assembly put his hands on his hips and glared disrespectfully at his lordship. The Assembly sent a letter to England describing Cornbury's abuses of power (including the dressing-up business) and calling him a "detestable magot." Cornbury sent his own explanation to the Crown, blaming his enemies for trumping up "Imaginary Grievances."

At the same time Cornbury's situation was crumbling in New Jersey, the inhabitants in New York were writing to London to complain. Cornbury had been just as corrupt on the other side of the Hudson, except that in the absence of Quakers he had persecuted Presbyterians.

In 1708 Queen Anne recalled Cornbury from the governorships of both colonies, enabling New Jerseyans to get back to the important business of fighting among themselves. Although the queen did not publicly reprove Cornbury, she is reported to have said that being her cousin "should not Protect him in Oppressing her Subjects." Before the ex-governor could sail for home, he was arrested and jailed in New York for nonpayment of his extensive debts.

But there was a happy end to Cornbury's story. News came while he was under arrest that his father had died, and Cornbury inherited the title of Earl of Clarendon. As a peer of the realm, he was wealthy enough to pay his debts, and he was released. Back in England, he went on to a distinguished public career, which included membership on the Privy Council. One suspects that as his ship sailed from New York harbor he thumbed his nose at the New World.

For the record, it should be noted that one modern historian, Patricia Bonomi, has said some nice things about Cornbury. She points out that the only evidence for the transvestite business comes from accounts by his enemies, and that a famous oil painting of an aristocrat in drag, long thought to be Cornbury, may be misidentified. Bonomi also suggests that Cornbury may not have been as bad an administrator as his opponents made him out to be.

There was also a happy ending for New Jersey. The experience with Cornbury helped to create a gulf between the Assembly and future royal governors. The legislators came to regard themselves as representatives of the people, and jealously kept an eye on the governors' powers and on the money appropriated for government.

A similar trend occurred as other colonies grappled with their royal governors, although none was ever as bad as the "detestable magot." Cornbury certainly did not start the Revolution (he took that first bribe seventy-two years before Lexington and Concord), but he helped create a sense of "us versus them" that enabled Americans to contemplate a break with the Mother Country.

1   *The First Bribe.* Lord Cornbury, First Royal Governor of New Jersey, was said to be a transvestite, and this engraving is taken from an oil painting reputed to show Cornbury in drag. There is some debate about the authenticity of this portrait; it may simply be an unidentified English noblewoman from the same period. (Special Collections and Archives, Rutgers University Libraries)

Edward Hyde Lord Cornbury.
afterw. 3rd Earl of Clarendon.

The Salem witch trials of 1692 comprise a famous and bloody chapter in American history. A good deal more obscure—and a lot more harmless—was a witch trial that took place in Mount Holly, then a Burlington County village, in 1730.

An account of the case first appeared in the *Pennsylvania Gazette* on October 22, 1730. The cityfolk of Philadelphia who read the *Gazette* that day found, amidst the news of ship arrivals and merchandise for sale an article entitled "A Witch Trial at Mount Holly."

The Witches
of Burlington
County

According to the article, a man and woman in the village had been suspected of practicing witchcraft, and it was decided to put them to a test. They agreed, but only if two of their chief accusers, also a man and woman, were subjected to the same ordeal.

On a Saturday in early October, 300 people gathered to watch. The first test called for weighing each person against a copy of the Bible, the assumption being that someone in league with Satan would not weigh as much as the word of God.

The male suspect was the first to be placed on the scale; a "huge great Bible" was placed on the other side. To the dismay of the villagers, he outweighed the Scriptures. So did the three others.

In the second test, the accused and accusers were to be thrown in the water, the assumption this time being that a witch would float while an innocent person would sink, since water—the instrument of baptism—would reject someone who had renounced God. The article described what happened next:

> A most solemn Procession was made to the Mill-Pond, where both Accused and Accusers being stripped (saving only to the Women their Shifts), were

bound Hand and Foot and severally placed in the Water, lengthways, from the Side of a Barge or Flat, having for Security only a Rope around the Middle of each, which was held by some in the Flat. The accused man being thin and spare with some Difficulty began to sink at last; but the rest, every one of them, swam very light upon the Water.

The trials appear to have ended on this inconclusive note, and no further word on the subject ever appeared in the *Gazette*.

This story, if true, is a historically important indication of folk belief in eighteenth-century New Jersey.

But is it true?

At first, the account was accepted. A contemporary publication, the *Gentleman's Gazette*, reported the story to its readers as fact. In the nineteenth and early twentieth centuries, many historians treated it as genuine. But there have been increasing doubts. In 1887, the historian John Bach McMaster pronounced it a hoax. Since then, educated opinion has swung in that direction.

What suggests that the story is false?

First, there is the absence of corroborating historical evidence. An event of this nature, one assumes, would have been mentioned in other records, such as diaries, letters, or church minutes. Unfortunately, court records for Burlington County in that period have not survived.

Second, the episode is out of synch with what we know of witchcraft in America. The most famous case, the Salem trials, occurred nearly forty years earlier. Twenty people were executed in Salem, and this gory excess helped to turn public opinion away from belief in witches. In England, the last legal execution of a witch took place in 1685. It would thus be unusual to find a case involving an entire village as late as 1730.

Third, the charges against the Mount Holly witches are atypical. In English and American history, witches were usually accused of bringing sickness and misfortune to their victims or causing some damage to their victims' property, such as a crop failure. In Mount Holly, the witches were charged with "making their Neighbours' Sheep dance in an uncommon Manner and with causing Hogs to speak and sing Psalms, etc., to the great Terror and Amazement of the king's good and peaceable Subjects in this Province."

Fourth, as the reader may have already noticed, there is the strong element of satire and broad farce in the *Pennsylvania Gazette* story. For example, the description of what happened when the first accused witch was placed on the scale is slapstick:

But to the great Surprize of the Spectators, Flesh and Bones came down plump, and outweighed that great good Book by abundance. After the same

Manner, the others were served, and their Lumps of Mortality severally were too heavy for Moses and all the Prophets and Apostles.

The explanation of why the women did not sink was in a similar vein:

It being the general Belief of the Populace, that the Women's Shifts and the Garters with which they were bound help'd to support them, it is said they are to be tried again the next warm Weather, naked."

In describing the weighing scene, the article noted that the scale was placed next to the home of the town's justice of the peace so that "the Justice's Wife and the rest of the Ladies might see the Trial without coming amongst the Mob."

And so on.

The final proof that the article is a hoax is the fact that the proprietor of the *Pennsylvania Gazette* was none other than the twenty-four-year-old Benjamin Franklin. The Mount Holly story has about it the sense of humor and the scorn of superstition that characterized Franklin throughout his long life.

Franklin, who wrote most of the copy for his paper, had a fondness for hoaxes of this sort. As a teenager in his native Boston, he had written satirical letters which he signed "Silence Dogood" and slipped into his brother's newspaper. Later in life he wrote a scientific paper explaining how flatus could be perfumed.

Though the Mount Holly story is probably a fraud, it is not without significance. It shows that, by 1730, an educated man like Franklin could attack belief in witches as laughingly old-fashioned.

And the *Gazette* article also deserves a footnote in history for another reason: In poking fun at the rural folk of Burlington County for his Philadelphia readers, it might be said that Franklin was telling the first New Jersey joke.

In Massachusetts, it was the Boston Massacre and the Tea Party that pushed the people toward Revolution. In Virginia it was the closing of the House of Burgesses and the fiery speeches of Patrick Henry. In New Jersey, the event that precipitated the break with the Mother Country was a burglary.

Like the Watergate burglary two centuries later, it was a crime that helped to bring down a government.

The Burglary

of the Treasury

The date was July 21, 1768, and the place was the Perth Amboy mansion of the wealthy Stephen Skinner. Hidden by the evening darkness, some person or persons unknown forced open a shutter and entered through a window.

The burglars managed to find the key to a locked money chest in a downstairs office, and made off with £6,750. This was a vast sum in those days, but what gave the crime earth-shaking dimensions was the fact that Stephen Skinner was the treasurer of East Jersey, and the money stolen from his house was virtually the entire public treasury, which he had locked up in his house for safekeeping.

When he discovered the robbery next morning, Skinner ran to tell his boss, William Franklin, the royal governor of New Jersey.

Like all royal governors in the American colonies, Franklin had a tough job. As the representative of the king, he was supposed to rule the colony in the interest of the British Empire. But George III was on the other side of the Atlantic; on this side Franklin had to depend on the popularly-elected Assembly to pass laws and raise taxes. It took a particularly adept tightrope walker to keep the government going without alienating the bigwigs in London or the smallwigs at home.

Franklin, who was the illegitimate son of Benjamin Franklin, had demonstrated his talents on this tightrope. He was widely respected as a conscientious governor who had earned the confidence of the people.

Said a satisfied Jerseyman: "Harmony reigns in a considerable degree." The ambitious Franklin knew that success in New Jersey could lead to bigger assignments within the Empire.

So Franklin acted quickly to head off the danger posed by the burglary. He ordered news of the robbery to be published in the press, offered a reward for information leading to the capture of the thieves, commanded the attorney general to get an accounting of the lost funds, and directed the chief justice to investigate the crime.

To the Assembly, he expressed his concern about the loss of public money and promised to support any measure passed by the legislature "to secure the Province from a like Disaster in the future." Skinner himself appeared before the Assembly in a suitably contrite manner.

But the Assembly was far from content. The loss of the East Jersey treasury was a severe blow to the poor and underpopulated colony. Then there was Skinner himself. In New Jersey there was an undercurrent of hostility between the east and west divisions of the colony, between Anglicans and other Protestant denominations, and between ordinary citizens and the wealthy proprietors.

It was galling that Skinner, an easterner, an Anglican, and a proprietor, had inflicted hardship on the colony because of his own negligence in safeguarding the public money. There were dark suspicions that Skinner may have been more involved in the robbery than he cared to admit.

The members of the Assembly decided to conduct their own investigation, and heard testimony from twenty witnesses and visited the scene of the crime. The legislators concluded that Skinner had not practiced the "Security and Care" necessary to safeguard the money in his keeping, and that he had to repay the colony.

Time moved slowly in that era, and just about nothing happened for several years. Perhaps out of a lingering wish not to antagonize the good relations between Governor Franklin and the Assembly, the matter was not pressed.

But in 1772, a newly-elected Assembly convened. This new legislature was different from its predecessors. Over half of the assemblymen were brand-new, and less inclined to patch things over. Goaded on by a Quaker delegate from West Jersey, James Kinsey, the Assembly pressed Skinner to pay up, despite the treasurer's plea that to do so would bankrupt him and turn his children into beggars.

The assemblymen took one critical step further: they called on Governor Franklin to dismiss Skinner, and threatened to hold back all appropriations for running the government until he did so. This was a portentous move because it impinged on a fundamental right of the governor—his exclusive power as the representative of the king to appoint and dismiss officials.

Franklin vowed that he would never surrender: "No consideration whatever shall induce me to give up that right but the King's express command"—even if the legislature should never again provide a farthing. He then dismissed the Assembly for a month.

But the anger of the assemblymen had not abated when they reconvened. As threatened, they took the momentous step of withholding all funds from the government, and they sent a petition over Franklin's head directly to the king.

New Jersey was now in a complete mess. All public business had been suspended. Public opinion, as expressed in petitions to the Assembly, had turned decisively against Skinner, and the whole miserable story was being exposed in the newspapers of New York and Philadelphia.

Franklin knew that his career was in jeopardy, and he gave in. Skinner sadly resigned—undoubtedly at Franklin's command. Franklin replaced him with the Assembly's choice for treasurer, and signed a law authorizing the new man to bring suit against Skinner if he did not repay the missing amount.

As it happened, Skinner never did pay up. By this time the thirteen colonies were swept up in the crisis of Revolution. Within a year the shooting war broke out at Lexington and Concord. Skinner and Franklin remained loyal to the king. The former treasurer fled to Canada and the former governor spent much of the war in prison and died in England.

The burglars were never caught, although there was some evidence that the crime had been committed by a criminal gang from the northwestern part of the colony.

The burglary of the East Jersey treasury was a pivotal event in the development of New Jersey's government. In the aftermath of the crime, the people of Jersey turned against a popular governor and stripped away his power. Like the Cornbury episode seventy years before, the crime helped to weaken the colony's allegiance to the Crown, and spread the idea that the authority of the people through their representatives was paramount.

In 1776, when the memory of the burglary was still fresh, New Jerseyans wrote a state constitution that turned the governor into a figurehead and gave the main power to the legislature, including the right to appoint the treasurer and other officials.

The voters of New Jersey can get awfully stirred up when they get hit in the wallet.

We tend to think of the Tories as aristocratic dandies with lace ruffles, clutching their silk hankies in terror at the sight of the Rebels. But they were nothing of the sort. New Jersey's Loyalists were a rough-riding, hard-fighting lot who, as they saw it, were battling to save their country from radicals who had illegally seized power.

Making allowances for the primitive technology of the eighteenth cen-

Tories

tury (the benefits of assault rifles and SAM missiles then being undreamed of), the struggle was every bit as bitter as any modern war in the Third World. Decades after the Revolution, a British general marching with his troops through the devastated French countryside of the Napoleonic Wars was reminded of the blasted landscape he had seen while serving in New Jersey.

New Jersey was fertile ground for the Tories. The colony had no large cities with their patriot mobs; no influential class of merchants who suffered from British regulations. Several groups within New Jersey were inclined toward the Loyalist side, notably the Anglicans and the Quakers. The Dutch Reformed church was split, with the conservative "conferentie" faction supporting the British.

A few Tories were wealthy, but most were ordinary farmers and shopkeepers who believed in law and order and obedience to the king. The actual number of Tories in New Jersey is hard to measure. As the war raged back and forth, men and women switched allegiances. Even a Jersey signer of the Declaration of Independence, Richard Stockton, took a loyalty oath to the king when the British army occupied the state and he was taken prisoner. The best guess is that over a third of New Jerseyans, roughly fifty thousand men and women, were Tories. Thousands of young men enlisted in the battalions of the Loyalist New Jersey Volunteers, perhaps the largest Tory military unit anywhere in the thirteen colonies.

During the war, Jersey's Tories were supported by British regulars who occupied New York and Philadelphia, and who spent much of the war battling Washington's Continentals back and forth across the state.

Reading the correspondence and journals of the state's patriot leaders, one gets the sense of a society in constant fear of Tory attack; in perpetual suspicion of secret enemies plotting against the government. In Monmouth County, the "Pine Robbers" welcomed British landing parties along the coast. In Hunterdon County, armed Tories battled the patriot militia. The residents of Essex County complained that the Tories in their midst were "Like the Snake in the Grass." In Perth Amboy, Loyalist spies passed along information to the British on Staten Island. From south Jersey, a correspondent wrote to General Washington, "This Country is in a miserable Situation the inhabitants afraid of every person they see."

The most dangerous region was the so-called "Neutral Ground" of the Hackensack Valley (present-day Hudson and Bergen counties) an exposed area accessible to raids from New York City and from British garrisons on the west bank of the Hudson.

The most effective of New Jersey's Tories was William Franklin, the last royal governor. Franklin, who we have already met, was an able leader who attempted to maintain British government even after the shooting war had begun. He was finally arrested in 1776 and sent to prison in Connecticut. After being exchanged two years later for a Rebel prisoner, Franklin went to British-occupied New York City, where he worked assiduously to subvert the Revolution. Deeply bitter about not being permitted to visit his dying wife while he was in captivity, he planned raids by Tories and British regulars into New Jersey and developed a network of informers.

Several New Jersey Tories emerged as guerrilla leaders, fighting behind Rebel lines. James Moody, a Sussex County farmer at the start of the war, became a feared marauder. Moody made raids to recruit Tory volunteers and to take military supplies. He was captured while on a mission to seize the rebel governor of New Jersey, but managed to escape. On another occasion, he said in his memoirs, he hid standing up for two days and nights in a corn stack while surrounded by Rebel soldiers.

Another bold Tory was Wiert Banta, a Bergen County Dutchman. Banta first made a name for himself by braving snowstorms to capture a Rebel militiaman who had killed an unarmed Tory. Shortly thereafter, Banta guided a group of raiders to a New York village occupied by Continental soldiers. He and his companions crawled up to a house, overpowered the sentries, and captured two high-level officers relaxing by the fire. Along with them he found the muster records of the Continental army. Banta galloped out of the village with his prisoners and his booty. "By this time the drums was beating, horns blowing and alarm guns firing in every part," he later recalled. He made his way to safety in a boat while Continentals fired at him from the shore.

The most mysterious Jersey Tory was a black man known as "Colonel Tye," who led raiding parties of blacks and whites on the Jersey shore. Tye may have been one of the hundreds of Jersey slaves who went over to the British. For them, ironically, the way to realize the freedom promised by the Declaration of Independence was to join the enemy.

Some of the Tory marauders were little better than outlaws, murderers, and horse thieves. In Bergen County, Tory bands roamed at night, seizing Rebels from their homes and whisking them to New York, where they were thrown into the infamous sugar warehouses that had been converted to prisons, with bitter cold and few rations. Or they were killed, like Captain Jonathan Hopper of the Bergen County militia. On April 21, 1779, Hopper came upon Tory raiders breaking open his barn to steal his horses. They shot and wounded Hopper, and followed him to his house where they broke open the door and bayoneted him to death.

In revenge for the execution of one Tory, outlaws murdered another Bergen County man, and left his wife a note saying, "We are determined to hang six for one, for the blood of the innocent cries aloud for vengeance."

The most infamous massacre occurred on the night of September 27, 1778, along the border between New York and Bergen County. Local Tories ran to inform British soldiers about a detachment of Virginia cavalry camped at nearby farm. Guided by the Tories, the British soldiers rushed the sleeping cavalrymen shouting, "No quarter to Rebels." After the Virginians surrendered, the British proceeded to kill fifty of them by bayonet.

Of course, not all the aggression was on the Tory side. Throughout the war, Continental soldiers and Jersey militia plundered and pillaged suspected Tories with gusto. The patriots also had the machinery of the state on their side. Laws were passed defining Toryism as high treason, requiring all officeholders to take a loyalty oath, and confiscating the estates of those who joined the British. The government established a thirteen-man Council of Safety that investigated persons suspected of Toryism and imprisoned or banished those found guilty.

At the end of the Revolution, the Tories fled to England and Nova Scotia. A few returned to New Jersey, where for years they encountered deep hostility from their neighbors.

The patriot side won the Revolution, but as everyone who lived through the upheaval knew, it was a very close call. It is fair to say that if the Loyalists of every state were as tough as New Jersey's, the War of Independence might have had quite a different end. If they had their way, July 4 would be just another workday and Washington, Jefferson, and company would be remembered as a gang of traitors.

On August 12, 1778, Major General Charles Lee of the Continental army was convicted by a military court of cowardice on the battlefield. The story of his disgrace is one of the most controversial incidents of the American Revolution, and it all happened in New Jersey.

General Lee was a strange figure of a man—tall, thin, and slovenly, perpetually surrounded by a pack of pet dogs. One observer described him as "a perfect original, a good scholar and soldier, and an odd genius,

Lee at

Monmouth

full of fire and passion, and but little good manners." A soldier of fortune, he had fought in Portugal, Poland, the Balkans, Turkey, and on the North American frontier. He lost two fingers in a duel with another officer in Italy. While in the American colonies, he was adopted into an Indian tribe and he married (more or less) the daughter of a chief. He left her and his two children when the army moved on.

Lee settled in the America at the time the Revolution erupted. Because he had more professional military experience than just about anybody in the colonies, he seemed to be the right man in the right place at the right time, and he was appointed by the Continental Congress as General George Washington's second in command. (Lee was, incidentally, no relation to the Lee family of Virginia.)

Lee evidently thought that he should have been appointed the commander in chief, and he made snide remarks in private about Washington. To a fellow general he wrote: "Entre nous [between us], a certain great man is most damnably deficient." But before he could prove himself, fate played one of its customary cruel tricks.

In December 1776, Lee was captured at a New Jersey inn by a detachment of British cavalry and held prisoner in New York for a year and a half before being exchanged. (There are those who say the best thing Lee ever did for the American cause was to get himself caught.)

Lee rejoined Washington's army at a critical moment. In the spring of

1778, Sir Henry Clinton and his army of 10,000 British and Hessians were marching through New Jersey. They had evacuated Philadelphia and were making their way to British-occupied New York City.

It was as hot, humid, and rainy as a Jersey summer can get, brutal for soldiers with eighty-pound packs and wool uniforms, and with faces swollen from mosquito bites. Sir Henry's march was slowed down by 150 baggage wagons and a contingent of camp followers.

George Washington seemed to hold the advantage. For once he was the pursuer and not the pursued, and for once the Continental Army was well trained and equipped, and supported by a strong force of New Jersey militia. Washington knew that if he could strike a knockout blow before Clinton reached the safety of Manhattan he had a chance to win the war. Washington put Lee in charge of an advance force of 5,000 men and gave him orders to attack the enemy until the rest of the American army could arrive.

Lee caught up to Clinton at Monmouth early on the morning of Sunday, June 28, and the fight began. When Washington arrived at midday with rest of the army, he was furious to discover American troops retreating in disorder in the face of the British, and he ordered his officers to stop the retreat. When Lee rode up to meet Washington, the commander-in-chief bawled him out in front of witnesses.

What did Washington say to Lee on that hot day, with the enemy advancing, the Americans in retreat, the cannon blasting, and the tape recorder not yet invented? Tradition has it that this was one of the rare occasions when the great Washington lost his self-control and swore in public.

Washington, according to Major General Charles Scott, "swore on that day till the leaves shook on the trees, charming, delightfully. Never have I heard such swearing before or since. Sir, on that ever-memorable day he swore like an angel from heaven."

An anonymous source had Washington saying, "In the Devil's name, Sir, go back to the front or go to hell."

According to an unidentified Virginia officer, Washington said, "Damn your multiplying eyes, General Lee! Go to the front, or go to hell, I care little which!"

The Marquis de Lafayette is reported to have said that Washington called Lee a "damned poltroon."

But the trouble is that these are second-hand and third-hand accounts, written many decades after the battle, and in the case of Scott and Lafayette, attributed to officers who were on a different part of the battlefield. According to the testimony of officers who were on the scene

THE BATTLE OF MONMOUTH, NEW JERSEY, ON JUNE 28, 1778.

2   *Lee at Monmouth.* When he found the American troops retreating at the Battle of Monmouth, George Washington is reported to have snapped, "What is the meaning of this?" at General Lee. Lee was later court-martialed and dismissed from the army. This 1858 engraving is from *Harper's Weekly.* (New Jersey Historical Society, Newark)

and who gave their accounts shortly after the incident, what Washington actually said in his anger was something like "What is the meaning of this?" Too bad for those who would like to see the man on the dollar bill unbuttoned a bit.

The battle raged on for the rest of the day. At the end 356 American soldiers and 358 British and Hessians were killed, wounded, or missing. Many of the deaths were from the sweltering 100-degree heat rather than musket balls. The Americans could be said to have won the battle since they took possession of the field, but they did not succeed in stopping the British from reaching New York.

After the battle Lee wrote angrily to Washington, claiming that the commander in chief was "guilty of an act of cruel injustice" and was misled by "the temporary power of office and the tinsel dignity attending it." He demanded a court-martial to clear his name. Washington obliged, and the trial began in New Brunswick on July 4. Five generals and eight colonels served on the court. The charge against Lee was that he had disobeyed Washington's order to attack, that he had made "an unnecessary, disorderly, and shameful retreat," and that he had shown disrespect to the commander in chief.

The court, after hearing testimony from officers present at Monmouth, found Lee guilty. He was suspended from the army, and died in disgrace four years later.

Was he guilty as charged? Lee claimed at the trial and for the rest of his life that he had not retreated, but instead had masterfully shifted his men to a better position in the face of a superior force and unfavorable terrain. "I manoeuvered my antagonists from their advantageous ground into as disadvantageous a one . . . without losing a single gun, a single color, or sacrificing a single battalion." He claimed that it was because of this brilliant tactical ploy that Washington was saved from a disaster. He maintained that Monmouth was the only real battlefield victory that the jealous and vindictive Washington could claim.

Lee had strong support. Sir Henry Clinton thought that Lee saved the American army from a perilous position. The old revolutionary Sam Adams and other leading patriots thought Lee had been railroaded, and there was a move in Congress to overturn the verdict of the court-martial. To this day, there are military historians who defend Lee's actions at Monmouth.

Washington's supporters then and now were convinced Lee was either a coward or a traitor. Alexander Hamilton, who was at Monmouth as a colonel on Washington's staff, wrote about Lee: "This man is either a driveler in the business of soldiership or something much worse."

Eighty years after the Revolution, evidence arose to give weight to Hamilton's suspicions of "much worse." A historian discovered that while Lee was a prisoner in New York, he gave his former British friends a strategic plan for crushing the Revolution. Lee's defenders say that it was an idle military speculation written by a bored captive—nothing that would actually aid the enemy.

So who was right and who was wrong at Monmouth? Who the hero and who the betrayer? The truth is as hard to grab hold of as a red-hot musket barrel on that unbearable New Jersey summer two centuries ago.

The taking of hostages might seem to be a modern invention of Third World terrorists, and America voices its righteous anger about the barbarous practice of holding innocent people captive for political purposes. But hostage-taking was not invented in the Middle East. A couple of centuries ago, our own country took a hostage and threatened to kill him.

It all grew out of a bloody feud between patriots and Tories in Monmouth County.

The Hanging of Captain Huddy

The story begins with Joshua Huddy, a captain in the Monmouth County militia. Huddy had a reputation as a fierce Tory hunter, and he was much hated by Loyalists he had driven out of the county. In March 1782, a Tory raiding party captured Huddy in an attack on a blockhouse he commanded in Toms River, and he was brought back as a prisoner to British-occupied New York City.

Six days later, another violent act occurred in Monmouth County. An infamous Tory, Philip White, was killed while in patriot custody. The Rebels said he had been shot while trying to escape; the Tories said he had been murdered.

When news of the death of Philip White reached New York City, a company of Tories pulled Joshua Huddy out of jail and set sail on a British ship for Sandy Hook, far behind American lines. The Tories rowed with their prisoner from the ship to a deserted stretch of beach. The leader of the Tories, Captain Richard Lippencott, gave Huddy a few minutes to say his prayers and write his will, and then hanged him from a makeshift gallows.

On Huddy's corpse his executors pinned a note vowing that for every Tory killed, they would hang another Rebel. The note ended with the words "UP GOES HUDDY FOR PHILIP WHITE."

At bottom, this was a local affair. Before the Revolution Huddy, Lippencott, and White had lived peacefully in and around Shrewsbury in

Monmouth County. But the war had thrown Huddy on one side, White and Lippencott on the other.

Now events transformed this unhappy local tragedy into an international incident. When Huddy's body was discovered, the residents of Monmouth County were outraged. They wrote to the commander in chief of the American army, George Washington, demanding vengeance.

Washington, after consulting with his officers and getting the consent of the Continental Congress, sent an angry letter to the British commander in Manhattan, Sir Henry Clinton: "To save the innocent, I demand the guilty.—Capn Lippencott therefore, or the officer who commanded at the Execution of Capn Huddy must be given up." If Clinton failed to surrender Lippencott, Washington warned darkly, "I shall hold myself justifiable in the Eyes of God and Man, for the Measure to which I shall resort."

Clinton had already heard of the hanging, and he too was angry. He ordered a court-martial for Lippencott, and he clamped down on the Tory military organization of which Lippencott was an officer, the Associated Loyalists. The president of the Associated Loyalists was that embittered New Jerseyan, William Franklin, the former royal governor.

But this was not enough for Washington, and he ordered that a British captain in patriot custody should be taken as hostage to force the British to hand over Lippencott. If the British refused, the captain was to be hanged to avenge Huddy's death.

The scene now moves to Lancaster, Pennsylvania. Thirteen British captains who had been part of the army that surrendered at the battle of Yorktown seven months before were brought under American guard from their prison camp to a room in an inn. An American brigadier general presided over a grim lottery. In one hat he placed thirteen slips of paper, each with the name of one of the captains in the room. In another hat were placed twelve blank slips of paper, and one slip inscribed "unfortunate."

A drummer boy drew a slip from the first hat and read out a name, and then drew a slip from the other. This continued until the eleventh try, when the "unfortunate" slip was matched with the name of Charles Asgill, a captain of the Foot Guards.

Asgill was nineteen years old, and by all accounts a likable young man. He was the only son of a wealthy and aristocratic London banking family. His father had been lord mayor of London.

Asgill was now brought under guard to "the place assigned for his execution," the camp of the American army near Morristown, where he was guarded by New Jersey Continental troops. Like a victim in some

Aztec ritual, he knew he was going to be sacrificed, since the British remained firm in their refusal to hand over Lippencott. How did he feel? How would you feel?

To save Asgill, the British seized on a technicality. It seems that when Cornwallis's army surrendered at Yorktown, a clause was put in the articles of capitulation stating that reprisals were not to be taken against the defeated army. The British protested that the seizure of Asgill violated the promise given at Yorktown.

To support their claim, the British appealed to the French military. After all, the French and Americans were allies, and at Yorktown Cornwallis had surrendered not only to General George Washington, but also to the French commander, General Jean Rochambeau.

From London, Asgill's mother wrote a heartbreaking letter to the Comte de Vergennes, minister of foreign affairs to King Louis XVI. Mrs. Asgill wrote of the suffering of her family while they waited to hear their son's fate: her husband was on his deathbed, her daughter was anguished. "A word from you," she wrote to Vergennes, "like a voice from Heaven will save us from distraction and wretchedness. I am well informed General Washington reveres your character; say but to him that you wish my Son to be released and he will restore him to his distracted family, and render him to happiness."

These events, of course, took place in the age before fax machines and satellite dishes, and it took months for letters and news to go back and forth between France, England, and America.

In the meantime, much was happening. The British court-martial in New York acquitted Lippencott of guilt on the grounds that he had only been obeying orders from the Associated Loyalists. Franklin, the president of the Associated Loyalists, concluded that it was a good time for him to leave America and seek refuge in England.

The enthusiasm for hanging Asgill seemed to be fading. The war was now virtually over, and there seemed to be no good purpose to snuffing out yet one more life. Washington himself began to waver. He had received piteous letters from Asgill and Asgill's British friends.

Washington, who seems to have had a soft spot for gallant young officers (his fatherly attitude toward the Marquis de Lafayette being the most famous example), seemed truly to pity Asgill. The general now turned to the matter over to the Continental Congress, asking it to "chalk a line for me to walk in this business."

After days of debate, a large majority of the members of Congress still wanted to hang Asgill. But in melodramatic fashion, on the very day on which the final vote was to be taken, a letter arrived from the Comte de Vergennes addressed to George Washington.

Vergennes reported that the king and queen of France had been moved to pity by the letter from Mrs. Asgill.

> The goodness of their Majesties Hearts induces them to desire that the inquietudes of an unfortunate Mother may be calmed and her tenderness reassured. . . . The danger of young Asgill—the tears and despair of his Mother—affects them sensibly, and they will see with pleasure the hope of consolation shine out for these unfortunate people.

Vergennes pointedly referred to the fact that although Asgill was a prisoner of the Americans, it was the king of France's army and navy that helped to put him there. The letter was respectful and polite on the surface, but it was clear that the French government was bringing heavy pressure on the weak, newborn American government.

Several more days of debate followed, as congressmen tried to balance their desire for revenge against their fear of antagonizing the mighty king of France. Finally, on November 7, 1782, almost half a year after Asgill's name was drawn from a hat, the Congress directed General Washington to set the Englishman free.

And so America's first hostage crisis ended. The aristocratic young Asgill had become sort of a sentimental hero in America, England, and France. The letters from his mother and Vergennes were read all over America and Europe. Asgill and his mother got to visit the king of France, plays were written about him, and he lived another forty-one years.

Forgotten in all this celebration, of course, was that crusty Jersey militiaman, Joshua Huddy, whose body lay moldering in his cold Monmouth County grave.

When they created the new American nation, the Founding Fathers debated fundamental questions about the relationship between the states and the federal government, about the protection of liberty, and about the separation of powers. They also debated whether the capital of the United States ought to be placed in New Jersey, on the Delaware River just outside Trenton.

Yes, reader, in the 1780s, New Jersey came within a whisker of being the location of the nation's capital. But for fortune, the Garden State

Trenton, N.J.,

Was Almost

Washington, D.C.

might now be the home of the White House, not to mention embassies, cabinet departments, spy rings, think tanks, and protest marches.

The shadow of the Washington Monument might have fallen on Route 1 Alternate and the Pentagon might have been built on the present site of the Quaker Bridge Mall. Grumbling American taxpayers might now be threatening to throw all the pointy-headed bureaucrats into the Delaware instead of the Potomac.

For most of the American Revolution (except when chased away by the British army), Congress had been located in Philadelphia. It was there that the Declaration of Independence was signed and that the Articles of Confederation were drafted. As the war came to an end, however, many delegates felt it was time to leave.

Philadelphia in the Revolutionary era had a population of 40,000. To us, this seems almost quaint—modern Montclair has about the same number of inhabitants. But to the eighteenth century, Philadelphia was an enormous megalopolis—probably the largest city in the English-speaking world after London.

And in America right after the Revolution, there was a great deal of suspicion about big cities. In contrast to the healthy, independent life of the yeoman farmer, cities seemed to encourage vice, corruption, epidemics, and the love of luxury. It was widely believed that throughout history, from ancient Greece and Rome to George III's England, liberty had been strangled by the growth of the city.

Philadelphia was also the center of the "nationalist" faction; merchants and investors who wanted a strong national government that could ensure a stable economy. Having just fought a war against a strong central government, most delegates wanted power to reside instead in the individual states. Moving out of Philadelphia, it was felt, would reduce the influence of the nationalists.

In the midst of the debate about moving the capital out of Philadelphia, in June 1783, an event occurred that gave force to the argument. A contingent of Pennsylvanian soldiers in the Continental army, angered by unfulfilled promises of back pay, marched to Philadelphia and demonstrated menacingly outside Independence Hall. The state authorities refused to provide military protection, and the delegates fled across the Delaware to Princeton.

Princeton, as it turned out, was quite nice. One foreign visitor had recently described it as "a pretty village where inns are handsome and very clean," with a "very handsome college." The delegates met in Nassau Hall, and the students treated their distinguished visitors with respect.

While in Princeton, the delegates began to consider a permanent location for the nation's capital. Proposals came in from states and towns eager to be the host. The town of Kingston, New York, was the first, with an offer of a square mile of land. The state of Maryland offered 300 acres in Annapolis, including existing government buildings and the promise of building thirteen official residences for the delegates from the states. Pennsylvania tried to woo the delegates back to Philadelphia, and New York also put in a bid.

The New Jersey legislature promised to provide £30,000 to any community in the state that petitioned to become the permanent seat of Congress, and several towns (including Newark, New Brunswick, and Elizabeth) applied.

Congress decided that the best alternative would be to build an entirely new city on vacant land, where the government could establish its own laws and authority. By October 1783 two such sites had emerged as the favorites: one on the Delaware River near Trenton, New Jersey, and the other on the Potomac River, near Georgetown on the Virginia-Maryland border.

The Potomac site was the clear favorite of southerners, not only because of geographical convenience, but because it would strengthen the region's influence in the new nation. Delegates from the middle states and New England tended toward New Jersey.

Apart from the fact that it was centrally located, New Jersey held a special appeal for those delegates who equated republicanism with agriculture. Because the state was thoroughly rural with no big city, it seemed that New Jersey would forever be free from the baleful influence of commerce and urbanization. (They should only see the New Jersey Turnpike at rush hour today.) Also in New Jersey's favor was the fact that it was the home state of the president of Congress, Elias Boudinot.

On October 7, 1783, a majority of the delegates voted to build the nation's capital on the New Jersey site. But the southern delegates refused to concede the issue, and threatened to block the two-thirds vote necessary to appropriate funds for construction of the new capital and to ally themselves with those nationalists who wanted to move back to Philadelphia.

To break this stalemate, Congress voted a few weeks later to repeal the earlier decision and to build two capitals, one on the Potomac and the other on the Delaware; the government would spend half of the year in each. It was further decided that until construction was complete, the Congress would alternate between Annapolis and Trenton. Those who favored limited government thought that the dual-capital scheme would prevent the growth of a bloated bureaucracy.

As planned, Congress left Princeton for Annapolis in November 1783, and thence to Trenton in November of the following year. Meeting in Trenton, the delegates began to reconsider the wisdom of their decision. There had been a great deal of criticism of the proposal. "To talk of building cities when they can scarcely furnish money to buy paper on which to draw a plan of them," wrote one observer, "appears to me something different from wisdom, prudence or policy." Other critics sarcastically suggested that Congress put sails on government buildings so they could float from city to city, or put Congress in a floating wooden statue of George Washington, or build a giant pendulum in the sky that would swing from the Potomac to the Delaware. More serious were reports that European powers were beginning to doubt the stability of American government.

Thus it was that the delegates changed their minds once again. They voted to establish a single capital, located on the Delaware, and authorized $100,000 to start construction. A committee was appointed to pick a site not more than eight miles above or below the falls of the Delaware. Until the new capital could be completed, it was agreed to move Congress and the government to New York City. Although Trenton had been hospitable (the French Arms Tavern on State Street had been renovated for the use of Congress), the small country town was too crowded to suit the delegates.

Before progress could be made on building the new capital, other matters got in the way—chiefly the growing dissatisfaction with the Articles of Confederation. The nationalists were pressing their campaign for a stronger central government, a campaign that led to the celebrated gathering in Philadelphia that produced the Constitution. Meanwhile, in Congress, the southern delegates, still anxious for a capital on the Potomac, blocked appropriations for construction on the Delaware site.

The most influential opponent was America's greatest hero, George Washington. "Fixing the Seat of Empire at any spot on the Delaware," he wrote, "is in my humble opinion, demonstrably wrong." The General's Mount Vernon home, not coincidentally, was a few miles downriver from the Potomac site.

The prospect of a capital located in their state was still alive in December 1787 when New Jerseyans overwhelmingly approved the new Constitution. But a deal was soon struck that left New Jersey out in the cold.

Alexander Hamilton, President Washington's secretary of the treasury in the newly-established federal government, needed votes in Congress for the administration's controversial fiscal policy. The South offered those votes, in exchange for a capital on the Potomac. Hamilton agreed, and that is how that swampy place of northern charm and southern efficiency, Washington, D.C., came to be.

So New Jersey missed out on some prestige and a source of steady jobs. And generations of presidents, senators, supreme court justices, generals, and admirals missed out on the joys of a real Trenton calzone.

On March 31, 1870, Mr. Thomas Peterson of Perth Amboy voted in an election. What made this a remarkable event was that he was a black man who was able to vote for the first time because the Fifteenth Amendment to the Constitution had just been adopted. Years later the people of Perth Amboy presented him with a medal with a picture of Abraham Lincoln on one side, and on the other an inscription noting that Peterson was "The First Colored Voter in the United States under The Fifteenth Amendment."

Free White

Males Only

Half a century later, it was women's turn. The Nineteenth Amendment to the Constitution had been adopted, and the first election New Jersey women could vote in under the amendment was the presidential primary on September 28, 1920. In the polling place of the eleventh district of the twelfth ward in Newark, the election officials presented a five-pound box of candy to the first woman who showed up to vote that morning, Mrs. Lulu Carter of Ferry Street, who was at the polling place when it opened at 8:00 a.m.

Mr. Peterson and Mrs. Carter were pioneers, but he was not the first of his race and she was not the first of her sex to vote in New Jersey. Years before, women and blacks had first won, and then lost the right to vote in New Jersey.

The New Jersey Constitution of 1776 was drafted in a hurry in the midst of the Revolutionary War and under the threat of British invasion. The Rebel leaders who had seized power desperately needed a blueprint for running the government. They drafted the document in two days, and hastily adopted it.

The new Constitution contained a clause stating that "all inhabitants of this colony of full age" who were worth £50 and who had resided in their county for a year were entitled to vote. What made this clause remarkable was that it did not exclude two groups who had never been permitted to vote before: blacks and women.

Did the authors of the Constitution deliberately intend to extend the right to vote so radically, or was it a mistake due to the haste with which it was written? Since there was no agitation expressed by any of the Rebels to allow blacks and women to vote, it does indeed seem to have been a goof.

New Jersey's Founding Fathers were evidently unaware that they were enfranchising two groups who were not permitted to vote anywhere else in the new nation, or for that matter just about anywhere else in the world.

The legislature eventually confirmed this right. A law passed in 1790 clarifying the issue confirmed that "all free Inhabitants of this State" could cast a ballot, and referred to the voter as "he or she." According to tradition it was a Quaker assemblyman who pushed this measure through.

How often did blacks and women actually vote? The records on this point are murky, but it does not seem to have been unusual, especially after 1790. Ironically, the best evidence is provided by complaints from white males about abuses. For example, it was alleged in 1793 that a black man who may have been a slave and a nonresident was permitted to vote; in 1800 it was complained that "negro wenches" on public charity were voting.

There were also frequent complaints that married women were voting, which was theoretically illegal since under the law a wife's property belonged to her husband. The implication is that single women and widows and free blacks could vote as long as they were residents of the state and met the property requirement. "Our Constitution," said an assemblyman in 1800, "gives this right to maids or widows *black or white.*"

Not everyone was so tolerant. Beginning in the 1790s, there was a rising chorus that the Constitution should be amended to restrict the franchise to white males. The debate over voting seems to have been somewhat split along party lines. Women and blacks were frequently accused of voting on the side of the Federalist party, and the loudest howls of complaint came from Republicans. A Republican paper in 1802 lampooned slaves marching to the polls with Federalist ballots, chanting "I be no more slave, 'cause I vote for a *fed.*"

Ironically, the textbook view of American history paints the Federalists as elitists and the Republicans, the party of Thomas Jefferson that evolved into the modern Democratic party, as the party of the common people. As sometimes happens, the people on the top and bottom of the ladder were allied against those in the middle.

The best-known instance of women voting occurred in 1797. In a

3   *Free White Males Only.* Because of a quirk in the New Jersey constitution of 1776, women and blacks were able to vote until 1807. This illustration shows women recording their votes under the scornful glare of male onlookers. (New Jersey Historical Society, Newark)

close race for the Assembly in Essex County, women rallied to vote for the Federalist candidate for the Assembly. His opponent, the Republican John Condict of Elizabethtown, managed nevertheless to win a narrow victory. Critics charged that the women were sent by their male sweethearts to the polls to vote for Federalists.

The *Newark Centinal* published a poem about this incident entitled "The Freedom of Election," with some smutty innuendos ("Their hands they laid on every maid") and a prediction that women ("metamorphosed witches . . . in coat and breeches") would take over the government.

The prize for rotten elections probably came in 1807 in Essex County. The issue to be decided was whether the new county courthouse should be built in Newark or Elizabethtown. This was a hot issue because the courthouse would bring prestige and business to the town in which it was located. Mass rallies were held by both sides on the eve of the election, and men from Elizabeth were beaten up in Newark.

In the election itself, men and boys voted over and over again, some of them allegedly disguising themselves as women to return to the polls.

Genuine women and girls, as well as blacks, also voted repeatedly. In one Essex County town thought to have about 350 voters, almost 1,891 votes were cast.

"A more wicked and corrupt scene was never exhibited in this State or in the United States" said the *New Jersey Journal.* So awful was the election that it was declared void by the legislature.

It should be noted that elections were unbridled affairs in those days, with ballots cast by "boys, beggars, foreigners," not to mention bribery, ballot box tampering, proxy voting, drinking, and rioting. Illegal voting by slaves and wives was only part of the problem.

Unfortunately, the notorious Essex County election occurred just at the moment when the Assembly was considering reform of the election law. A bill had been introduced to limit the franchise to "free, white, male citizens." When opposing legislators pointed out that the bill contradicted the Constitution of 1776, supporters replied that New Jersey's Founding Fathers had never really meant to extend the right to vote.

The 1807 bill passed by an overwhelming majority, with both Republican and Federalist votes. Historians have found no evidence that women or blacks complained at the time of being disfranchised.

In 1844, the state adopted a new Constitution that included the "free, white, male" clause.

But the fact that the door had once been opened was not forgotten. In the decades that followed, blacks and women campaigning for the vote in New Jersey were able to ask for a right that had been removed—not for an entirely new right.

It took 63 years after the 1807 bill before Thomas Peterson was able to vote in Perth Amboy and 113 years before Lulu Carter could vote in Newark. Proof once again, as if any more were needed, that history does not move in straight lines.

Sylvia Dubois may have been born in March 1768, but she was never quite sure. "They didn't used to keep a record of the birth of niggers," she said, "they didn't no more keep the date of a young nigger than they did of a calf or a colt. The young niggers were born in the fall or in the spring, in the summer or in the winter, in cabbage time, or when cherries were ripe, when they were planting corn, or when they were husking corn, and that's all the way they talked about a nigger's age."

She Never

Lost Her

Scars

Sylvia Dubois was a slave who survived slavery. We know something about her because, unlike countless other blacks who lived in bondage and perished without leaving any record of their lives, she lived into advanced old age.

In 1883, when she was reputed to be 115 years old, she was visited by Dr. Cornelius W. Larison, a local physician and amateur historian. Dr. Larison, who was white, wrote down the story of her life as she told it. It is not an uplifting story—there is ample demonstration of human cruelty, and her life left Sylvia an angry and bitter person.

But it is nevertheless a chronicle worth retelling. Dubois's story tells us something about what life was like in the time of slavery, and how one indomitable woman endured it.

She was born the daughter of the slave of a hotel keeper in Somerset

4   *She Never Lost Her Scars.* Sylvia Dubois was a former slave who described her experiences in bondage in 1883, when she was said to be 115 years old. (Special Collections and Archives, Rutgers University Libraries)

SILVIA DUBOIS,
BORN MARCH 5th, 1768.

County. While still an infant, she and her mother became the property of Minical Dubois, who owned a nearby farm. Early in Sylvia's childhood her mother went to another owner. At age fourteen Sylvia moved with the Dubois family to western Pennsylvania, where her master operated a farm and a tavern on the Susquehanna.

She recalled good times and bad. She remembered the food—"nigger butter"—two parts of lard with one part butter, spread on hard bread. She remembered the clothing, coarse woolen stockings, and stout shoes. She remembered the whippings: her own mother had been beaten for losing her grip on a hog while her master tried to yoke it.

She remembered small triumphs, like the fact that the slaves were warmer sleeping next to the kitchen fireplace than were the whites in the other parts of the house. She remembered slave frolics where she excelled at dancing. "When I was young, I'd cross my feet ninety-nine times in a minute and never miss the time, strike heel or toe with equal ease and go through the figures as nimble as a witch," she said.

She remembered how she would help her master make brandy, and how once, when no one was looking, she drank an enormous quantity of it from a keg until she was dizzily drunk. She knew that she would be whipped if she was discovered, so she pretended to be desperately ill. Her mistress began to fan her. "My God, thought I, if you only knew what I am doing, you'd throw that fan away and give me hell."

She remembered how she would earn money by ferrying people across the river. "The folks who were acquainted with me used to prefer me to take them across, even when the ferrymen were about." She would land her ferry near a rival, Captain Hatch, and load up passengers before he could. "I would hurry them into my boat and push off from the shore, and leave him swearing."

She became adept at steering a skiff across the river. "They say that in using the skiff I could beat any man on the Susquehanna, and I always did beat all that raced with me," she remembered with pride.

She regarded Minical Dubois as a good master. "I tried to please him, and he tried to please me; and we got along together pretty well," although there was an occasional beating.

But it was a different story with Elizabeth, the wife of Minical. "I did not like her," Sylvia DuBois said, "and she did not like me; so she used to beat me badly. Once she knocked me till I was so stiff that she thought I was dead. Once after that, because I was a little saucy, she leveled me with the fire shovel." The blow from the shovel left a break in Sylvia's skull. Dr. Larison reports that he found a depression in her cranium into which he could bury a part of his index finger.

Sylvia Dubois struck back. It was in the tavern, she remembered, one day when the master was away. The mistress was scolding Sylvia for not scrubbing the barroom properly, and struck her in front of the tavern customers.

> Thinks I, it's a good time to dress you out, and damned if I won't do it. I set down my tools and squared for a fight. The first whack I struck her a hell of a blow with my fist. I didn't knock her entirely through the panels of the door, but her landing against the door made a terrible smash and I hurt her so badly that all were frightened out of their wits, and I didn't know myself but that I'd killed the old devil.

Sylvia Dubois ran away, but later returned to her master. "He didn't scold me much; he told me that my mistress and I got along so badly, if I would take my child and go to New Jersey, and stay there, he would give me free." She left the next morning and walked for days, carrying her freedom papers and her one-year-old child back to New Jersey.

Why was her master so generous? Possibly because Sylvia was so intractable, possibly because slavery was gradually being abolished in the North.

And perhaps there was more. It occurs to the modern reader that Minical Dubois had a sexual relationship with Sylvia Dubois, which would explain his leniency, his wife's savagery, and perhaps even the child that suddenly appears in the narrative.

Once back in New Jersey Sylvia Dubois was accosted by a white man. "Whose nigger are you?" he asked.

"I'm no man's nigger," she replied, "I belong to God."

When the white man demanded to know where she was going she put down her child and shook her fist at him: "That's none of your business. I'm free; I go where I please."

Sylvia Dubois found her mother laboring as a slave in New Brunswick, and went to work there and in Princeton as a household servant.

She eventually inherited a tavern, a seedy establishment secluded in the mountainous woods on the way to Hopewell. Put's Old Tavern had a notorious reputation. According to Dr. Larison it was the scene of cock-fights, fox chases, prizefights, and prostitution. "There were scenes," Dr. Larison wrote, "of lewd men, of the basest passion, fired by whiskey and hilarity, in an atmosphere entirely free from decency and shame."

It was also one of the few places where blacks and whites could mingle freely.

Sylvia Dubois operated the tavern until 1840, "when them damned

Democrats set fire to my house, and burned up my home and all that I had." She went to live with a daughter in a cabin in the Sourland Mountains of western New Jersey. It was there that Dr. Larison found her late in her life.

Dr. Larison characterized her as an impulsive, profane woman. "Less restraint I never saw in any person," he wrote. She was superstitious, and saw supernatural forces at work in every wood and swamp. She was belligerent, with contempt for her neighbors.

And she was a cold person. "To children she was not very wooing," Dr. Larison wrote, and she took a perverse pleasure in frightening them.

Sylvia Dubois carried scars inside her skull, as well as outside.

But she survived.

T he little ghosts, goblins, and witches who come to your door on Halloween are pale reflections of ancient magical beliefs. In English villages and towns centuries ago there flourished a world of astrology, charms, spirits, alchemy, witchcraft, and fortunetelling. It was part of the mental baggage that the colonists took to America.

One corner of this magical world was the connection between the occult and underground treasure. It was widely believed that supernatu-

The Buried

Treasure Hoax

ral forces could be used to find hidden booty. Snow White's dwarfs with their underground gold mine and the leprechaun guarding his pot of gold are the surviving fragments of this ancient folk tradition.

The belief in buried riches is not completely far-fetched. In the age before our modern, safe, savings and loan industry, people frequently did bury their valuables in the ground.

All of which brings us to New Jersey at the close of the eighteenth century, when an enterprising con man named Ransford Rogers convinced a sizable number of the citizens of Morristown that he could conjure the spirit world to reveal the location of buried treasure.

Rogers appeared in Morristown in 1788. He was a native of Connecticut who had been a schoolteacher in upstate New York. Rogers had a reputation for having occult powers, and he seems to have been persuaded to come to Morristown by a group of men who wanted his help in finding treasure, and who got him a job teaching school.

The treasure in question was gold and silver that was said to have belonged to the Tories at the time of the Revolution. Before they fled the state, the story went, the Tories had buried their valuables somewhere on Scholey's Mountain, a range of desolate hills twenty miles outside Morristown. (As late as 1900, Morris County residents were still searching for Revolutionary War gold.)

Rogers began his work with a group of eight Morristown men meeting late one night in an isolated house far outside town. He told the group how he could summon the spirits of the dead to lead them to the Tory gold. As he spoke, a loud thumping was heard from the roof and the sides of the house. "Press forward," said an unearthly, disembodied voice.

This was the first of many nighttime meetings held by Rogers. Eventually the secret society of followers grew to forty men, all eager to press forward to find the treasure.

Rogers was a good showman, and he varied the routine of the gatherings with special effects. The account of one meeting says that it took place in a deserted field late at night, illuminated only with candles. Rogers had inscribed occult circles and symbols in the ground, and his followers were told to stay within them. At Rogers's command came explosions and flashes of fire in the air. Ghostly white figures appeared in the distance, groaning and shouting in nonhuman voices.

The night meetings were run like church gatherings, with the congregation facing Ransford, and with much prayer and exhortation. Unlike a church, however, the services were said to have begun with the drinking of large quantities of applejack, which was powerfully effective in encouraging the spirits to appear.

As time went on, the spirits conveyed messages through Rogers. They revealed that they were the shades of honest, godly men. The faithful were instructed that they too had to lead pure, unblemished lives in order to be worthy of getting the treasure.

Further, the spirits revealed, the faithful had to demonstrate their sincerity by making an offering of cash. The ghosts at first asked for £12 currency from each person, which had to be in hard coin and not inflated New Jersey paper money. Later the spirits passed the message that they were willing to accept less—times were tough in New Jersey just then, even for the dead.

The money was delivered by leaving it under a tree during the night meetings. The devout would bow their heads and pray; when they looked up the money was gone.

After several months of this, a great deal of money had been collected, and the faithful were beginning to get impatient. Rogers promised that the location of the treasure would be revealed at a forthcoming outdoor night meeting. But at that meeting the spirits refused. As interpreted by Rogers, they were angered by the wicked lives of the congregation and their lack of faith. More offerings and more followers were needed. It was all a visibly frightened Rogers could do to prevent the ghosts from smiting the trembling Morristown men.

Now, from the perspective of larceny, Rogers probably should have taken the money and run long before. But he was evidently under pressure to keep the scheme going a while longer. Two of his helpers, who had been responsible for the rapping, fireworks, and ghostly appearances, wanted to expand beyond Morristown in a sort of franchise arrangement. And Rogers may have been confident enough to think he could keep the scam going a bit longer.

But some of the members of the secret society had by now become skeptical. It is reported that the wife of one of Rogers's followers goaded her husband into going with her to examine the ground where the spirits had appeared the night before. The couple found the impression of a man's shoes, leading off to a trail of horseshoe prints.

The realization that they had been duped spread quickly among Rogers's followers. He was arrested, but managed to escape while out on bail. As they say in fairy tales, he was nevermore seen in Morristown.

Now comes a nagging thought. Is the whole story of Ransford Rogers itself a fairy tale? It seems almost too theatrical, with the credulous followers drinking applejack and the skeptical wife discovering footprints. Could forty upstanding citizens have been so gullible as to fall for a few magic tricks? It is suspicious that virtually all of what we know about the case comes from an anonymous 1797 pamphlet entitled *The Morris Town Ghost Diliniated*. Perhaps the pamphlet was a satire.

Evidence that the Morristown story is true is the fact that Ransford Rogers actually existed. There are independent accounts that after his escape from Morristown he appeared in Pennsylvania, New England, and throughout the South, in each place running a variant of his treasure scam. In Exeter, New Hampshire, he raised money from the locals to buy a magic divining rod that would lead to underground treasure. Of course, he absconded with the cash.

Another confirming bit of evidence lies in the legal records of Morris County from 1789 to 1790 showing Rogers's indictment for fraud and conspiracy, his bail jumping, and the division of the property he left behind among his creditors.

Perhaps the most convincing proof is that there are plenty of people around today who are every bit as gullible as Rogers's followers in Morristown. The Morristown and vicinity phone book lists six astrologers, and the local paper carries a horoscope column. The local bookstores have a section of New Age books, with their pseudoscientific claptrap about spirit channeling, ESP, and crystal healing. The supermarket in Morristown carries tabloids that tell of people abducted by aliens who meet Elvis Presley in a UFO.

And there are doubtless people in Morristown who, like the rest of us, search for the mystical numbers that will unlock the treasure buried in the Pick-6.

So we live our little suburban lives in New Jersey today. We have our little triumphs: a promotion, a wedding, a new house. And we have our little tragedies: the car breaks down, the property tax goes up.

Sometimes there is a real tragedy—the biopsy comes back positive, a son uses drugs, a parent dies. But even here, everything is muted and softened by institutions: the hospital, the social worker, the funeral

Aunt Polly among the Indians

home. Rarely do the curtains ever part to give us a glimpse of the real terror and violence of our world.

Not so for Mary Kinnan, a New Jersey woman who survived hell.

She was born Mary Lewis in Basking Ridge in 1763. In the middle of the American Revolution, when she was fifteen years old, she married a sergeant in the militia, Joseph Kinnan. After the war, Mary and her husband packed up their children and moved to the frontier, settling in the Tygart Valley in what is now West Virginia.

We can almost imagine the scene on the evening of May 13, 1791, in that isolated valley farmstead: smoke rising from the chimney, chickens in the yard, children running about. Mary's brother, Jacob Lewis, had come from Basking Ridge to stay with the family.

At that moment the door burst open and three Shawnee Indians armed with muskets entered. Mary's husband tried to talk to them and was shot; she remembered ever after how he groaned as he fell. Mary grabbed her youngest child, a daughter about two years old, and tried to flee. The Indians caught up with her. She broke loose, leaving her daughter behind in their hands.

As she was running away, she heard her child calling for help. She turned and raced back; one of the Indians knocked her down with a tomahawk.

She was carried back to the house. As she later recalled in a written account: "Gracious God! what a scene presented itself to me! My child, scalped and slaughtered, smiled even then; my husband, scalped and weltering in his blood, fixed on me his dying eye, which ... still expressed an apprehension for my safety and sorrow at his inability to assist me." Her brother had escaped with the other children.

The Indians ransacked the house. They then tied Mary's hands behind her back and led her away with them. They marched all night, through the rain. When they stopped the next evening, the Indians used the time to trim the scalps they had taken.

The march continued the next day through rough terrain. Mary was repeatedly beaten and threatened with death for not moving fast enough. Exhausted and numb, she thought of committing suicide.

Then came a chance to rest: one of the Indians was bitten by a rattlesnake, and his companions waited for nineteen days while he recovered. They crossed the Ohio River on a raft, and traveled through wild country. The Indians feared being detected, so for much of the time they did not build a fire. They hunted as they went along, and forced her to eat.

After a month and a half of traveling, they came to an Indian village. Her captors painted her and presented her to the members of the tribe, who proceeded to beat her until she fainted. Mary was sold to a squaw, and worked as a slave, chopping and carrying wood.

Was she raped? An early twentieth-century Somerset County minister and amateur historian who studied the story of Kinnan, Rev. Oscar M. Vorhees, stated that the Indians "never did violence to her as a woman," but his source for this statement is unclear.

Mary was in the northwestern frontier, what is now Ohio. It was a wilderness claimed by the Americans, the British, and the Indians. Mary frequently had to move with the tribe to evade an American army, which was intent on exterminating the Indians. In the fall of 1791, the Americans were defeated in battle, and Mary saw the scalps of the dead soldiers brought back to the village.

Mary was not a learned woman, but she had a sharp mind. She observed the customs of the Indians, and noted the beauty of the Northwest Territory. She kept track of the calendar, and was able to mark off the days of her captivity.

And she continued to plan her escape. Although a war was going on, traders sometimes visited the village. Through one of them, Mary sent a letter to Basking Ridge pleading for help.

It took three months for the letter to reach New Jersey; according to one account, the messenger died of yellow fever in Philadelphia, and the letter, along with his personal effects, was buried in order to disinfect it. When the danger of infection had passed, the letter was unearthed and sent on to Basking Ridge where it was read to the congregation of Mary's former church. A collection was taken up, and her brother Jacob, who had returned to Basking Ridge with Mary's surviving children, set out for the Northwest Territory to rescue her.

In the meantime, Mary continued to be a captive, with no idea that help was on the way. She suffered from frostbite, and was racked by fevers and pains.

At last, to her joy, a trader brought her a letter from Jacob, who had arrived in British-occupied Detroit, about 140 miles away. He could get no closer because of the war, and they could communicate only by letters carried back and forth by traders. Jacob worked as a woodchopper to support himself.

Six months after arriving at Detroit, Jacob joined a party of British and French traders and managed to make his way to the camp where his sister was being held. When Mary caught sight of him she was so astonished that she cried out, then quickly jabbed herself with a needle to explain the scream to nearby Indians, and pretended not to notice Jacob.

Through another trader, she arranged to meet her brother that night. But they missed each other in the darkness. They tried again the next night, and were successful. It took them several days to make their way out of Indian territory and on to Detroit, Mary sometimes hiding in the brush and sometimes disguised as a man.

Friendly boatmen passed the brother and sister across Lake Erie, up the Niagara River, and over Lake Ontario to western New York. From there, with Mary on horseback and Jacob walking beside her, they made their way to Basking Ridge where she was reunited with her children. She had been in Indian captivity for three years.

Mary spent the rest of her life in Basking Ridge, living to the age of eighty-five, and becoming known to everyone as "Aunt Polly." It was said that every year, on the anniversary of her capture and the slaughter of her family, she would spend some time alone in the woods.

The "captivity narrative" was a popular form of literature in that age (like romance novels today), and an Elizabeth printer, Shephard Kollock, published Mary's story in 1795 as *A True Narrative of the Sufferings of*

Mary Kinnan. Although written in the first person, it is likely that Kollock made Mary's words a bit more flowery, and added some items to give the story more popular appeal, such as an attack on Great Britain for inciting the Indians. (It is doubtful that Mary would say "O Britain! How heavy will be the weight of thy crimes at the last great day.")

But the real Mary Kinnan comes through when she talks of her horror at seeing her husband slain and her joy at seeing her brother. We also know that Mary's story is genuine. There is an account of the attack in Tygart Valley written by a neighbor who was at the Kinnan home at the time, and Jacob Lewis, who later settled in Ohio, wrote about his adventures. A copy of Mary's letter to Jacob, pleading for help, was found by a historian among the papers in the pension application Mary sent to Washington in 1836. Early in the twentieth century, Mary's granddaughter and grandniece recalled hearing the story from the old woman's lips.

So imagine the aged Aunt Polly, on her front porch in Basking Ridge. Her modern counterparts are those aged Jewish grandmothers who, as young girls, went through the Nazi Holocaust. Like them, Aunt Polly sits and rocks, and in her head are horrors we can only imagine.

Nineteenth
Century

On July 11, 1804, the most famous bullet in New Jersey history left the barrel of Aaron Burr's pistol. Traveling at 600 feet per second, it entered Alexander Hamilton's abdomen, just above the hip.

The occasion, of course, was the duel between Hamilton and Burr on the heights at Weehawken. The opponents were two of the most famous men in America. Hamilton was the former secretary of the treasury and brilliant leader of the Federalist party. The Newark-born Burr was vice

Alexander Hamilton in the Emergency Room

president of the United States and leader of a Republican faction in New York politics. The two men were political rivals and bitter personal enemies.

Burr and Hamilton met at 7:00 on that summer morning at the popular dueling grounds on the Jersey side of the Hudson River. In accordance with the dueling code, they exchanged shots at each other from ten paces apart. Hamilton missed; Burr did not. (There is some evidence that Hamilton deliberately aimed away.)

Much has been written about this duel: about the tragic waste of a brilliant man's life, about the folly of duels, about the rascality of Aaron Burr. Today, however, let us look at the affair from a different angle—that of trauma care. Forget that the victim was the famous Alexander Hamilton, and look at him instead as an emergency room gunshot case: white male, age forty-eight.

We have the testimony of Hamilton's friend and physician, Dr. David Hosack, M.D., who was present at the duel and who later wrote a detailed letter describing his efforts to save Hamilton's life.

Dr. Hosack ran to the fallen Hamilton right after the shots were fired. "His countenance of death," he recalled, "I shall never forget." Just before he became unconscious, Hamilton was able to say, "This is a mortal wound, Doctor," which turned out to be a pretty accurate self-diagnosis. Hosack stripped off his friend's clothes, and discovered the bullet hole in the abdomen. There was very little loss of blood.

Hosack could feel no pulse, and feared Hamilton was dead. He helped carry him to a barge for the trip back to Manhattan. Once on board, Hamilton revived. "My vision is indistinct," he said. He complained of pain when Hosack pressed his side, and said that his lower extremities had lost all feeling.

From the Manhattan wharf Hamilton was carried to a nearby house and placed in bed. Hosack administered some diluted wine, and later an ounce of laudanum, a type of morphine. He applied pain-killing compresses to the wound. Hamilton was in excruciating pain, but was able to get some sleep. The next day the pain decreased.

Throughout much of the time, Hamilton was conscious and able to talk. Among his visitors were his wife and children, to whom he bade a sad farewell, and the bishop of New York, who discussed with him the morality of dueling and who administered communion.

One wonders, however, if Hamilton was really this talkative, or if his friends embellished the bedside scene a bit to fit the stereotype of the fallen hero. Did the dying Hamilton really greet the bishop with "My dear Sir, you perceive my unfortunate situation and no doubt have been made acquainted with the circumstances which led to it."

Hosack consulted with other doctors, including a well-known physician from Columbia College and with surgeons from a French warship in the harbor who had experience in gunshot wounds. All agreed that the victim could not survive.

Hamilton died at about 2:00 p.m. on the day after the duel; he had lived for about thirty-one hours.

An autopsy performed by Hosack indicated that the bullet (or to be technically accurate, the ball) had struck a rib, passed through the liver and the diaphragm, and splintered a vertebra at the base of the spine. There was about a pint of blood in the abdominal cavity.

It is revealing that Hosack never gave any specific cause of death. Given the state of medical knowledge in 1804, it was enough for him to tell his readers that the wound was in some "vital part."

We now turn to another medical man, Stanley Trooskin, M.D., director of Trauma Services at Kings County Hospital. Dr. Trooskin, who has had experience treating gunshot wounds, has kindly consented to provide an opinion on the Hamilton homicide from the perspective of modern medicine.

Since the duel took place a century and a half before Dr. Trooskin was born, he obviously did not get the chance to examine the patient; he also must work on this case without the standard diagnostic tools such as blood pressure, CAT scan, EKG, and x-ray. Dr. Trooskin's opinion, then, comes from his reading of Dr. Hosack's 1804 letter.

The fact that Hosack saw no heavy external bleeding and that the autopsy turned up little internal bleeding indicates to Trooskin that there was no damage to a major blood vessel. The wounds to the rib, diaphragm, and liver would not be immediately life-threatening, but could lead to infection. The absence of labored breathing indicates that the lungs were not injured. There was evidently no injury to the bowels, although the hole in the diaphragm could mean later intestinal problems.

The real problem was the spine. The absence of feeling in the legs, the loss of muscular control, and the evidence from the autopsy proves it was injured. Hamilton's weak pulse, unconsciousness, and blurred vision when he was first wounded are signs of spinal shock.

Spinal shock is dangerous because blood vessels in the extremities lose their tone and thus their ability to deliver enough blood through the body. Death comes gradually as the cells perish from lack of oxygen-bearing blood. Blood was still flowing to Hamilton's brain, however, as indicated by the fact that he was conscious almost to the end.

The cause of death that Dr. Trooskin would have put on the death certificate: "cardiac arrest secondary to spinal shock following a gunshot wound."

Could Hamilton have been saved today? Dr. Trooskin believes that his survival would have been a reasonably safe bet in a modern trauma center—with its electronic diagnostic and monitoring equipment and with its team of specialists. In Hamilton's case, the specific treatment would have been intravenous fluid plus medication to restore tone to the blood vessels, as well as antibiotics to prevent infection.

One thing that modern medicine still cannot cure, however, is a severed spinal chord: Had he lived Hamilton would have been a paraplegic in a wheelchair.

What about Dr. Hosack's treatment? By the light of early nineteenth-century medicine, he did the best he could. The one questionable treatment from a modern perspective is morphine: Although it does relieve pain it also dilates the blood vessels, making a bad condition slightly worse.

And so, we in the modern world can take pride in the miracles we can perform of saving lives that would once have been lost. We can also take pride in the fact that dueling is no longer an accepted method for settling disputes. But let us not be too smug. In the most recent year for which we have statistics, there were 350 reported murders in New Jersey.

It was Hamilton, of all the Founding Fathers, who was most pessimistic about human nature. "Take mankind in general," he said, "they are vicious." Alas, the old boy was on to something.

L ook, each of us has different talents. Some are brain surgeons, some are carpenters, some write columns. All of which provides a jumping-off place, so to speak, for the story of Sam Patch, the Jersey Jumper.

Like many New Jerseyans, he migrated to our state from outside, and like many New Jerseyans, he had to go to New York to make a splash. But New Jersey was his home during his brief adult life, and it was here he first tasted fame.

Jumping
to the Wrong
Conclusion

To be specific, Sam Patch first came to public attention on September 30, 1827, in Paterson, New Jersey. A crowd had gathered on that memorable day to watch the erection of a new bridge over the Passaic Falls. In front of the assembled citizens, and despite of the efforts of constables to stop him, Sam leaped over the falls and into the Passaic River. Reporters who had come to write about the new bridge described the daredevil feat in the newspapers.

Who was Patch? He was about twenty years old, an employee of the Hamilton cotton mills in Paterson. He had moved to the city from Pawtucket, Rhode Island, where as a young mill hand he had entertained his friends by jumping from bridges and factory roofs into the Pawtucket River.

The notoriety he earned from his Paterson leap convinced Patch that he could turn his skill at jumping into a career. He went from place to place, jumping from any height into any body of water. Sometimes he was paid to perform, sometimes he passed the hat. Sometimes he used a tame diving bear to add variety to the performance.

In the summer of 1828, he appeared before a crowd of 500 people in

Hoboken, where he jumped from the mast of a ship ninety feet into the Hudson River.

A group of hotel owners in Buffalo invited Patch to jump off Niagara Falls as part of a publicity stunt that also involved dynamiting rocks and sending a ship over the falls. He arrived too late for the festivities, so he scheduled another leap which he announced in a poster:

I shall, Ladies and Gentlemen, on Saturday next, Oct. 17th, precisely at 3 o'clock, P.M., LEAP AT THE FALLS OF NIAGARA, from a height of 120 to 130 feet (being 40 to 50 feet higher than I leapt before), into the eddy below. On my way down from Buffalo, on the morning of that day, in the Steam-Boat Niagara, I shall, for the amusement of the Ladies, doff my coat and Spring from the Mast head into the Niagara River.

Sam Patch of Passaic Falls, New Jersey

On the appointed day, he appeared on an island at the edge of the falls. While the crowd watched from the American and Canadian sides, he climbed onto a high, swaying platform supported by ropes. There he waited for ten minutes, while suspense increased. He then waved to the crowd, kissed an American flag, and jumped into the water, more than a hundred feet below him.

For an agonizing moment, there was no Sam Patch to be seen. Then, to the cheers of the assembled, he reappeared and swam to the shore. The crowd on the bank rushed forward to shake his hand. "There's no mistake in Sam Patch," he joyfully announced.

More jumps followed in upstate New York. At Rochester, he announced that he was "determined to astonish the natives of the West before returning to the Jarseys." And astonish them he did by a leap over the Genesee Falls. Said a local newspaper, "It was a frightful leap, but he performed it gracefully and fearlessly."

Sam decided to provide yet one more thrill before his return to New Jersey by jumping again at Rochester. The poster read:

HIGHER YET
Sam's last Jump
"Some Things Can be Done as Well as Others"
There is no mistake in
SAM PATCH!

The claim that this was to be Sam's last leap turned out to be prophetic.

Seven thousand people from as far away as Oswego and Canada

came to watch the feat that day, November 13, 1828. Sam was dressed in an outfit that included white pantaloons and a black silk sash. He gave a speech in which he observed that Napoleon and Wellington were both great men, but neither man could jump the Genesee Falls. "That was left for me to do and I can do it and will."

With that he climbed a platform 125 feet above the river. In his previous dives he had always entered the water straight as an arrow; but this time he hit the water at an angle with arms and legs akimbo. This time he did not come to the surface.

There was some speculation that on the morning of the dive he had consumed a great deal of alcohol at a local tavern.

Four months later a farmer found Sam's body under the ice in the frozen river, six miles distant from the falls. The autopsy showed he had burst a blood vessel and dislocated his shoulders. A crude wooden marker was placed over his grave: "Here lies Sam Patch, Such is Fame."

Sam Patch was dead, but he was not forgotten. In the years after his death he became a part of nineteenth-century American folklore.

For serious-minded Americans, Patch was a tragic figure. In sermons his fatal leap was used as a metaphor for the danger of trusting in human pride instead of in God. A Newark doctor wrote a turgid poem describing Patch as a "martyr of science," and a peer of Newton and Galileo. Nathaniel Hawthorne mused on how Patch threw away his life in pursuit of empty fame.

But most Americans did not take such a gloomy view. For them Sam Patch exemplified the comic, boastful, daredevil American hero—like Davy Crockett, Casey Jones, and Pecos Bill.

As with many heroes, there were rumors that he had not died, but was only hiding somewhere, waiting to come out and dive again.

Fabulous stories about his early life were invented, such as the account that as an infant he had jumped into the washtub and how as a schoolboy he skipped over hard words. One tall tale relates how the Jersey Jumper popped up in the South Seas, where he explained to a passing Yankee sea captain, "In that Niagara dive I went so everlasting deep, I thought it was just as short to come up t'other side, so I came out in these parts."

A comic actor named Dan Marble played the hero in two immensely popular plays that toured the country for years: *Sam Patch, or The Daring Yankee* and *Sam Patch in France, or The Pesky Snake*. As part of his act, Marble would jump some forty feet over a fake Niagara Falls into a pretend raging river.

There were also doggerel poems and mock ballads:

> Poor Samuel Patch,—a man once world renounded,
> Much loved the water, and by it was drownded.
> He sought for fame, and as he reached to pluck it,
> He lost his ballast, and then kicked the buck-it.

And then there were the awful italicized puns, about how on the fateful day he had taken a *drop* too much, endured a sad *fall,* and a *precipitate* loss. There were laments like "Ah, cruel Death, thus to dis-*patch* him," and cracks about how he had proved himself a genuine *descendant.*

Even modern scholars of folklore who study Patch cannot help but make winking references to such things as his vaulting ambition and his search for loftier challenges.

This column, of course, would never sink to such depths.

A century and a half ago, the place to go in New Jersey during the summer was the unpolluted waterfront at Hoboken and Weehawken. There, a short ferry ride from Manhattan, day-trippers could stroll and picnic in the scenic countryside.

On a pleasant day in the summer of 1841, however, this innocent amusement was shattered by the discovery of the bound and bruised corpse of a young woman floating offshore. It turned out to be the body of one Mary Cecelia Rogers, about twenty-one years old, who had been

The Beautiful

Cigar Girl

missing for three days from her mother's boardinghouse in Manhattan.

The "Mysterious Murder at Hoboken" became headline news. The newspapers seized on the fact that the victim had at one time worked behind the counter of a Broadway tobacco store, something a bit racy in that era. Mary became "The Beautiful Cigar Girl," and the press published page after page of interviews, speculations, and rumors about her death, and accounts of her attractive face and figure.

One news item was the fact that more than two years before the murder, Mary had disappeared from home for two weeks. The *New York Herald* reported the rumor that she had been with a lover, a naval officer stationed in Hoboken.

More than a month after the discovery of the body, an important witness came forward. Mrs. Frederica Loss, proprietress of "Nick Moore's House," a Weehawken inn, said that on an afternoon around the date of the murder she had served lemonade to a girl in the company of a "dark complexioned young man." The girl fit the description of Mary Rogers.

The couple had left the inn after half an hour. In the evening, Mrs. Loss had heard screaming coming from the woods. She assumed it was just some drunken gang members fighting—it was common for rowdies to loiter in the area.

Some time later, Mrs. Loss said, she discovered shreds of clothing in a nearby thicket—clothing that she said had been worn by the girl at the inn. The authorities confirmed that the garments were Mary's.

The best guess about the murder was thus that Mary had been strolling on the Hudson waterfront when she fell into the clutches of a gang who had taken her to a secluded spot, raped her (the press used the term "violated"), strangled her, tied her with strips torn from her clothes, and carried her dead body down to the river to cover up the crime.

And so the case seemed to resolve itself at the close of 1841. Now enters Edgar Allan Poe, the melancholy genius of American literature. For Poe's role in this mystery, we are indebted to John Walsh's intriguing 1967 book, *Poe the Detective*.

At the time of the murder, Poe was in the midst of his long, tortured decline—out of work, in need of money, and hitting the bottle. He was living in Philadelphia with his consumptive young wife and his mother-in-law. Like other Philadelphians, he read the accounts of the Rogers case.

It probably had a special meaning for him, since he had a few years before lived in New York, not far from the tobacco shop. He may even have known Mary Rogers, but there is no evidence for that romantic notion. (One modern writer has fancifully suggested that Poe was the murderer.)

Poe hit on an idea for raising cash. He wrote to publishers, offering a fictionalized account of the case that would present a solution to the mystery. The New York *Ladies' Companion* bought the story, which it published as "The Mystery of Marie Roget."

The story transfers the scene of the crime to France: Weehawken becomes a secluded neighborhood in Paris, the Hudson River becomes the Seine, Mary Rogers becomes "Marie Roget," Mrs. Loss becomes "Madame Deluc," the *New York Herald* becomes "*Le Mercurie* and so on. Although the locale has changed, the story closely parallels the events in New Jersey.

In his story, Poe claims that the dark-complexioned man seen at the inn was the naval officer, who murdered Mary/Marie in a fit of passion in the notorious thicket. Why the naval officer? Because the murder coincided with the arrival of his ship in port and the cloth strips binding the corpse were tied with a sailor's knot.

Or at least, this was how Poe intended the mystery to be solved. The story was supposed to appear in three installments in the *Ladies' Companion*. The first installment, in the November 1842 issue, had already hit the stands and the second, aimed for December, was in press when fragmentary reports of new developments in New Jersey began to appear.

It seems that the innkeeper, Mrs. Loss, was accidentally shot by one of her sons. In interrogating the dying Mrs. Loss and her sons, the local justice of the peace discovered that the innkeeper had lied about her role in the Rogers murder. Mary Rogers had actually come to the inn with a physician to obtain an abortion (a "premature delivery" said the press).

She had died during the operation, and those present had covered up the crime by throwing the body in the Hudson and hiding the clothes. The inn, the justice said, was "one of the most depraved and debauched houses in New Jersey." (All of which gives the story a certain contemporary relevance.)

Now Poe had a problem. The solution to the mystery he had been building toward in the first two installments was clearly wrong. It was too late to call back the story, but he was able to postpone the publication of the third and final installment long enough to rewrite it to include the new developments. The final installment, which came out a month late, kept the naval officer, but fudged enough to include the possibility that the victim had met her death in a "fatal accident" at Madam Deluc's inn.

Walsh speculates that Poe made the six-hour trip from Philadelphia to New York to make the revisions. As supporting evidence, Walsh cites a fact that has long puzzled Poe scholars: the report of an old girlfriend that Poe had visited her in Jersey City one day in 1842. What was he doing there when he was supposed to be living in Philadelphia? Walsh thinks that the writer dropped by while he was in New York correcting the manuscript. One hopes that this is true—the image of Edgar Allan Poe roaming the streets of Jersey City has a great deal of charm.

"The Mystery of Marie Roget" was republished in 1845 as part of a collection of Poe stories. In this collection, Poe revised the text still further to fit the revelations about Mary's abortion. He then tacked on a long footnote claiming that the story had first been published in November 1842, and that evidence uncovered "long subsequent to the publication" confirmed that he had been right in making the inn the scene of the crime.

This supposed feat of detection was long accepted by the critics. But thanks to Walsh, it is now clear that Poe performed a neat sleight of hand to enhance his reputation. Like most tricks, it worked because the audience wanted to believe in magic.

So ends the story of poor Mary Rogers. She was taken advantage of by a lover, butchered by a clumsy doctor, manipulated by Poe to make himself appear a masterful detective, and exploited by writers of cheap sensationalism (including yours truly) to sell newspapers.

There is no monument to Mary. The site of the inn and the thicket have long since been paved over as part of the entrance to the Lincoln Tunnel.

In the years before the Civil War, New Jersey was a cheapskate, backwater state. One demonstration of that fact was the way the state cared for the insane. While elsewhere enlightened policies were taking hold for the treatment of the mentally ill, in New Jersey the insane were dumped into poorhouses and jails; sometimes they were farmed out to the care of householders who offered the lowest bid.

Reformers in New Jersey had tried in vain to move the legislature to follow other states and build a state mental hospital. But the legislature

Dorothea Dix

Visits the

Lunatics

stoutly resisted on the grounds that it would cost too much.

So it was that in 1844, the forty-two-year-old reformer Dorothea Dix came to New Jersey to lead the fight for a state asylum. She was well known for her successful agitation on behalf of the insane in Massachusetts, Rhode Island, and New York.

Dix traveled around the state to witness at first hand the condition of the insane. Her account of what she saw is as grim and grotesque as the portrait of underworld of Victorian London being painted in the same decade by Charles Dickens.

At the Salem County Poorhouse she found "several epileptics and persons of infirm minds," plus eight insane. The keeper of the poorhouse told Dix a story about one of the inmates, a madman who had been chained up for twenty years:

> Going up to his room not long since, in order to shave him, my hands both being full, as I came near, he suddenly sprang upon me, and dealt a violent blow at my chest; his being chained, alone, prevented his killing me. I knew I must master him now or never: I threw down the shaving tools, caught a stick of wood from the entry and laid upon him until he cried for quarters: I beat him long enough to make him know I was his master, and now he is too much afraid of a thrashing to attack me; but you had better stand off, ma'am, for he won't fear you.

At the Shrewsbury poorhouse the wife of the keeper told Dix that one inmate would wander in the woods, returning only when he became hungry; for the past three months he had not been back and nobody was quite sure where he had gone.

At the Piscataway poorhouse, she found a raging maniac who reminded her of an caged tiger. The madman was "chained, naked except a straitjacket laced up so as to impede the motion of the arms and hands, exposed and filthy." To prevent him from starting a fire, he was chained on the opposite side of the dark room from the stove.

At the Essex County Jail in Newark, she found men and women, adults and children, sane and insane, thrown together. The inmates amused themselves, one informed her, by "telling good stories of our adventures and escapes—oh, that is good fun." Observed Dix, "our county jails, in effect, are the primary schools, and the normal schools for the state-prisons."

In the Morris County poorhouse she found that the violently insane were kept in basement cells, "dark, damp, and unfurnished, unwarmed and unventilated—one would not hesitate, but refuse to shut up here a worthless dog even." Some time before an inmate had been accidently killed when he tried to escape by thrusting his head through a hole in the cell.

At the Trenton poorhouse, she found a violent madwoman. "In a bed next to hers, separated by a slight partition-screen, is a helpless paralytic woman, and her husband, who is quite feeble, occupies the same room...so here are these poor invalids at the mercy of this often furious and noisy mad-woman, who rends off her garments and utters imprecations and obscene language that appall all within hearing." The mistress of the house confessed "we are afraid to make her angry, and let her have her own will pretty much."

Dix described what she had seen in a report submitted to the state in January 1845. Because she was a woman, she could not appear before the legislature to speak; her report had to be introduced as a memorial by a state senator sympathetic to her cause.

Like the New England schoolmistress she was, Dix used her report to lecture the legislators on the backwardness of their state. In most of the civilized world, she said, insanity was considered a malady that could be cured. But in New Jersey these people were caged up like prisoners; as unjust a practice as jailing a person with consumption. "It is more than time this un-Christian abuse should cease."

She appealed to the frugality of the legislature. The establishment of a state asylum would reduce the expenses faced by counties and towns to house the mentally ill. And the state would be spared other expenses caused by the insane: "what sums are consumed by their uncontrolled habits of destructiveness, what are lost by their crimes when under frenzied impulses they fire buildings, take human life, and make wreck of all social and domestic peace and happiness?" An asylum would be able to cure the insane and restore them to productive lives.

Dix sounded a warning to the legislators: Have pity on the insane, she said, "their grievous, forlorn estate may be shared by yourselves or your children."

Dix pressed her cause. She wrote letters and articles for the newspapers. She also lobbied the legislators by inviting them to her rooms in a Trenton boardinghouse, where she argued with them for hour after hour. In a letter to a friend, she told how she had encountered a gruff assemblyman who opposed helping the insane. After she lectured to him for an hour and a half, he rose to his feet.

> Ma'am, I bid you good-night! I do not want, for my part, to hear anything more; the others can stay if they want to. I am *convinced;* you've conquered me out and out; I shall vote for the hospital. If you'll come to the House, and talk there as you've done here, no man that isn't a brute can stand [against] you. . . . The Lord bless you!

There was some opposition. One assemblyman called the planned asylum as extravagant as an "Egyptain Collosheum."

But in the end Dix won. On March 25, 1845, the measure passed by 18–0 in the Senate and 41–8 in the Assembly. The New Jersey State Lunatic Asylum, as it was called, was built in Ewing Township, where it still stands.

Dix spent the rest of her life in the service of the insane and the sick, and was responsible for the establishment of asylums and hospitals all around the country. During the Civil War she achieved fame as the supervisor of the Union's nurses.

The crusader, who never married, proudly called Trenton asylum her "first-born child." Thirty-six years after her triumph in New Jersey, she became gravely ill while on a visit to the asylum. The staff invited her to remain as a guest in a comfortable apartment in the building, and she died there six years later.

In the end, the child cared for its parent.

Today we venerate Abraham Lincoln to such a degree that it is hard to imagine that anyone, at least in the North, could have despised him while he lived. But of course, that was not so. Lincoln aroused tremendous hostility among many of his fellow citizens, and nowhere in the Union was that more in evidence than in New Jersey.

Even before the Civil War began, the state had been sympathetic to the South. New Jersey bordered on the the slave state of Delaware, and a portion of New Jersey then, as now, stretched below the Mason-Dixon

Getting Wrong with Lincoln

line. The city of Newark did an enormous trade in manufactured goods with the South, and New Jersey provided a profitable railroad link between the South and the Northeast. New Jersey was also one of the free states with the most disdain for the abolitionist movement.

New Jersey's opposition to the new, anti-slavery Republican party and its standard-bearer Abraham Lincoln thus came quite early. In the election of 1860, New Jersey was the only free state where Lincoln did not carry the popular vote. Indeed, the word "Republican" was so unpopular in New Jersey that the state party officially called itself the Opposition party in that election.

When southern states began to leave the Union after Lincoln's election, there was some sentiment that New Jersey should join them. The *Newark Journal* argued that such a move would make the state a manufacturing center of the Confederacy and would make Perth Amboy a major seaport for the new nation. Former governor Rodman M. Price wrote a public letter arguing that joining the South would augment "our prosperity, progress, and happiness."

Even those who did not go that far believed that the South was the aggrieved party and that the North should yield to southern demands.

5   *Getting Wrong With Lincoln.* The New Jersey brigade was one of the first units of Union soldiers to reach Washington in the early days of the Civil War. Here, in an engraving from the May 25, 1861, *New York Illustrated News,* the brigade passes before Abraham Lincoln. Despite this show of patriotism, New Jersey was the northern state most opposed to the war and to Lincoln. (New Jersey Historical Society, Newark)

Although President-elect Lincoln was welcomed by large crowds when he passed through New Jersey in February 1861 on his way to Washington, there was an undercurrent of dislike. In jest, one assembly-man in Trenton offered the resolution "That when this house shall have seen Abraham Lincoln, they will have seen the ugliest man in the country."

With the firing on Fort Sumter, opposition to Lincoln became muted. In the eyes of many Jerseyans, the president was now the defender of the Union against southern aggression.

Volunteers from New Jersey flocked to the colors, and when Jersey regiments first reached Washington, the *New Jersey Mirror and Burlington County Advertiser* reported, Lincoln himself had welcomed the troops and had remarked "that New Jersey, according to her population, had pre-sented a fuller and more completely equipped body of men, than any other State." The report continued: "Every man felt proud that he was Jerseyan, and especially a Jersey volunteer."

But the early euphoria faded rapidly as the Union lost battle after battle, as the casualty figures increased, and as war taxes rose. A series of "peace meetings" were held in the state following the defeat at Bull Run, and some person or persons unknown unfurled a Confederate flag in Hackensack.

In September 1861, federal authorities arrested a prominent New Jerseyan, James W. Wall of Burlington, who had written anti-Lincoln editorials and who had helped to organize peace meetings. Wall was jailed for almost two weeks without warrant or indictment, and his case was seen as an example of the high-handed, dictatorial methods of the Lincoln administration.

The Emancipation Proclamation also outraged many Jerseyans, who saw it as shifting the purpose of the war from preserving the Union to freeing the slaves. In July 1863, a Newark mob protesting the newly-enacted draft law smashed windows and destroyed property.

As the war progressed, the Democratic party in New Jersey divided into two factions. One consisted of the War Democrats, led by the party's gubernatorial candidate Joel Parker, who supported the war effort but who felt that the Republican administration was losing the conflict and violating the Constitution.

The members of the other faction, called Peace Democrats by their friends and Copperheads by their enemies, wanted an immediate end to the war. The "martyr" James W. Wall was a leading figure in this wing of the party. Some extreme Copperheads crossed the line between dissent and treason by actively working for a southern military victory.

But whatever their opinion, the Democrats were united in dislike of Lincoln and a desire to turn him out of office. They were supported by anti-Lincoln newspapers across the state, such as the *True American,* the *Bergen Democrat,* and the *Newark Journal.* The *Journal* was a particularly bitter Copperhead organ, which described Lincoln as "a perjured traitor" who "betrayed his country and caused the butchery of hundreds of thousands."

In the New Jersey election of 1862, the Democrats won a great victory, capturing four out of five congressional seats, both houses of the legislature, and the governorship. The new legislature that convened in January 1863 immediately passed a set of notorious "Peace Resolutions," which, while professing a desire to have the Union restored, protested the conduct of the war and called for immediate negotiations with the Confederacy.

The legislature then elected the Copperhead James W. Hall to the Senate in Washington.

As the presidential election of 1864 approached, New Jersey Democrats found a champion who could challenge Lincoln on the national level—General George B. McClellan, the dashing former commander of the Union army of the Potomac who had been dismissed by Lincoln and who now resided in Orange. At its national convention that year, the party nominated McClellan for president and adopted a platform that echoed the New Jersey Peace Resolutions.

In American politics, the issues separating the parties often get fudged in order to win elections. But in 1864 the differences were about as clear as they could be. On one side stood Lincoln and the the Republicans, calling for military victory over the South. On the other side were McClellan and the Democrats, for whom the war was a disaster.

When the voting was over, McClellan had won a victory in New Jersey, with 68,024 votes to Lincoln's 60,723. But New Jersey was almost alone: only the slave states of Kentucky and Delaware joined it in voting for the Democratic ticket. In the rest of the Union, the Republicans won strong majorities in both houses of Congress and there were Republican governments in every northern state except you-know-where.

(New Jerseyans did not forget McClellan; he was elected governor in 1877.)

It does not take much thought to realize how disastrous it would have been if the Democrats had won and peace negotiations with the Confederates had been undertaken. It is hardly likely that the South would have reentered the Union without insisting that slavery be protected and that the federal government be made subordinate to the states.

And even if nothing had come of the negotiations, a cease-fire would have provided the South with a chance to regroup its military force, and undoubtedly the war would have gone on much longer.

Fortunately, Lincoln won, and the nation conceived in liberty and dedicated to the proposition that all men are created equal prevailed— and New Jerseyans retained the right to be stubbornly in the wrong when they so choose.

I n 1889, Jefferson Davis, the first, last, and only president of the Confederate States of America, died peacefully at age eighty-one. What does this have to do with New Jersey history, you ask? Had it not been for one independent-minded Jerseyan, Jeff Davis's life might have ended a lot sooner and a lot more unpleasantly, possibly with a rope around his neck.

When he was captured in a Georgia cornfield in May 1865, Davis was undoubtedly the most hated man in the United States. As leader of the

Jeff Davis

and the

Jersey Doctor

rebellion, he was held responsible for the deaths of hundreds of thousands of Union boys on the battlefields and in the prison camps of the South. It was believed that he had personally ordered the assassination of Lincoln. Even southerners had contempt for Davis as the failed leader whose blunders had lost the war.

Davis was taken to Fort Monroe in Virginia, an impregnable prison with walls ninety-five feet thick and a moat eight feet deep. The commander of the fort was Major General Nelson A. Miles, twenty-six.

The young general was determined that the war criminal Davis would not escape his custody, even by suicide. He had Davis placed in leg irons in a damp cell overlooking the moat. A lamp was left burning all night in the cell. Guards stationed in the cell watched everything the prisoner did, twenty-four hours a day. The only possession allowed him was a Bible.

And then into that grim cell came John J. Craven of Newark. The forty-two-year-old Craven was an interesting character—the embodiment of the restless, inquisitive Yankee of the nineteenth century. As a young man in Newark, Craven became fascinated with the new marvel of the age, the telegraph. Working in his kitchen he invented a method for insulating wires that made it possible to run cables underwater. When he failed to get a patent for his discovery, he quit the telegraph business and went to the California gold fields. He found no fortune, but judging from his letters to his wife, he thoroughly enjoyed his adventures in the Wild West.

Back in Newark, he decided to become a doctor. In the manner of the day, he spent time with a practicing physician, Dr. Gabriel Grant on Market Street, until he learned enough to open his own office. Then he got himself elected coroner of Newark.

With the outbreak of the Civil War, Craven joined up as an army surgeon. When other New Jersey doctors protested that he did not have adequate training, he went directly to Abraham Lincoln, who gave him permission to take an examination for army doctors. Craven passed, and he spent the war as a medical officer in hard-fought military campaigns up and down the Atlantic coast of the Confederacy.

Craven was the chief medical officer at Fort Monroe when Davis arrived, and Miles put the prisoner under the care of the New Jersey doctor. From Miles's point of view, it turned out to be a mistake.

When he first walked into Jefferson Davis's dismal cell on May 24, Craven found the prisoner emaciated and feverish. Over the next few months, according to Craven's account, the doctor petitioned Miles for improvements in the patient's condition: removal of the leg irons, better food, regular exercise, removal of the guards from the cell, a screen for privacy, and finally, transfer to healthier quarters. These improvements were granted, although sometimes grudgingly—it took an order from the War Department to remove the chains.

Perhaps Craven's greatest gift was simply to talk to Davis as a human being. The rebel and the Jersey Yankee carried on conversations about everything from the life of the sea turtle to the events of the war. The two men clearly liked each other.

The grateful Davis described to his wife the help he had been given by Craven: "I am deeply indebted to him and can assure you that while I am under his charge you need have no apprehension that anything which is needful will be wanting."

But Craven overstepped the boundaries. Without asking Miles's permission, the doctor wrote to Davis's old tailor in Washington to order some warm clothing, including a coat. Friends of Davis heard of this, and contributed their own money to make the coat more luxurious.

The scandal made the newspapers, and Craven was reprimanded with the order that all future conversation with the prisoner "be confined strictly to professional matters." Shortly thereafter he was mustered out of service. He had served as Davis's physician for slightly over seven months.

Although Davis had been made more comfortable at Fort Monroe, his future was still not promising. Plans were underway to put him on trial for treason. One Confederate officer, the commandant of Andersonville prison, had already been hanged for war crimes.

Craven, now back in Newark, performed one more great service for his patient. With the help of an old army buddy who had become a journalist in New York, Charles G. Halpine, Craven published *The Prison Life of Jefferson Davis.*

The best-selling book portrayed Davis as a devout Christian, a devoted husband and father, and a prisoner who had suffered at the hands of his captors. The Davis of *The Prison Life* was a sympathetic figure, far from the monster that the North imagined him, and the book did much to arouse public opinion in his favor.

Davis was released on bail less than a year after the book was published, and the treason charges were dropped nine months later. Davis spent the rest of his years in honor and dignity as the representative of the Lost Cause. It was unquestionably Craven's book that made it all possible.

As for Craven, he kept up his interest in tinkering, and ultimately formed a company to market his inventions, among them an improved method of refrigeration for shipping meat in trains and ships. He died a wealthy man in 1893.

Ah, but there are a few dark clouds behind this touching story. From the time the book was published, questions were raised about how much was written by Craven and how much by his journalist friend Halpine. It was even been alleged that Halpine, a fervid Democrat, wrote the whole thing himself as a blow against radical Reconstruction and as a way of reviving the prewar coalition between the northern and southern wings of the Democratic party.

Craven defended himself by saying that although he had paid Halpine to help him put the book together for publication, it was his own work compiled from notes he took at Fort Monroe.

Interestingly, Jefferson Davis obtained a copy of the book while he was still in prison and scribbled his own comments in the margin. Especially next to sentiments of a political nature attributed to him, he wrote things like "false," "not so," and "bah!" He left other passages stand or made minor corrections. It is clear from these penciled notes that he never said many of the statements attributed to him.

All of this suggests that the Newark doctor provided the basis for the book, and that the New York journalist enlarged and dramatized it. This may well be the first example of the "as told to" genre of book publishing.

Let us make one other nasty observation. *The Prison Life* was an important step in reconciliation between North and South; it was one of the first books to cover the Civil War in the fog of nostalgia and can thus be considered a progenitor of the sentimental *Gone With the Wind* view of the South.

Obscured in the magnolia-scented claptrap about the Lost Cause and the Gentleman's War was the fate of the newly freed slaves. In extending its hand to the defeated Confederates, the North withdrew its protection of southern blacks, and left them to fend for themselves. This was a lapse for which we are still paying.

Perhaps the nation should not have been so quick to forgive and forget.

I f you are one of those people who cling to the notion that fiction is stranger than truth, let me introduce you to the story of the Jersey City treasurer and the Mexican bandits.

The whole saga is sort of a Jersey City version of *Les Misérables.* The part of Jean Valjean is played by the Republican treasurer of Jersey City in the early 1870s, a man with the quite unexpected name of Alexander Hamilton (not for a minute to be confused with the Founding Father).

The Treasurer

and the Bandits

The part of the pursuing policeman is played by Inspector Benjamin Murphy of the Jersey City police force.

The story can be found in the classic exposé of New Jersey politics, *Modern Battles of Trenton,* written in 1895 by the ever cynical William Sackett. The details are confirmed in newspaper accounts from New Jersey, Texas, and New York.

It seems that Hamilton fell in love with one Winetta Montague, an actress appearing in Jersey City. He needed a great deal of cash in order to keep Winetta in the style to which she hoped to become accustomed. Put yourself in the shoes of the lovestruck Hamilton. If you were the treasurer of Jersey City, where might you look for cash?

Hamilton left his Jersey City office on Friday, January 23, 1874, saying that he had business in Trenton. On Monday, a telegram arrived from Boston saying he had been called there on an urgent matter. When Hamilton failed to report to work, an investigation discovered that not only was the treasurer missing, but so was a major portion of the treasury. In fact, Hamilton had run off with about $86,000 in cash and negotiable bonds. The only things he left behind were his wife and four children. The city fathers put out an alarm and elected a new treasurer.

The Boston telegram was a ruse; Hamilton was actually headed for the Wild West where he planned to slip over into Mexico. In Corpus

Christi, Texas, where he claimed his name was Morgan, he announced that he wanted to be taken across the border. "My business is urgent," he declared, "and I must reach Mexico at once if it costs a fortune."

This talk attracted the attention of Thomas Parker, the police chief of Corpus Christi. Parker realized that the fugitive was the missing Jersey City treasurer and telegraphed the Jersey City authorities, offering to make an arrest if a suitable reward was offered. When Jersey City failed to come across with the promise of money, Parker decided on another way to cash in.

He and his friends agreed to take Hamilton to Mexico, but once they were forty miles outside Corpus Christi they extorted $7,500 from him. The thieves then turned Hamilton over to a character named "Pedro the Mexican," who took the fugitive over the border.

Parker, incidentally, got into trouble when word of his caper got out. He was dismissed from his job of police chief and drummed out of the Corpus Christi Council of the Friends of Temperance for "conduct unbecoming an honorable man, a good citizen, a Friend of Temperance." (I am not making this up.)

After taking Hamilton over the border, Pedro the Mexican made his way to Brownsville, Texas, where he bragged about how the gringo from New Jersey had been persuaded to part with some of his loot. He was overheard by a woman who bore a grudge against Pedro simply because at some time in the past he had killed her husband.

The woman contacted a law officer in Brownsville who sent a telegram to the Jersey City police chief, Benjamin Champney. Champney, in turn, assigned the case to one of the keenest men on the force, Inspector Benjamin F. Murphy, who quickly caught a train to pick up Hamilton's trail in Texas.

Murphy knew he was on the right scent when he chatted with a ferryman taking him over the river to Corpus Christi. "The other night I had the valise of the Treasurer of New Jersey, with a million in it, for a pillow," said the boatman. "If I'd a' known on it, there'd a' bin another cap'n on this ferry to-day."

The fleeing treasurer, meanwhile, was discovering that Mexico was not the haven he expected. He found it necessary to pay bandits to protect him from other thieves and from the law. Pedro the Mexican passed him on to an outlaw known as Happy Jack, who in turn passed him on to a sinister character named Cortinas in Matamoras, a city just across the Rio Grande from Brownsville. By now Hamilton had lost a fair portion of his loot.

And speaking of fair portions, what happened to Winetta Montague? A reporter found her at a hotel in Philadelphia, where she said that Hamilton had been only a passing acquaintance, who had never given her clothes or jewelry, and that she had nothing to do with his embezzlement. Did she start to run away with Hamilton and then change her mind?

A report published in a Texas newspaper said that at the time he was robbed by Parker, the treasurer was traveling in a group that included a woman. Was this Winetta? This aspect of the story is one of those impenetrable mysteries, like the reason for the disappearance of the Maya Indians or the origin of the statues on Easter Island.

Inspector Murphy managed to track Hamilton all the way to Matamoras, where he found that Cortinas and his band had just taken over the local government and were ensconced in city hall. Murphy, who had faced his share of bad men in Jersey City, found the Mexican banditti to be the most "desperate-looking thugs and cut-throats" he had ever seen in his life—men who walked about with pistols at the ready.

Murphy wisely decided he needed help, so he got the commandant of Fort Brown in Texas and the United States consul to go with him to Cortinas's adobe hut. Although Cortinas maintained he had never heard of Hamilton, Murphy suspected that the treasurer was at that selfsame moment hiding in the back of the hut. Murphy nevertheless gave up any expectations of arresting Hamilton and returned to Jersey City empty-handed.

What happened next is described in Sackett's book: "A couple of months later, the bell of Murphy's house door rang, and the servant announced that a man with the aspect of a tramp wanted to see him. When Murphy stepped to the door, who should be there but Hamilton, shabby and broken-spirited, and come to surrender himself into the hands of the law!"

It seems that the Mexican bandits had taken his last Jersey City dollar, and had then thrown him on a boat to Brazil to get rid of him. He had somehow struggled back to New Jersey.

Once in court, Hamilton admitted that he had taken the money. In July 1874, he was sentenced to three years at hard labor in the state penitentiary, plus a $1,000 fine. The judge told Hamilton he would not lecture him on the enormity of his crime, since the ex-treasurer's conscience would speak louder than the court ever could.

One suspects that Hamilton's conscience, a withered and underused organ, probably had very little to say. But as he lay in his cell at the state pen he had time to reflect with some sadness how his hopes of a life with Winetta Montague in sunny Mexico had turned to ashes.

There is some redeeming social significance to this sorry story. Hamilton was a member of a ring of hack politicians who had been appointed to run Jersey City by the Protestant, Republican legislature over the wishes of the growing Irish-Catholic, Democratic population of the city. His crime helped to discredit the ring and return city government to the voters.

Thus, in spite of himself, Hamilton managed to do some good. The thought of it must have driven him crazy.

J uly 4, 1873, was a summer day at the height of the Victorian era. In London, the shah of Persia visited the architectural wonder of the age, the Crystal Palace. In Long Branch, New Jersey, President Ulysses S. Grant arrived at his elegant seaside cottage for the Independence Day holiday. And in Jersey City, the Reverend John Stuart Glendenning allegedly seduced Miss Mary Pomeroy in the back parlor of her parents' home.

The story of Mary Pomeroy's seduction and downfall, a sort of Jersey

Poor

Mary Pomeroy

City version of *The Scarlet Letter,* is as much an artifact of the Victorian age as the gingerbread cottages of Long Branch and the Crystal Palace in London.

John Glendenning was the minister of the Prospect Avenue Presbyterian Church, one of the most fashionable houses of worship in the city. Glendenning, a bachelor in his thirties, had come to the church's pulpit directly from Princeton Theological Seminary.

Mary Pomeroy was a woman in her mid-twenties. As befitting this morality tale, she was an orphan, who had been adopted by her cousin James Miller and his wife Ethelinda. Mary lived in the comfortable Miller household, and earned a bit of money as a music teacher.

She and Glendenning struck up an acquaintance when she got a part-time job playing the organ at the Prospect Avenue Church. The young minister began to visit Mary at the Miller home as often as three times a week to sing hymns and chat. Soon he was bringing her gifts, including a watch, earrings, and a locket.

The Millers would go up to bed, leaving the couple alone in the parlor. "I always had confidence that Mr. Glendenning would do nothing but what was right," Miller said later. It was widely thought in the church that the couple were engaged, or soon would be.

But the expected engagement never took place, and eventually the minister stopped going to the house. Then, one summer day in 1874, Mrs. Miller discovered that Mary was pregnant with the minister's child.

Said Mrs. Miller: "I asked her whether she was married and after a great deal of hesitation she gasped out 'yes'; I then told her to go and get her certificate at once; she faltered and fell across my knees; 'Oh, my God!' I said, 'you are not married."

When Mr. Miller learned of the business from his wife, he was outraged that such a scandal could occur under his roof. He had Glendenning arrested and brought to his house by a policeman. There, in front of witnesses, Miller demanded that the minister wed the young woman. Glendenning refused, and denied that he was the father. Mrs. Miller fainted; Mary sobbed.

Glendenning was charged with bastardy and released on bail. Mary gave birth to a baby girl she named Ella Stuart Glendenning, and then fell deathly ill. From her sickbed she confessed all to her family and friends.

She said that the minister had first seduced her in the back parlor on a July 4th one year previously while the Millers were away, and that for months thereafter they had continued to be intimate. Glendenning told her they were not doing anything wrong; she was his "little wife."

But when she became pregnant he turned away from her. She claimed that on one occasion when they were alone he pulled a pistol from his pocket and threatened to kill her if she did not sign a paper absolving him of blame.

Mary passed away on August 18, 1874. Reportedly, her last words were: "God forgive him for his wrong to me. I loved him. I trusted him foolishly; God have mercy on me; I have told the truth." She then kissed her baby and died. According to the doctor who attended her, the cause of death was congestion of the lungs, hastened by "anxiety of mind."

An enormous crowd attended her funeral, including the mayor of Jersey City. The sermon was given by the Reverend Tunison of the Methodist Church, who spoke about how "one, single mistake broke a heart that was full of joy, and destroyed a life."

"I am a father," said Reverend Tunison to the weeping mourners, "and I speak to fathers and mothers. I would rather see the mangled and lifeless remains of my daughter stricken down by the hand of the midnight assassin, brought to my door, than to see her robbed of her honor and her virtue." (Is there a parent in the nation today who would prefer his daughter to be dead than to be unchaste?)

Glendenning was widely regarded as a cad, and there was talk of tar and feathers. He managed to escape civil prosecution because the child was not being placed on the public charge, but on October 14 he went on trial before the Presbytery of Jersey City.

The case was handled like a courtroom trial, with witnesses, cross-examinations, and evidence. Presbyterian ministers served as prosecuting counsel and defending counsel. Reporters and spectators were allowed to attend, but not anybody under age twenty-one.

Witnesses for the prosecution testified movingly about the pure character of Mary, and that the only person she had ever been intimate with was the Reverend Glendenning. Neighbors testified that they had seen the minister leaving the Miller house late at night.

The defense painted a different picture of the relationship between the pair. Supporters of Glendenning came forward to say that Mary had forced herself on the innocent minister. They charged that Mary had kept company with other men, and it was hinted that Mrs. Miller's brother had fathered the illegitimate child.

Horace Dean, superintendent of the Sunday School at Glendenning's church, testified that "Miss Pomeroy was not attractive in any way, either in education, manner, or ability." (Note how unattractiveness served as proof of moral failure.) Glendenning's aged mother testified that her son never stayed out late.

The climax of the trial occurred when Glendenning himself took the stand. He resolutely maintained that he had never had intercourse with Mary, never promised to marry her, and never threatened her with a pistol. His friendship with her reflected only the concern of a minister for one of his flock.

On December 8, the Presbytery announced its verdict. The elders ruled that although the charge of bastardy could not be proved, Glendenning had "compromised his Christian character by making Miss Pomeroy so many valuable presents, visiting her so frequently and at such unseasonable hours and living on such intimate terms with her as to occasion public suspicion of impropriety." On these grounds he was discharged as minister.

The case had aroused enormous attention, including a lurid pamphlet entitled *Poor Mary Pomeroy! The Unfortunate Music Teacher.* The pamphlet summed up public opinion: "Mary Pomeroy's name has been added to the long list of unfortunates, whose trusting love and belief in the promises of a scoundrel, a lying, lecherous coward worked their ruin."

Today we live in a world awash in condoms, abortions, premarital sex, and X-rated movies. The saga of John and Mary is so remote from our lives that it seems to reflect not another age, but another planet.

But we should not forget that for all the Victorian rhetoric, Mary Pomeroy was a real person, who suffered and died.

Ask Americans today to identify the name Garfield and most would probably think of the cat from the comic strips. But at one time the name meant the martyred president whose slow, agonizing death at the Jersey shore a century ago transfixed the nation in horror and pity.

All of which shows that one generation's tragedy is another's comedy.

Had Garfield lived he might have been one of the better presidents of the nineteenth century. Like Lincoln, he had been born in frontier

A

President Dies

in Jersey

poverty. He had risen to become a teacher, a lawyer, a Civil War major general, and a nine-term congressman from Ohio. A well-educated, brainy man, he could perform the neat trick of writing Latin with one hand and Greek with the other. In 1880, he was elected the twentieth president of the United States on the Republican ticket.

On July 2, 1881, Garfield was walking arm in arm with Secretary of State James G. Blaine through the ladies' waiting room of the Baltimore and Potomac train depot in Washington. The president was on his way to catch a train for a tour of New England. A madman named Charles Guiteau fired two shots at the president with a .44 caliber revolver. Garfield fell bleeding to the floor. (This was an age in which men could walk arm in arm and when unescorted women stayed in their own waiting room.)

A prominent local physician, Dr. D. Willard Bliss, was summoned to the scene by the secretary of war and asked to take charge. The secretary of war, incidentally, was Robert Todd Lincoln, the son of the president who had been assassinated sixteen years before. Dr. Bliss found that one of the two bullets merely grazed Garfield, but the other had entered his back. The president seemed to be dying. His pulse was weak, he vomited frequently, and he complained of pain and tingling in his feet. Bliss poked a metal probe into the wound to see if he could find where the bullet was located.

Under Bliss's direction, Garfield was taken by horse-drawn ambulance from the train station to an upstairs bedroom in the White House. Bliss assembled a team of prominent medical men to assist him in the care of the president: Philip S. Wales (the surgeon general), J. J. Woodward and Robert Reyburn of Washington, D. Hayes Agnew of Philadelphia, and Frank H. Hamilton of New York. Dr. Bliss and his colleagues were prominent physicians and surgeons who could be expected to employ the latest medical and scientific knowledge to save the president's life. (Bliss's first name, curiously, was "Doctor." His parents must have been quite ambitious).

The doctors' main concern was locating where the bullet lodged to find out if an organ had been damaged. They continually searched for it with their fingers and with probes. As part of the state-of-the-art treatment, the famous inventor Alexander Graham Bell came to the White House to use his electric "induction balance"—a primitive sort of metal detector—to find the bullet. Bell's device confirmed the opinion of the doctors that the bullet was "in the front wall of the abdomen, immediately over the groin, about five inches below and to the right of the navel."

The doctors also were desperately worried about keeping the president nourished. He had difficulty keeping down food and his weight fell from 210 pounds to 130 after six weeks. Again using advanced medical techniques, the doctors administered enemas containing beef extract, whiskey, and tincture of opium. He was also fed milk from a cow tethered on the White House lawn.

It was a typically unbearable summer in Washington, and the doctors feared that the stifling heat was contributing to the president's continued fevers. Yankee ingenuity was put to use to construct what was probably the first air conditioner used in America. The device drew air from a fan through a box filled with ice, with wet towels acting as a sort of filter. This contraption actually lowered the temperature in the President's room by fifteen degrees.

But this was not sufficient to ward off fever, and the doctors concluded that Garfield had to be moved to a cooler climate. On September 5 the president was tenderly taken on a special train to Elberon, New Jersey. Volunteers from the Jersey shore had constructed a three-quarters-of-a-mile spur of track from the Elberon station to a seaside cottage donated by a wealthy New Yorker. Local residents stood by the track, with heads bowed in respect, as the president's rail car trundled by. The New Jersey press expressed hope that the state's balmy sea breezes would help the president's recovery.

From the moment Garfield was shot, the public was caught up in the details of his case. Wrote an observer about the day of the shooting: "In every city, in every town, in every village of the United States groups formed about the telegraph and newspaper offices and other centers of information, and discussed in excited fashion the terrible news."

State governors proclaimed days of public prayer for the president's survival. New Jersey was slow getting around to this; perhaps because Governor George C. Ludlow, a Democrat, was reluctant to call on the Lord to help a Republican.

The doctors issued daily bulletins for the newspapers, and the public could read about changes in the president's temperature and pulse, along with details on the hours he slept, the pus he discharged, the bowel movements he made, and the medication he received. Never before had the public been bombarded with so much medical information. There were days of hope when the fever abated and when it appeared that the president would survive, followed by despair when he sank close to death.

Suggestions came from around the country on how Garfield could be saved. One writer proposed that the doctors hang the president upside down so that the bullet would fall out.

The newspapers also contained affecting accounts of his wife and young children at the bedside, and of his bravery in the face of suffering.

And in fact, Garfield does seem to have been brave. Although often feverish and in great pain, he maintained good humor. It is reported that shortly after the shooting, he asked Secretary Blaine about the motive of the man who attacked him. Said Blaine: "Indeed I do not know, Mr. President. He says he had no motive. He must be insane." Garfield smiled: "I suppose he thought it would be a glorious thing to be a pirate king." You have to admire a man who can quote Gilbert and Sullivan after being shot in the back.

But for all his spirit and for all the efforts of the doctors, the president died. The end came in Elberon at 10:35 p.m. on September 19, eighty days after the shooting in the train station.

6   *A President Dies in Jersey.* President James A. Garfield was shot by an assassin in a Washington train station. Doctors tried in vain for eighty days to save him. In his last days he was taken to Elberon, on the Jersey shore, where he died. This illustration, from *Harper's Weekly,* shows him being comforted by his wife. (New Jersey Historical Society, Newark)

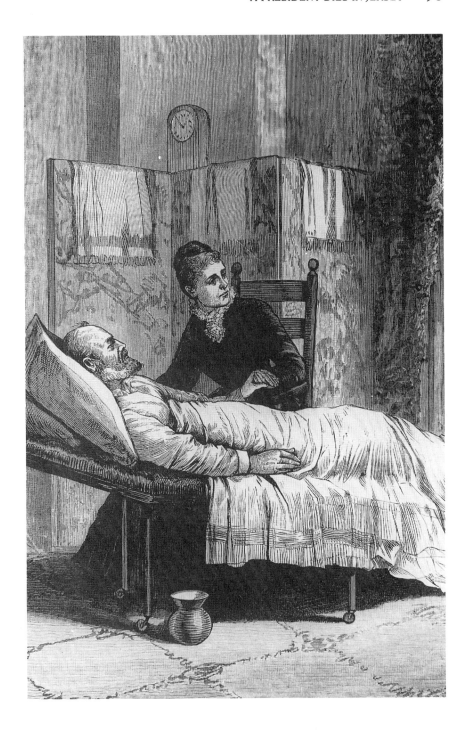

Even before he died, there was criticism about the medical treatment he was given. For the rest of their lives, the matter was a blot on the careers of the White House doctors. When they presented their bill to Congress, the legislators slashed away at their claims: their request for $91,000 was reduced to $27,500. Bliss refused to accept his reduced share.

The doctors stoutly maintained that they had done everything they could to save the president's life. But even they were plagued by doubts. Thirteen years after the assassination, Dr. Reyburn confessed in an article in the *Journal of the American Medical Association* that he had spent countless "weary days and wakeful nights" arguing with himself whether he could have saved the president's life if he had done something different.

We can now look back from the twentieth century and conclude that Dr. Bliss and his colleagues did indeed err; Garfield could have been saved.

Modern doctors who have studied the case are convinced that the cause of the president's death was massive sepsis—blood poisoning. Whence arose this sepsis? Undoubtedly from the unsanitary fingers and probes shoved in the wound by the doctors in their search for the bullet. Two physicians who studied the case in 1951, Robert W. Pritchard and A. L. Herring, Jr., noted the irony: "It is apparent that the many weeks of his treatment were essentially directed against complications of the treatment itself." Pritchard and Herring argued further that had Garfield been an ordinary citizen, and not the president of the United States, he would not have been subjected to the unceasing probing of his wound. There were, after all, countless Civil War veterans walking about with bullets lodged in their bodies.

Ironically, for all their probing, and despite Alexander Graham Bell's induction balance, the doctors were wrong about the location of the bullet. The autopsy proved it had lodged near the spine.

Dr. Stanley Trooskin, director of Trauma Services at Kings County Hospital, believes that with modern treatment, Garfield would have been fully recovered and back in the White House in four weeks.

Today the average Cub Scout and Brownie knows more about the need to keep wounds clean than the eminent doctors assembled around the president's bed in 1881.

But it is more than a little unfair to criticize Bliss and his colleagues from the perspective of the twentieth century. After all, the Cub Scouts and Brownies of the late twenty-first century will probably know things about healing that the Harvard Medical School can't even guess at today.

It is fair, however, to ask if there was an alternative available in 1881 that might have saved Garfield.

And, in fact, there was. At the time of Garfield's death, there were doctors who were aware of the new theories of sterilization, first advanced by the Englishman Joseph Lister in the 1870s. A Prussian disciple of Lister's, Dr. Johann Friedrich August von Esmarch, followed the case from Europe. After the president's death, von Esmarch wrote a devastating attack on the failure to use antiseptic methods. But in America, the majority of doctors were blissfully unaware that bacteria causes infection, and Garfield's doctors were part of that mainstream.

None other than the lunatic Charles Guiteau summed things up at his trial. When accused of killing the president, Guiteau protested: "The doctors did that. I simply shot at him."

C ornelius Wilson Larison, M.D., of Ringoes, was many things: a writer, a doctor, a publisher, a reformer. But above all he was a world-class eccentric, one of the most bizarre in the history of the Garden State.

Larison (1837–1910) is chiefly remembered today as an advocate of spelling reform. Like many other thinkers, from Benjamin Franklin to George Bernard Shaw, Larison was appalled by the confusion of the English language. At his home in the rural village of Ringoes, Larison

The Great

Eccentric

established the Fonic Publishing Haus which produced books, magazines, and pamphlets advocating simplified phonetic spelling. Under his scheme, "language" became "langwag" and "laugh" became "laf."

The principal product of Fonic Publishing Haus was *The Jurnal of American Orthopei,* which was published bimonthly from 1884 to 1909 and which was written, mostly by Larison, in phonetic spelling. The press also published twenty-four books by Larison, including two autobiographies, a "text buk" on "geografy," local history and genealogy, and philosophical speculation. Among the titles were *A List of Wurds Hwich Ar Not Alwaz Pronounst in the Sam Wa, Reminissensez ov Scul Lif,* and *Speling-Reform Jemz.*

Larison's writing tended to be a bit wordy. One critic observed:

> If brevity is the soul of wit,
> The Doctor often misses it.

Typical of the kinds of articles published in the *Jurnal* was a series by

7   *The Great Eccentric.* Dr. Cornelius W. Larison, a physician in Ringoes, was known for his unconventional views on medicine, education, nutrition, and other causes. He is best remembered as an exponent of spelling reform. Written on the back of this photo is the caption "Taken on the Tenth ov Janyari, 1907." (Special Collections and Archives, Rutgers University Libraries)

Miss Mary B. Rudebock, in which she described her travels to colleges and teachers' conventions around the state to observe how English was being taught to young people. She attended a convocation at Rutgers College in New Brunswick in 1887 and observed that the president of the college was a terrible orator. "With such a pattern az this at the hed of an Institushun," she wrote in the *Jurnal,* "it iz not licli that the students wil ever becum fin lingwists."

Mary B. Rudebock (or, in phonic spelling, Meri B. Rudeboc) was one of three unmarried women who comprised the staff of the Fonic Publishing Haus. The other two were Mary W. Prall and Susan M. Fillips. At one point a young German, Gustav W. Yensen, joined the staff as a bookbinder. After he returned home to Germany, Gustav wrote to thank Dr. Larison for teaching him English.

Larison's reform activities did not produce much money. His journal had few subscribers and his books few readers. But fortunately, Larison did have an income as a physician (or rather, "fysician"). He fits the classic image of the beloved old country doctor, traveling about in a horse and buggy to treat the common folk. His account ledgers show that his charges ranged from twenty-five cents for pulling a tooth to five dollars for delivering a baby.

He dispensed nostrums such as strychnine, opium, morphine, turpentine, and dried bearberry leaves, and he seemed cheerfully willing to experiment on his patients, giving whiskey to a seven-year-old child suffering from the croup and nitrous oxide to a woman with tuberculosis.

As this suggests, he did have some curious views of medicine, which he disseminated in *The Jurnal of Helth,* another publication of the Fonic press. The magazine was not a great success; it had a total of thirty-one subscribers and folded after twelve issues. Its publication was interrupted for a time because the entire staff came down with influenza.

In the pages of the *Jurnal,* Larison provided tips on how to combat influenza, poison ivy, baldness, and other ills. He warned that vaccination was "a dangerous, loathsome practice," and that taking at least three baths or showers a day would prevent disease.

He advocated various types of food, particularly the tomato. With the use of tomatoes, "the liver becums toned up and activ, the glands of the small and large intestines becum activ, the hole alimentary tract becums activ, constipation disappears, digestion and assimilation becums activ, flesh accumulates, the movements becum more elastic, the port is nearer erect, the eys are efflugent with animation and good nature, and he who so long has been a regular visitant to sum celebrated fysician's office, thanks to tomatoes! now begins to feel wel."

Cabbages, in contrast, were unhealthy. Larison described the case of a pregnant woman under his care who developed an uncontrollable craving for the vegetable. She gave birth to a deformed child, Larison reported, that strikingly resembled a cabbage.

He believed in the benefits of fresh air, although he was accused of causing the death of three young patients suffering from scarlet fever and three suffering from measles by insisting that their windows be kept open in the winter. This was probably not as bad for Larison's income as one might think, since he also ran the local cemetery.

Larison was also an educator, and he served as principal and chief instructor of a private school at Ringoes. The school song ran

> We'l proudli bost
> That we wer wuns
> Girls and boiz at Ringoz

The school never enrolled a large number of students, but it provided a stage for Larison to explore his wide-ranging interests. He taught zoology, physics, chemistry, botany, and geography.

He delighted in taking the students on field trips around New Jersey, to natural sites like the Pine Barrens and artificial wonders like the County Clerk's Office in Monmouth. At Sea Girt on the first Wednesday in August he brought students to witness a local custom known as "sheep washing day" when inhabitants from the area came to bathe. At the wealthy resort of Long Branch he pointed out to his students the fact that idle rich people were "ugly, awful, squelching, withering, hideous, monstrous, tremendous, enormous."

Larison was also an amateur historian. It was he who interviewed the aged former slave, Sylvia Dubois, described elsewhere in this volume.

Then there were the experiments. Larison had some interesting ideas about the nature of life and death (see *Hwot iz the Sol? Haz the Dog a Sol?* Fonic Publishing Haus, 1902). On one occasion that must have been long-remembered by his students, he placed a black snake in a container of water and left it out overnight in freezing temperature. The next morning he pounded the frozen snake in the block of ice into small bits. When he warmed up the pieces of snake and exposed them to electrical current in front of his class, the pieces jumped.

Along the same line of inquiry he demonstrated how a decapitated eel placed in a hot frying pan squirmed. There were experiments of a similar nature with a turtle and a dog, but it is probably wise to draw the curtain on these.

As an avid scientist, he embraced Darwin's evolutionary theory. He looked forward with enthusiasm to the cataclysm that would end the age of humankind and would result in newer, higher life forms.

Larison died at age seventy-three in his beloved Ringoes. Today we laugh at his bizarre beliefs. But he had spent a long and interesting life, taking a cold shower every morning, having a nap after lunch, and eating a lot of tomatoes.

At his death he was mourned by his loving wife and children, by his devoted staff of unmarried women, by his surviving patients, by his attentive students, and by a small but committed band of spelling reformers that stretched from Ashtabula, Ohio, to Hetton-le-Hole, England. He was utterly convinced of the rightness of his cause and the soundness of his beliefs. How many of us will be able to die with as much confidence?

Maybe old Doc Larison deserves the last laf.

I t was a front-page courtroom drama that pitted religion against modern secularism, that tested a community's right to keep out unpopular opinion, and that brought a big-city lawyer to challenge small-town America.

The 1925 Scopes evolution trial in Dayton, Tennessee? No, the 1887 Reynolds blasphemy trial in Morristown, New Jersey.

The story begins in Boonton, New Jersey, in the summer of 1886, when one Charles B. Reynolds came to preach his version of the truth.

Blasphemy

on Trial

Reynolds was a former Methodist minister who had turned away from his faith. He had become an itinerant freethinker who used the techniques of the ministry to attack religion, holding tent meetings and distributing tracts.

His anti-religious message outraged the devout people of Boonton, especially the Methodists and the Catholics, and a mob descended on his tent. A reporter described what happened: "They pelted Reynolds with ancient eggs and vegetables. They chopped away the guy ropes of the tent and slashed the canvas with their knives. When the tent collapsed the crowd rushed for the speaker to inflict further punishment by plunging him in the duck pond."

The attempted duck pond baptism drove Reynolds out of town, but it did not silence him. He surfaced in Morristown, where he distributed his pamphlets again, this time with an allegorical cartoon inserted in them. The illustration showed him at his tent in Boonton, literally throwing pearls before a herd of swine while a priest with a bucket labeled "Catholic swill" and a minister with a bucket labeled "Methodist slop" looked on. (Nobody ever accused Reynolds of being overly subtle.)

The authorities in Morristown decided to use the law to shut Reynolds up. The grand jury indicted him on an old colonial-era law making blasphemy against religion a crime punishable by a maximum penalty of $200 and a year in prison.

The story might have ended here with a quick conviction. But then came a startling development: Reynolds was to be defended by the famous Robert G. Ingersoll.

"Colonel Bob" Ingersoll was the son of a Calvinist minister (Freudians take note) and a veteran of the Civil War who had become one of the most successful attorneys in the nation and a power in the Republican party. What made him famous, however, was his position as America's leading agnostic. His books, speeches, and debates attacking religion were the gospel for freethinkers across the country and in Europe.

On the morning of May 19, 1887, the plump, baldish Colonel Bob arrived at the Morristown train station, from where he was brought by coach up the dusty hill past a throng of gawking onlookers to the courthouse. Judge Francis Child's courtroom was packed with spectators—women in the balcony and men downstairs. Local ministers sat prominently in the audience, but there was at least one local freethinker: a man who jumped up in the middle of court and shouted "Thr' cheers fo' Bob Ing'sul." He was removed by the sheriff.

After the jury had been selected, the prosecution presented sixteen witnesses who claimed they had received the pamphlets from Reynolds. Ingersoll limited himself to a few questions, mostly asking witnesses if they had actually read the offending material. In response to Ingersoll's questions, a baker admitted that even though he had read the pamphlet he was still able to make good bread. When it came time to present the defense, Colonel Bob announced that he would not call any witnesses, but that he might make a "few remarks" after the lunch recess.

The promise of a powerhouse speech by Ingersoll attracted even more spectators to the courtroom in the afternoon. (This was an age when public speaking was a popular art form, an age long before the attention span of the average American was reduced to the length of an MTV rock video.)

Ingersoll rose to address the jury. "The question to be tried by you," he said, "is whether a man has the right to express his honest thought."

Over the next two hours Ingersoll gave a masterly performance in defense of free speech, ranging over history, philosophy, theology, and constitutional law. He recalled the persecution of heretics throughout

8   *Blasphemy on Trial.* In 1887, the famous agnostic lawyer Robert "Colonel Bob" Ingersoll appeared in a Morristown courtroom to defend a man accused of anti-religious blasphemy. This Chicago pamphlet contains Ingersoll's powerful address to the jury on freedom of speech. (Special Collections and Archives, Rutgers University Libraries)

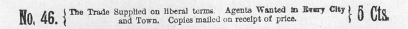

No. 46. { The Trade Supplied on liberal terms.   Agents Wanted in Every City } 5 Cts.
          and Town. Copies mailed on receipt of price.

COL. R. G. INGERSOLL'S LECTURES.

THE GREAT JERSEY HERESY CASE
IN FULL AND COMPLETE.
SPEECH IN THE TRIAL OF THE REV. CHARLES B. REYNOLDS
FOR BLASPHEMY,
AT MORRISTOWN, NEW JERSEY, MAY 22, 1887.

THE TRADE SUPPLIED BY
G. S. BALDWIN,
LOCK BOX 287, CHICAGO, ILL.

history, how kings and tyrants had crushed dissent with torture and murder.

He cited the new science of the nineteenth century. Darwin's works, he said, had given more benefit to the world than "all the sermons ever uttered." England placed Darwin's remains Westminster Abbey; in New Jersey he would have been placed in the penitentiary.

Ingersoll presented heart-rending images (a Dark Ages wife weeps as her husband is burned at the stake) and stirring language ("To enslave the minds of men, to put manacles upon the brain, padlocks upon the lips—that is blasphemy").

He appealed to the local pride of the jury: "For the sake of your State— for the sake of her reputation throughout the world...say to the world that New Jersey shares in the spirit of this age."

"I sincerely hope," he thundered at the end, "that it will never be necessary again, under the flag of the United States—that flag for which has been shed the bravest and best blood of the world—under that flag maintained by Washington, by Jefferson, by Franklin and by Lincoln— under that flag in defense of which New Jersey poured out her best and bravest blood—I hope it will never be necessary again for a man to stand before a jury and plead for the Liberty of Speech."

But Ingersoll lost. He had based his defense on the idea that the blasphemy statute violated the constitutions of the United States and of New Jersey. Judge Child instructed the jurymen that they could not rule on the constitutionality of a law; they could only decide whether the defendant was guilty as charged.

The jury found Reynolds guilty and the judge fined him $25 plus $50 in costs, which Ingersoll promptly paid (he also waived his legal fee). On his way out Ingersoll answered a reporter's question about the blasphemy statute: "The law was made up by the bigoted baboons of the past and enforced by the religious donkeys of the present," he said.

Unlike the Scopes trial almost four decades later, the press was on the side of the prosecution. "Reynolds is a crank of blackguardly instinct" who had to learn that liberty is not license, an editorial in the *Newark Daily Advertiser* said. The *New York Times* called Reynolds "a noisy and offensive blackguard," who was rightfully suppressed because he had disgusted and revolted the community.

If Reynolds showed up today in New Jersey with his pamphlets, we would surely show greater tolerance. After a century of changing interpretations of the First Amendment we are much more accustomed to the idea that free speech is to be defended even when it is offensive.

At least up to a point. Right now there are a great many Americans who regard burning the flag as blasphemy rather than as free speech, and who are willing to amend the First Amendment of the Constitution to punish the blasphemers. Even Ingersoll, who was more of an agnostic than a libertarian, might have balked at seeing his beloved flag dishonored.

And in other parts of the world, in places like Iran and China, there are governments willing to kill people who say unacceptable things in unpleasant ways.

There is still a lesson to be learned from Reynolds and the Boonton duck pond.

Who is the best known fictional character from New Jersey? Is it the Jewish-American princess of Philip Roth's *Goodbye Columbus*? The Hoboken longshoreman of *On the Waterfront* ("I coulda been a contender")?

Probably the New Jersey name most recognizable to readers around the world is a character who appeared in one short story written in England a century ago, and since then reprinted countless times and in countless languages. The character's fame is due to one sentence in that

"To Sherlock Holmes, She Is Always the Woman"

tale: "To Sherlock Holmes, she is always *the* woman."

The character is Irene Adler, and the story is "A Scandal in Bohemia" by Arthur Conan Doyle, published in the *Strand Magazine* in July 1891. This was the third Holmes adventure, and the first in short story form. It has joined the other fifty-five short stories and four novels in the Holmes canon.

The story begins one night at 221B Baker Street as a mysterious masked client arrives. It is the king of Bohemia, Wilhelm Gottsreich Sigismond von Ormstein, who needs Holmes's help in a delicate matter.

His Highness recently ended a love affair with the beautiful and celebrated Irene Adler. But she has kept a photograph of the two together. (Not, evidently, the kind of photograph taken by detectives in motels in the twentieth century. Remember that this was the Victorian era.)

If the photograph were to become public, warns the king, an impending royal marriage will be called off, and Europe will be plunged into crisis. Holmes agrees to take the case. The detective takes down from the shelf his collection of newsclippings and reads about Adler to Watson and the king:

> Hum! Born in New Jersey in the year 1858. Contralto—hum! La Scala, hum! Prima donna Imperial Opera of Warsaw—Yes! Retired from operatic stage— ha! Living in London—quite so!

The next day, Holmes disguises himself as a Cockney laborer, and spies on Adler's London villa. He catches a glimpse of her: "A face that a man might die for," he tells Watson.

The detective returns to the villa that evening, this time in the guise of a simple-minded clergyman. Using a ruse he is invited into Adler's home. At a signal from Holmes, Watson (who as usual has only a dim conception of what his friend is up to) throws a smoke bomb through the window.

Holmes knows that "when a woman thinks that her house is on fire, her instinct is at once to rush to the thing which she values most." Thus, in the confusion of the smoke, Holmes sees Adler check on the safety of the photograph in a secret compartment in the wall. He now knows the hiding place.

As Holmes and Watson are returning to 221B Baker Street after their evening adventure, "a slim youth in an ulster" hurrying by says, "Good night, Mister Sherlock Holmes."

The next morning Holmes, Watson, and the king go to the villa to seize the photograph, only to find that Adler has fled earlier that morning to the Continent. Inside the secret compartment is a letter from Adler to Holmes. She explains in the letter that she suspected the detective had been behind the smoke bomb, and she had followed him in disguise back to Baker Street to make sure.

The letter goes on to say that once she knew Holmes was on her trail, she realized that she could be safe only if she fled England, taking the photograph with her for future protection. But she promises never to reveal it. "The King may do what he will without hindrance from one whom he has cruelly wronged," she writes.

The king understands that Adler will keep her word, and his secret is safe. He offers to pay Holmes, but the detective asks for only one thing— a photograph of Adler. The story ends with Holmes lost in admiration for the clever and beautiful woman. "The daintiest thing under a bonnet on this planet," he describes her.

The story ended here, but the life of Irene Adler does not. The Sherlock Holmes tales have attracted a passionate group of followers known as the Baker Street Irregulars. The Irregulars play a peculiar game. They begin with the assumption that Sherlock Holmes actually lived, and that his good friend Dr. Watson was writing fact, not fiction. Doyle, in this universe, is simply the literary agent who published Watson's writings.

And not only are Holmes and Watson alive, so are the whole pantheon of characters—the genius of crime Professor Moriarty, Holmes's corpulent brother Mycroft, the long-suffering housekeeper Mrs. Hudson, and the insufferably dense Inspector Lestrade, to name a few.

Irene Adler is a prominent part of this universe. She was also one of the few adversaries, male or female, to outsmart the great detective. And then there is the curious statement of Watson's about Irene being *the* woman to Holmes. Does this mean that the aloof Holmes was actually in love?

Watson's remark has spawned endless Irregular speculation about the relationship between Holmes and Adler. The most intriguing theory concerns the disappearance of Holmes from 1891 to 1894, after he fell over the Reichenbach Falls with Professor Moriarty. Did Holmes go into hiding, as he told Watson, to escape the revenge of Moriarty's gang, or did he have another purpose in mind? The theory goes that Holmes and Adler had an affair, and that Adler bore a son who grew up to become the famous New York city detective Nero Wolfe.

Irregulars have also been concerned by the fact that there was no such monarch as the "king of Bohemia," and they have spent much time debating the actual identity of the client. Was Watson covering up the fact that the masked nobleman was actually the notorious rake Prince Edward Albert (later King Edward VII), the son of Queen Victoria?

Then there is the business of the husband. At one point in the story, Adler rushes off to church with her beau, a handsome young lawyer named Godfrey Norton, to get married. Holmes theorizes that she has tied the knot so that Norton can protect her against the king (a Victorian sort of idea). Irregulars claim that there was something, well, irregular about this episode, and that the marriage is a fake.

Another mystery lies in the fact that Watson refers in the beginning of the story to the "late" Irene Adler. It may be that the king of Bohemia finally had her murdered to keep her quiet, but most Irregulars refuse to accept this sad end.

So the story of Irene Adler continues to intrigue Sherlockians. But a question remains: Why did Doyle give his character a New Jersey origin?

It is likely that the real-life model for Irene Adler was Lillie Langtry, a famous and beautiful nineteenth-century English actress, among whose lovers was Prince Edward Albert. Born on the Isle of Jersey in the English Channel, she was known as the "Jersey Lily." Consciously or unconsciously, Doyle translated Langtry's Jersey into Adler's New Jersey.

And in so doing, Doyle gave our state a small but not insignificant connection to the most popular literary figure of all time, Sherlock Holmes.

After two hundred years and forty presidents, New Jersey has yet to put one of its own in the White House. Woodrow Wilson and Grover Cleveland don't count, since Wilson did not move to New Jersey until he was thirty-three and Cleveland moved away when he was four.

The closest a native, life-long Jerseyan has come to being president was Garret Augustus Hobart, who was the twenty-fourth vice president

President Hobart?

It Might

Have Been

of the United States. Vice presidents tend to become president more often than, say, movie actors; of the forty men who have served as president, fourteen had previously occupied the number-two slot. So Hobart had a reasonable shot at becoming the first real New Jerseyan in the White House.

Hobart (known to his friends as "Gus") was only a heartbeat away from the presidency; but alas for New Jersey, it was his heart that failed first. It is a story filled with might-have-beens and there-but-for-fortunes.

Hobart was the quintessential insider. He was born in Long Branch on June 3, 1844. He graduated from Rutgers College in 1863 and studied law under a Paterson attorney with the picturesque name of Socrates Tuttle. Hobart took a time-honored career step: He married the boss's daughter, Jennie.

Hobart rose steadily in the cozy world of Jersey politics in the Gilded Age. He became city counsel of Paterson in 1871, a master in chancery and a member of the Assembly in 1872, Speaker of the Assembly in 1874, state senator in 1876, chairman of the Republican State Committee in 1880, and president of the Senate in 1881–82. He was his party's candidate for the United States Senate in 1884, and in the following year he organized the successful campaign of his friend John W. Griggs for governor, thus recapturing the governorship for the Republican party for the first time in two decades.

At the same time he was cutting a formidable figure in politics, Gus Hobart was amassing a personal fortune. He was an enormously successful lawyer, with an interest in dozens of banks, railroads, utilities, and other companies.

As an insider in the worlds of government law and business, he was a powerful man in New Jersey. But he had larger ambitions, and in 1896, when he boarded the train to St. Louis as a delegate to the Republican convention, Hobart was being mentioned as a strong contender for the vice-presidency.

The 1896 campaign was an important one, pitting the populist Democrat William Jennings Bryan against the conservative Republican William McKinley. The Republican kingmakers knew that they needed an easterner to balance the ticket with the midwesterner McKinley. And since McKinley had no experience in the world of business, they needed a man who could convince Wall Street of the party's devotion to sound monetary policy. And it didn't hurt to have a man on the ticket who could guarantee New Jersey's electoral votes.

Hobart was clearly the number-one man for the number-two job, and the Republican leaders saw to it that he received the nomination. As it turned out, he did what was expected of him. His worshipful biographer says Hobart had "the confidence of men of large capital," and he helped to raise a fair share of the unprecedented $10 million spent by the Republicans.

Hobart actually developed something of a popular following during the campaign. A Republican mother and father named their twin daughters Hoberta and Garretta. His biographer notes that the overwhelming vote for Hobart in New Jersey "shows what the intelligent, right-thinking conservative citizens can do when aroused."

With McKinley's victory, Hobart went to Washington. He purchased a lavish bluestone house on Lafayette Square, which became the scene of many parties, including a celebrated dinner for the Prince of the Belgians.

Hobart also had a serious side, and it is reported that McKinley frequently took an evening stroll from the White House across Lafayette Square to Hobart's house, where they would discuss important matters of state "over boxes of fragrant perfectos." He served quite ably as president of the Senate during the crisis of the Spanish-American War, and an admiring senator stated that Hobart "restored the Vice Presidency to its proper position" (although this remark could be subject to several interpretations).

Hobart was instrumental in appointing other Jerseyans to high office. His old friend John Griggs was named attorney general, and another friend, William M. Johnson of Hackensack, became the first assistant postmaster general.

Hobart was not an unattractive character. In the style of the day, he was portly, and in the style of politicians always, he was a friendly, back-slapping fellow, much involved in civic and charitable work.

Now, let us indulge in a bit of historical "what if."

It is quite likely that the popular Hobart would have been renominated for vice president in 1900 and would have won a second term under McKinley. It was during the first year of that second term that McKinley was assassinated. Hobart would then have ascended to the presidency, and the course of American history would have been different.

Never mind here the effect on foreign and national affairs; let us imagine what might have happened in New Jersey. Highways would have been named after him, Rutgers would have been renamed Hobart University, his home would be a presidential library, and New Jersey children would learn about a native son who made it to the top.

But all this was not to be. His health began to fail in the spring of 1899 and he died, apparently of heart failure, in New Jersey on November 21, 1899. His place on the ticket was taken by a newcomer to Republican politics, Theodore Roosevelt.

A statue of Hobart was erected in Paterson; it stands in the City Hall plaza next to Alexander Hamilton (who, incidentally, also died in New Jersey, at the hands of Jersey-born Aaron Burr).

Hobart's beautiful estate on the hills above Paterson is now the site of William Paterson College. His house contains the admissions office, and the carriage house now holds the college's computer lab. One visiting the campus can almost imagine where the Hobart Presidential Library might have been situated.

9   *President Hobart? It Might Have Been.* Garret A. Hobart, a wealthy Republican lawyer, was elected vice president under William McKinley in 1896. Hobart died in office, and his place on ticket was taken by Theodore Roosevelt. (Special Collections and Archives, Rutgers University Libraries)

Twentieth
Century

At the turn of the century, the silk city of Paterson was perhaps the most polyglot city in the nation, with settlements of immigrants from all over Europe.

The Italians among them were skilled textile workers from northern Italy who had come to Paterson to earn higher wages in the silk mills. Along with the cultural baggage these Italians brought to America—their church, their cuisine, their language—some came with an enthusiasm for the revolutionary doctrine of anarchism.

Paterson

Man Kills

King

Anarchists wanted to build a socialist utopia. Not the state-controlled socialism of Karl Marx, but a vastly more democratic, decentralized, individualistic socialism that would make humanity truly free. The more extreme among them believed that the way to awaken the proletariat to build this new society was by using bombs and guns against the ruling classes.

As usually happens with fringe groups, the Italian anarchists of Paterson spent more time fighting among themselves than with the capitalist oppressor. In smoky restaurants, in meeting halls, and in newspaper offices they would endlessly debate the correct path to world revolution.

In the midst of one such debate at an Italian saloon in West Hoboken, a member of one anarchist faction shot and wounded the leader of an opposing faction. Fortunately, a young man in the crowd, Gaetano Bresci, grabbed the would-be assassin and subdued him before he murdered his opponent.

The thirty-year-old Bresci had emigrated from Milan two years before. He was a silk weaver at the Hamil & Booth Mill on Spruce Street in Paterson, where he was regarded as "a good worker who never caused trouble." He had married an American woman from Chicago, Sophie

Neil, and had a daughter. Sophie later described him as "a loving husband and father."

The good worker and loving husband was also an adherent of the extreme, violent wing of anarchism. As a boy he had seen his own family in Tuscany pushed into poverty. In Paterson, he had read about how King Umberto had ordered the Italian army to put down a protest riot in Milan, and how hundreds of Milanese had been killed or wounded as a result. King Umberto had awarded a medal to the general in charge of the massacre. The king, Bresci decided, had to die.

Bresci bought a 9mm Harrington and Richardson pistol from a Paterson hardware store. On outings to the countryside, he would practice shooting while his wife and daughter picked wildflowers. He quit his job at the mill, and on May 22, 1900, he departed for Europe on a French steamship.

On the evening of July 29, he was in a crowd in the pleasant suburban town of Monza, near Milan. King Umberto had just presented prizes at a gymnastic exhibition, and was in his carriage, waving to a great throng of loyal subjects. Bresci fired three shots at the king, who breathed "it is nothing" as he fell dead. The outraged crowd tried to beat Bresci to death before the police pulled him away.

There was astonishment when the news reached New Jersey that the assassin came from Paterson. The authorities tried to reassure the public. Mayor John Hinchcliffe of Paterson told a reporter: "We are ready to put down the Italians at the first sign of trouble. Paterson has a police force of 104 men, and I have every confidence in their ability to control the situation. So far the foreigners have given us no trouble."

Governor Foster M. Voorhees of New Jersey declared: "There is one thing I want to say, and that is the plot to kill King Humbert was not hatched in New Jersey. I am sure it was made up in New York if plotted in this country at all."

But despite the governor's statement, the press, the secret service, and Italian consular officials came to Paterson looking for evidence that the city was the hub of a world-wide anarchist terror network.

There were reports of defiant Paterson anarchists conspiring to assassinate the leaders of Europe and America, and there was melodramatic talk of mysterious characters, like a beautiful anarchist woman, "La Bella Teresa" and a sinister newspaper editor, Errico Malatesta. (Teresa was imaginary; Malatesta was real.)

Bresci's wife, Sophie, was interrogated by police, and the apartment searched. She later moved to Cliffside Park, but continued to be the object of suspicion by the authorities. "I suppose that I will be hounded in every place I go, and branded as an Anarchist," she said. "People would like to see me driven to the poorhouse and left there to die." She eventually returned to Chicago.

The fear of conspiracy in America was fed by the authorities in Europe. The Italian police questioned passengers who had been on the ship with Bresci, and jailed three of them. One of the three was a nineteen-year-old girl who was having an affair with Bresci. (Evidently he was not such a loving husband after all.) On a tip from the Italian authorities, two Italians were arrested at a New York City pier and charged with sneaking into the country to assassinate President Mckinley.

Eventually the search for conspiracies died down as police were unable to find any evidence. The public seemed reassured by the fact that most Italians in the state were genuinely outraged by the assassination, and memorial services for the king attracted crowds of sorrowing Italians in Newark, Jersey City, and even Paterson.

At his trial a month after the assassination, Bresci himself stated that he had acted alone, and his claim seemed to be accepted by the authorities.

Bresci was sentenced to life imprisonment. He was found hanged in his cell less than a year later. It was suspected that he had been driven to suicide by the torments of his guards, or perhaps that they killed him and made it look like suicide.

One side effect of this sad story was that for perhaps the first time, newspapermen visited the Little Italy section of Paterson to report on the wretched conditions of the immigrant silk workers.

The lament of a young anarchist woman was printed in the *Newark Evening News:* "They have run us out of Italy, where to have stayed would have been to have starved. We have come here. Things are no better here. We are treated like dogs in the mills. We are not considered human by Americans. We do not starve, but there is a worse death than starvation. It is neglect."

The trolley car traveling north on Clifton Avenue was jammed with teenagers on their way to high school that cold winter morning. The city was covered in snow, and the kids were having fun, chatting and singing to each other. The trolley was packed so tightly that students were standing in the aisles and on the front platform.

When they came to the Orange Street stop, the kids laughed because there was no room for people waiting there to get on. The few adult

The

Clifton Avenue

Horror

passengers on board were enjoying the students' high spirits.

After crossing over Orange Avenue, the car began to descend a gentle slope, at the bottom of which the trolley track crossed the Lackawanna railroad line. The kids laughed because the trolley seemed to be coasting down the icy track. "Slide, Kelly, slide," a boy said, quoting a popular baseball song.

But just then the gate in front of the railroad track went down, indicating that a train was coming. The trolley motorman applied the brake, but ice on the track prevented the car from stopping. The passengers screamed as the trolley crashed through the wooden arm of the gate and collided with an oncoming locomotive.

From blocks away people could hear the sound of smashing woodwork, metal, and glass, and then the cries of the injured.

It was a little after 8:40 a.m. on February 19, 1903, in Newark, New Jersey. Nine high school students were killed, another thirty passengers were injured.

The people of Newark were filled with shock and grief. For days the papers published pictures of the young boys and girls who died, and accounts of parents visiting the city morgue to identify the bodies of their children. The high school, reported the newspaper, was "transformed into a house of mourning," and the mayor declared Sunday as an official day of mourning for the city. Along with this sorrow came anger and a desire to punish those responsible.

After an investigation, the Essex County Grand Jury concluded that the operator of the trolley line, the North Jersey Street Railway Company, was to blame. The seven members of the executive committee of the board of directors and four top officers of the firm were indicted for manslaughter.

The trial began on August 31. The *Newark Evening News* said later that because the case tested the limits of corporate liability, it was "by far the most important that has ever been tried in the courts of Essex County or of the State of New Jersey, indeed the most important in some of its features that this country has ever known."

The presiding judge was the chief justice of the New Jersey Supreme Court, William S. Gummere; the case against the company was presented by the county prosecutor, Chandler Riker. The prosecutor argued that the company had been negligent in three ways: First by allowing the trolley to become so overcrowded that the brake would not work, second by not clearing the ice off the track, and third by not installing an automatic derailing device at the dangerous crossing.

On the first day of testimony, a sister of one of the victims was called as a witness. Said a reporter, "Her sorrowful face and the deep mourning in which she was clad seemed to symbolize the grief that came to so many families with the disaster and awoke the minds of those who saw her to an appreciation of the full meaning of the trial."

But four days after the trial began, Justice Gummere announced that he was dismissing the case. He ruled that there had been no criminal negligence. No human effort could ever have made the intersection completely safe, he said, and the management had taken reasonable safety precautions: "As the case is presented, it cannot be said that any of the defendants failed in his plain duty." Gummere instructed the jury to return a verdict of not guilty, which they promptly did.

Prosecutor Riker shrugged off the defeat: "There isn't much to say. We presented all the facts to the jury, and we insisted on the law as we understood it. The court did not agree with us as to the law and its application to the facts in the case."

And so the matter rested until, four and a half years later, there came a startling front-page revelation.

It was an election year, and one of the Republicans seeking his party's nomination for governor was Chandler Riker, the former prosecutor.

Riker was stoutly opposed by a group of Republican reformers, one of whom was Alden Freeman of Orange. Freeman had been a member of the Grand Jury that indicted the trolley company at the time of the accident.

In the midst of the campaign, Freeman issued a statement. He charged that right after the accident, tremendous pressure had been brought to bear on the grand jurors not to indict the North Jersey Street Railway Company directors. Said Freeman:

> Different members of the jury told me ... that they were being approached from the outside. One man told me that he was offered fifty $1,000 bills by the son of one of the officers of the company to use his influence to quash the indictment. The same man told me of loans called by financial institutions of Newark and contracts held up.

Freeman alleged that Prosecutor Riker and Justice Gummere did everything they could to prevent the indictment: Riker had even taken the irregular step of having the grand jurors meet with Gummere in the judge's office so that he could try to dissuade them.

According to Freeman, the grand jurors had resisted the pressure and had voted that the directors should stand trial. But at that trial, he said, Riker and Gummere had conspired to weaken the case, exclude the damaging evidence, and dismiss the charges. After the defendants had won, said Freeman, he had observed one of them shake the prosecutor's hand with a hearty "Thank you, Chan!"

To Freeman, this was all part of the alliance between big business and politicians against the people of New Jersey. Reformers like Freeman had long been hostile to the trolley companies for their monopolistic practices. In many Jersey cities, the owners had managed to obtain perpetual franchises and enormous tax exemptions.

We do not know today if there was in fact a conscious conspiracy of the scope that Freeman alleged. But it is certainly fair to say that politics, business, the press, and the legal profession in New Jersey in that era were dominated by a clubby elite, spanning Newark and Trenton. The trolley company board represented the most powerful corporations in the state, and among the defendants were E.F.C. Young, president of the North Jersey Street Railway Company; A. J. Cassatt, president of the Pennsylvania Railroad; and Leslie D. Ward, vice president of the Prudential Insurance Company. They were defended by a former governor of New Jersey, George T. Werts.

These men had equally powerful friends who had invested in the trolley company and who attended the trial to show their support—men like U.S. Senator John F. Dryden, the founder of the Prudential, and Thomas McCarter, president of the Public Service Corporation and former state attorney general.

The establishment view of the case was expressed in an editorial by the *Newark Evening News* the day after the trial, which spoke of "the high personal character, the eminent responsibility and the immense wealth of the persons put on trial as common criminals for a crime no one of them could conceive of committing and for which none would ever hold them directly responsible."

It is likely that Prosecutor Riker and Judge Gummere shared that point of view. They too were members of the state's elite. Riker himself was an early investor in trolley stock and Gummere had once been a lawyer for the Pennsylvania Railroad.

Whether Freeman's charge was true or not, it seems to have had an effect: Chandler Riker dropped out of the race for the Republican gubernatorial nomination. Three years later, in 1910, it was widely touted in Washington that Justice Gummere was going to be nominated by President Taft to fill a vacancy on the U.S. Supreme Court. Progressives opposed to Gummere's nomination published the old trolley allegations in a leading reform journal, *LaFollette's Weekly Magazine,* and no more was heard of Gummere's candidacy.

Memories of what was called the "Clifton Avenue horror" have abated. The parents and friends of the dead teenagers are themselves long dead. The trolleys too are gone and the tracks torn up. To us, in fact, trolleys seem nostalgic, and we think of them chugging and tooting through picturesque turn-of-the-century main streets.

But there is still something chilling about the image of that trolley, crowded with laughing children, as it begins its slow descent down the hill toward death.

I f you think New Jersey suffers from a poor image in the national press today, you should have been around in 1905 when *McClure's Magazine* hit the stands with an article entitled "New Jersey: A Traitor State" by Lincoln Steffens.

To say that the two-part article (the first half ran in April, the second in May) was critical of our state is to understate the matter. Steffens was furious. "New Jersey is selling out the rest of us," he charged. The state shows "plainer than any other state or city, how we are all betraying one

The Traitor

State

another." He spoke of the "stench of the vice graft," and of a state whose citizenship was "mean, narrow, local."

New Jersey "deserves all the punishment we can give her," Steffens declared, "I'd like to see the citizens of this selfish state pickle in the corruption of Hudson County and Essex, of Camden, and Passaic, and Middlesex, and Ocean." But on second thought that was unfair. "I know my feeling about punishing Jersey is wrong: It is too Jersey-like."

Steffens, thirty-eight years old, was America's preeminent muck-raker—what we would call an investigative reporter. His specialty was exposing municipal corruption, and he was the author of the celebrated exposé *The Shame of the Cities*. He wrote in fierce, clipped sentences, describing an American public at the mercy of corrupt, entrenched interests. His picture of good locked in a struggle with evil in the cities and states of America is startling to those of us who have learned to accept a bit of compromise in our lives.

In his article on New Jersey, Steffens traced the state's wickedness back as far as Alexander Hamilton, that most undemocratic of the Founding Fathers. According to Steffens, Hamilton recognized New Jersey's potential as a small state strategically located between New York City and Philadelphia, a state which business interests could dominate.

Then came the railroads. The first in the state, the Camden & Amboy, obtained a monopoly on rail service and a generous tax exemption from the legislature. The line brought revenue into Jersey by charging higher rates for passengers and freight originating outside the state's borders. This was the beginning of a tradition: New Jersey was able to profit at the expense of the rest of America.

But New Jersey paid a price. To preserve its privileged position, the Camden & Amboy (and its successor the Pennsylvania Railroad) routinely bribed state officials. Before long, New Jersey's state legislators, governors, congressmen, and senators became servants of the special interests. When rival railroads wanted to build lines in the state, they had to buy their own politicians.

Before long the state was well advanced in graft. The Republican party represented the Pennsylvania Railroad; the Democrats represented the racetrack interests, the liquor lobby, and the Baltimore and Ohio Railroad.

All of this was merely a prologue to the real corruption that began in the late nineteenth century: the selling out of America that came when New Jersey decided to become a refuge for the trusts.

The national climate had turned against these trusts—giant corporations that dominated the economy and squeezed competition. A canny young lawyer, James B. Dill, with the cooperation of leading politicians and businessmen, established the Corporation Trust Company of New Jersey. For a fee, the company would assist businesses to incorporate in the state, even furnishing New Jersey residents to serve on boards of directors to satisfy the law.

To attract trusts, the state passed laws shielding them from regulation and legalizing giant "holding companies." When New Jersey corporations were being investigated by the New York legislature, the New Jersey legislature quickly passed an act protecting state corporations from any legal action authorized by "the statutes or laws of any other state."

This arrangement brought some interesting examples of greed. The law required businesses incorporated in New Jersey to meet from time to time within the state. Hotels on the Jersey side of the Hudson and the Delaware rivers thus developed a lively trade. Businessmen could travel over on the ferry from New York or Philadelphia in the morning, hold the required meeting, and then return home in the afternoon. Steffens alleged that some of the hotels catered to prostitutes in the evening, completing the picture of New Jersey as a red-light district for America's business.

It was a marvelous idea. The trusts could free themselves from bothersome interference from other states, and the taxes paid by these corporations swelled the New Jersey treasury. The only losers, as Steffens pointed out, were the people of the United States.

Steffens imagined New Jersey speaking to the corporations: "The other states have made your business a crime; we'll license you to break their laws. We'll sell out the whole United States to you, and cheap; and our courts are 'safe' and our legislature is 'liberal,' and our location is convenient."

The legacy of all this chicanery for New Jersey, Steffens claimed, was a deep-seated corruption that ran through the state at every level. Trolley companies and other utilities grabbed monopolies from municipal governments, and cities were squeezed for revenues because of generous tax exemptions granted to railroads by corrupt legislators.

Steffens's muckraking provided encouragement to a movement of Jersey reformers within the Republican party which came to be known as the New Idea. Steffens wrote glowing articles for his magazine about the New Idea leaders such as Mark Fagan, mayor of Jersey City, Everett Colby, state senator from Essex County, and George L. Record, a reform-minded attorney. To Steffens, these men were heroes battling on behalf of the people to smite corruption.

Although the New Idea men were ultimately defeated at the polls, the reform impulse did not die in New Jersey. When Woodrow Wilson ran for governor in 1910, he promised to tame the corporations. Once in office, he pushed through seven bills—the so-called Seven Sisters—aimed at taking New Jersey out of the incorporation business. The Seven Sisters put strict controls on New Jersey corporations; any violation was punishable by depriving the corporation of its charter and prosecuting its directors.

If only the story had ended here, it would be an uplifting tale of how a reporter alerted New Jersey to danger; how the people of the state responded by seizing power; and how Woodrow Wilson brought the corporations to heel.

But alas, real life does not always provide the uplift we would like to see. What happened next is sadly predictable.

With New Jersey out of the trust business, other states now saw the potential for moving in on this lucrative trade, and speedily liberalized their incorporation laws. Established business moved out of the Garden State and new businesses chose to incorporate elsewhere. New Jersey lost millions of dollars in filing fees and taxes to states such as Delaware.

In 1920, the state repealed the Seven Sisters, and was back in business at the same old stand, albeit with some real competition. The cynic might say that the legacy of Steffens was not to make New Jersey into a good apple, but rather to make some of the other apples equally rotten.

But Steffens was not around to witness what had transpired in New Jersey. A short time after the article came out, he quit his job at *McClure's* and began a quixotic search for answers to the mysteries of life. For a while he explored applying the Golden Rule to social conflict. He then flirted with radicalism, and traveled to witness the revolutions in Mexico and Russia. After interviewing Lenin, Steffens uttered the classic idealistic line about the Soviet Union: "I have seen the future; and it works." Still later he was favorably impressed by that Italian man of action Mussolini.

No doubt there is a lesson to be learned from all of this, but it is probably not a very inspiring one.

Mrs. Helen Prickitt Buchanan wrote a letter to this column a while back, asking for information on the 1908 murder of her grandfather, the Reverend Samuel Prickitt. Mrs. Buchanan witnessed that murder when she was five years old. She is now almost ninety, and the memory of that event has stayed with her all these years.

With the help of Mrs. Buchanan's recollections, we can recount the story of this long-ago crime. It was not a famous New Jersey murder, like the Hall-Mills case or the Lindbergh kidnapping, but it is an interest-

A Minor

Murder

ing story of murder and madness from the early years of the twentieth century.

On July 15, 1908, five-year-old Helen Prickitt was at her home on Clive Street in the quiet village of Metuchen. "I remember that my brother, Charles Norris Prickitt (then ten years old), another boy from the neighborhood, and I were in the yard of our home when we spotted Grandpa leaving his home on the other side of the orchard that separated the two houses. I usually watched for him and walked with him down the street."

Grandpa was Samuel Prickitt, a sixty-eight-year-old retired Methodist minister, much admired by his neighbors in the village. After leaving the pulpit, he had served for a brief time as a local magistrate. In the course of his duties he had sentenced one Archibald Herron to thirty days in the county jail for being drunk and disorderly. Archie Herron, a short, bald, intense man in his late forties, was a town neer-do-well who lived in poverty with his wife and retarded son, both of whom he was accused of abusing.

Meting out justice to unfortunates like Herron did not suit Prickitt, and he eventually resigned as magistrate. But Herron continued to bear a grudge. He would tell anyone who would listen that Prickitt had wronged him; that he had not been drunk, but only suffering from too much sun. He would mutter about how he would get even, and at least once he threatened Prickitt to his face. Now, two years after his sentencing, he took a pistol and went to Prickitt's home.

He caught Prickitt on Clive Street, as the grandchildren looked on. When Prickitt saw Herron he asked, "What's the matter? What are you going to do now?" Herron fired a shot into the minister, saying, "That'll finish you. You'll die."

Helen's father carried her fatally wounded grandfather to the front stoop, where the old man died. Helen's mother (the minister's daughter-in-law) ran from the house and tried to stop the murderer from escaping. He brushed her aside, and calmly walked away.

A posse led by two Metuchen constables surrounded Herron's Durham Street home. The killer surrendered with the pistol still in his hand. A crowd of 200 people gathered outside, and there was talk that Herron should be strung up. He was hustled into the mayor's automobile and taken to the New Brunswick jail. In the car, Herron ranted, "I didn't do it. If I did it, I didn't know it."

"Kills Old Minister in Village Street" was the blunt *New York Times* front-page headline next day.

The trial began in New Brunswick on July 27; Judge James J. Bergen presided. There was no doubt that Herron had killed Prickitt; the only question was whether or not he was sane. "Electric Chair or Madhouse" said the headline in the *Home News,* and public opinion clearly favored the former destination.

The prosecutor argued that the crime was premeditated. Metuchen residents took the stand to describe Herron's hatred of Prickitt, and how, shortly before the murder, he had boasted "I will put a hole in somebody." Witnesses testified that Herron had gone looking for Prickitt that day. Helen's father and brother described the shooting. (Helen was considered too young to take the stand.)

Defense attorney Charles T. Cowenhoven produced two psychologists (called "alienists" in those days) who testified that the defendant suffered from "paranoic insanity" or "alcoholic paranoia." They said that Herron was not able to distinguish right from wrong. The prosecutor ridiculed this claim.

The jury foreman appeared to observers to be crying as he delivered the verdict that Herron was guilty of murder. The *Home News* speculated that the foreman "could not bring himself to say the words that meant death to a fellow human being." Judge Bergen pronounced the sentence: Herron was to die at Trenton State Prison during the week of September 7.

In an editorial, the *Home News* expressed its approval: The execution "should have a salutary effect upon the community, which has had far too many crimes of violence of late."

In the days after the trial, the charge that Herron was insane seemed to be borne out. A reporter who saw him being taken by guards from the New Brunswick jail to Trenton State Prison described him "as cheerful as if going on a day's outing." An article about Herron on death row said: "He does not appear to be in the least worried concerning the gravity of the crime which he committed, and fails to realize that his time on earth is short. He is under the impression that he will be given his liberty."

While in jail Herron wrote a letter to Theodore Roosevelt, asking the president to help get him released. "Let me hear from you by return mail," Herron warned Roosevelt. The prisoner also wrote letters to Judge Bergen, saying that as soon as he got out of jail, he would get revenge. All of his letters were confiscated by the warden, who expressed the opinion that Herron was mentally unbalanced.

Defense attorney Cowenhoven continued to fight for his client. A week before Herron was to be strapped in the electric chair, Cowenhoven persuaded the state appeals court to reconsider the verdict. The governor of New Jersey granted two reprieves while the court debated the case.

The appeals court upheld the conviction, and once more Herron was scheduled to die.

But again came a reprieve. The judge who had originally sentenced Herron to die, James J. Bergen, was now a justice on the New Jersey Supreme Court. At the urging of Cowenhoven, he ordered the execution postponed until the experts could determine whether Herron was sane enough to be electrocuted.

Ironically, the court order to stop the execution was brought by Cowenhoven to the warden of Trenton State Prison the same afternoon the perplexed warden received an order from the governor stating that Herron should be executed. (The governor did not know about Justice Bergen's action.) It was, said the *Home News,* "another chapter of remarkable legal confusion."

When Cowenhoven went to Herron's cell to give him the good news that his execution was postponed, the prisoner was lying on the cot. "What in thunder are you doing here?" he said to the attorney, "I don't want you to bother so much. What can the courts do for me and what do I care for the courts?" He went on to tell Cowenhoven that once he was released from jail he would punish all his enemies.

The experts deliberated over Herron's sanity for years without any resolution. Then, fifteen years after the murder, Justice Bergen died. A technicality in the law required that in the case of an execution, the sentencing judge had to sign the death warrant, something that under the circumstances was now impossible. Archie Herron had beaten the hot seat.

But was he therefore entitled to be released from prison? Was he supposed to be transferred to an insane asylum? Nobody was quite sure, and Herron simply remained in Trenton State Prison for the rest of his life.

Most of that time he spent lying on his cot. He rarely spoke to the other prisoners, never went to the prison yard, and ate his meals in his cell. He never saw a movie and did not hear a radio until 1934. Newspapers ran stories about the hermit of state prison, reputedly the oldest man on death row in America. When he finally died in 1948 at the age of eighty-eight the *New York Times* obituary said that he was regarded as a "kindly, gentle old fellow."

And now, Mrs. Helen Buchanan is the last person alive who sorrows over the death of the Reverend Prickitt.

One of the most dramatic political battles in New Jersey history began in November 1910, when the Boss went down to Princeton to pay a call on the Professor.

The Professor in question was Woodrow Wilson, an angular, aloof, Virginia-born scholar. The Boss was Jim Smith, a portly, backslapping, Irish politician from Newark.

Wilson had just won the governorship of the state of New Jersey. He owed much of this success to Smith, who ruled the state Democratic

The

Professor and

the Boss

party from his base in Essex County. It was Smith who, months before, had approached Wilson, then the president of Princeton, about running for the governor's chair. Although Wilson had never had anything to do with state politics, Boss Smith realized that the Professor's national reputation as an educator might appeal to the electorate.

After persuading Wilson to run, Smith twisted the arms of skeptical Democratic party professionals to place the newcomer at the head of the ticket.

On election day, Wilson won by the enormous margin of 49,056—the first Democrat in fifteen years to win the governorship. Democrats riding his coattails unexpectedly won a majority in the Assembly. Boss Smith and his neophyte candidate had done better than anyone could have imagined.

Now, a few days after the election, Smith had come to visit Wilson to claim his reward. The Boss believed he was entitled to become New Jersey's next United States senator, and he told Wilson that he intended to have the incoming Democratic-dominated legislature send him to Washington.

(Prior to the adoption of the 17th Amendment in 1913, senators were elected by the members of the legislature, and not by the voters. Since the Democrats were now a majority in the legislature, Smith was assured of being elected.)

But there was one problem. In a primary election held before the November election, Democratic voters had selected one Joseph Martine of Union County as the party's choice for U.S. senator. Martine was a political eccentric on the fringe of the Democratic party who for forty years had been running unsuccessfully for every sort of public office. Smith had not bothered to run in this nonbinding primary.

Smith's statement that he now wanted to push Martine aside put Wilson in a difficult position. The Professor was elected on his claim that he would never kowtow to the bosses. But he felt a sense of obligation to Smith, and he regarded Martine as an embarrassing buffoon. At the meeting in Princeton, Wilson tried without success to persuade Smith to step aside gracefully. The Boss politely refused.

In the aftermath of the meeting, word of Smith's senatorial ambition leaked out. Progressives around the state complained that it looked like politics as usual; that for all Wilson's campaign oratory, the old party bosses still controlled the statehouse. Wilson heard this talk, and he knew his credibility as governor and his future political prospects were at stake.

Behind the scenes, the governor-elect met quietly with influential Democrats to try to head off Smith's candidacy. He visited Smith in Newark to make one last plea for the Boss to step aside.

When Smith refused to budge, Wilson finally decided to bring the fight for the leadership of the party out into the open. As the world would discover in a few years, when the Professor made up his mind on an issue he became a fierce, uncompromising warrior. A month after the gubernatorial election, Wilson announced to the newspapers that he would support the election of Joseph Martine: "I know that the people of New Jersey do not desire Mr. James Smith, Jr., to be sent . . . to the Senate."

Wilson's lobbying became intense. He invited Democratic legislators to Princeton to cajole them into supporting Martine, and he traveled to Trenton and New York to meet with others. The Professor offered these politicians not the usual reward of patronage, but instead asked them to take an ethical stand to save the party from being repudiated by the voters.

The press and public opinion swung to Wilson's side. A well-known columnist for the *Jersey Journal*, George L. Record, declared that Wilson's declaration of war against Smith was "the most powerful, far reaching and epoch-making utterance ever made by a public man in New Jersey. It fairly makes one rub his eyes to make sure that it is true."

One of Wilson's close allies in the fight was a young Hudson County politican, Joseph P. Tumulty. It was Tumulty who helped persuade Wilson that he should go directly to the party rank and file through mass meetings.

On January 5, Wilson spoke at a rally, arranged by Tumulty, for Martine at St. Patrick's Hall in Jersey City. It was a magnificent speech, one that electrified the audience. Wilson linked Smith to the powerful business and railroad lobbies in the New Jersey, and to corrupt government in general. He described Smith and bossism as "a wart on the body politic," and he promised to be the man to cut off the wart.

Wilson knew that he, the Virginia-born son of a Presbyterian minister, was calling on his largely Catholic audience to go to battle against the Catholic Jim Smith. In the course of his speech in Jersey City he cannily praised Catholics on his side, including young Tumulty, whose conduct reflected "the teachings of the great church of which they are members." (Tumulty ultimately became Wilson's chief aide in Trenton and the White House.)

A week later Wilson addressed another rally in Newark, where he linked his battle against Smith to "the age-long struggle for human liberty." Once again the crowd rose to cheer him.

Smith fought back bitterly. He accused Wilson of deceit and ingratitude, and he worked through the old network of county Democratic political bosses to keep the legislators loyal to him.

The rest of the nation was watching the struggle in New Jersey. This was the height of the Progressive Era, when the mood in America had swung toward reform. Wilson's fight was linked to the popular campaign for the direct election of senators, and he was being increasingly mentioned as a leading candidate for Democratic presidential nomination.

Wilson was inaugurated as governor on January 17, 1911. A week later the new legislature met to select a senator. Smith supporters from Essex County traveled by train to Trenton to boost their candidate, bringing with them a brass band. A boisterous rally for Smith was held on the steps of the Trenton Opera House.

But when the final vote was taken, Martine had 47 votes and Smith 3. It was a crushing defeat for the Boss.

In a letter to a friend, Wilson described what happened to Smith.

The minute it was seen he was defeated, his friends began to desert him like rats leaving a sinking ship. He left Trenton (where his headquarters had at first been crowded) attended, I am told, only by his sons, and looking old and broken. He wept, they say, as he admitted himself utterly beaten.

Wilson emerged from the fight at the undisputed leader of the Democratic party in New Jersey and as one of the nation's leading progressives.

Smith later exacted a bit of revenge: In the next election he worked behind the scenes to make sure that Republicans retook the legislature. But it was too late; by that time Wilson was the favored candidate to win the Democratic presidential nomination in 1912.

When he finally made it to the White House, Wilson told a visitor from Trenton, "everything I know about politics I learned in New Jersey." Maybe, but it seems that the Professor could teach a lesson or two of his own.

Movie theaters used to be called nickelodeons because the price of admission was only five cents. So imagine the chagrin of Mrs. Minerva Miller when, on a September evening in 1911, she was charged a quarter to see a movie at "The Paterson Show," a theater at 136 Market Street.

Why was she being charged so much? she asked.

"We charge a quarter for colored people," the cashier replied.

As it turned out, Mrs. Miller was a New Jersey version of Rosa Parks,

Mrs. Minerva

Miller Goes

to the Movies

the determined black woman who refused to give up her seat to a white person on a bus in Montgomery, Alabama, in 1955, and so helped to spark the civil rights movement.

Like Rosa Parks, Minerva Miller decided she had enough. Mrs. Miller decided she was not going to pay her twenty-five cents; instead she was going to sue.

Mrs. Miller's legal action against The Paterson Show caused a stir. The front-page headline in the *Morning Call* expressed the town's astonishment: "Want White Folks' Rights: Colored Woman Sues Proprietors of Moving Picture House."

The black citizens of Paterson held a mass meeting to express support for Mrs. Miller, who was the daughter of a prominent minister.

The trial was held in November at the Passaic District Court. In the audience were black supporters of Mrs. Miller. The reporter for the *Passaic Daily News* who covered the case said it was "one of the most dramatic ever to be tried in the city."

Except for Mrs. Miller, all of the main actors in this drama were white: her attorney Robert F. Buckley; the attorney for the owners of The Paterson Show, James F. Carroll; and Judge Walter Carrington Cabell. This was not a jury trial; Judge Cabell would render the verdict.

The Virginia-born Cabell had recently been appointed to the bench by another native Virginian, Governor Woodrow Wilson, a life-long segregationist. Early in the trial, attorney Buckley seemed to sense that Judge Cabell was hostile to Mrs. Miller, and he tried to prod His Honor into making a decision quickly so the case could be appealed. The judge snapped back that he refused to be rushed. It was not an encouraging sign.

It got worse. Mrs. Miller's case was based on a New Jersey statute of 1884 which stated that all persons residing in the state were entitled to "full and equal enjoyment" of theaters, inns, and other public places. Similar federal civil rights laws had been invalidated by the United States Supreme Court, and as the trial began Judge Cabell expressed some doubt about whether the state law could be applied to this case.

Mrs. Miller was the first one to take the stand. She told how she had gone with friends to The Paterson Show, how she had been charged extra, how the cashier had told her it was the policy set by the boss, and how the cashier refused to let her in.

Her story was corroborated on the stand by a white acquaintance of Mrs. Miller's, one Thomas Praxton, who she encountered outside the theater that evening.

Defense attorney James F. Carroll tried a clever move. If he could prove the light-skinned Mrs. Miller was actually white, her case would collapse. The attorney asked Praxton how he knew his friend was colored.

"I can tell she's colored by looking at her," said Praxton.

"Well, how do you know she's a colored woman?" persisted Carroll.

"I am sure she's not a man," replied Praxton.

Carroll was not ready to give up. He recalled Mrs. Miller to the stand and asked her if she was black. "Yes, I am a negro and you can tell it by my flat nose and kinky hair," she said.

Carroll tried another move: he asked for the case to be dismissed because it should have been brought against the cashier and not the owners; Judge Cabell refused the motion.

Now came to the stand the cashier herself, a Mrs. Lena Moore. She said that she did not remember whether it was Mrs. Miller who she argued with that night, since to her all colored people looked alike. One imagines that Mrs. Moore smiled a little smile to herself at this witticism.

The ingenious defense lawyer, Carroll, now played one last card.

Under his questioning, the cashier, the manager of the theater, and a patron said that the theater was filled to capacity that evening. Mrs. Miller had thus been kept out not because she refused to pay twenty-five cents but because there were no more seats.

To refute this claim, Mrs. Miller's lawyer called to the stand a series of black witnesses who testified that on other evenings they too had been charged a quarter.

Now came the summations. Buckley's concluding speech, said the *Morning Call,* was "one of the most eloquent, convincing and stirring summings-up heard in the Passaic District Court." From a modern perspective, it is indeed stirring, and yet a bit patronizing.

> The members of the African race, born or naturalized in this country, are citizens of the states where they reside and of the United States. Both justice and the public interest concur in a policy which shall elevate them as individuals and relieve them from oppressive or degrading discrimination, and which shall encourage and cultivate a spirit which shall make them self-respecting, contented and loyal citizens, and give them a fair chance in the struggle of life, weighted as they are at best, with so many disadvantages.

Courts kept longer hours in those days, and it was close to 9 p.m. when at last came Judge Cabell's time to render a verdict. Cabell launched into a long-winded oration about the law. He talked of the New Jersey statute of 1884 and the U.S. Civil Rights Act of 1875, he referred to the United States Supreme Court, and to cases in New York, Michigan, Mississippi, and elsewhere. He discussed the merits of an argument made by the defense that under common law, a proprietor could exclude anyone he wished from his establishment.

No doubt Mrs. Miller, the theater owners, and their assorted friends and enemies in the courtroom fidgeted impatiently as they waited for the judge to get to the point. He finally did. He found the owners of the theater guilty, and fined them $500, the maximum the law would allow.

The cynical reader will doubtless note that this was a small victory; that the only thing decided was that a theater could not charge extra to people of a particular race; it would still have been perfectly legal for the theater to segregate people of that race once they were inside. No civil rights revolution flowered from Judge Cabell's decision.

Indeed, the issues raised by Mrs. Miller have still not been entirely settled in our own era. Only recently did the New Jersey Supreme Court ban male-only eating clubs at Princeton, and a vice president of the United States can still play golf at whites-only country clubs.

But no doubt Mrs. Minerva Miller, as she left the court that evening, felt the same sort of quiet pride in herself that Rosa Parks experienced decades later. If she was of a mathematical bent, perhaps she calculated that the fine of $500 could pay for 10,000 admissions at the rate of five cents each.

The Adamses, the Kennedys, the Rockefellers, the Fords: these are among the family dynasties that have provided America with generations of leaders in politics, industry, and philanthropy.

There is one family dynasty, however, that comes from the bottom of the pile. A family that produced not leaders, but prostitutes, thieves, alcoholics, and other species of low life. We are speaking about a New Jersey family whose baleful influence allegedly stretches from the Revo-

The Crime

of the

Kallikaks

lutionary era to the twentieth century: the notorious Kallikaks. Whether their story is true is another matter.

It was Henry H. Goddard (1866–1957), the head of the research department at the Vineland Training School, who brought the clan to public attention in his 1912 book *The Kallikak Family*. Goddard, a pioneer American psychologist, believed that just as the color of one's hair is genetically determined, so is one's intelligence. Moreover, he believed that there was a natural tendency for those of subnormal intelligence to fall into lives of crime and vice.

To prove his case, Goddard selected a "feebleminded" family he dubbed Kallikak (the name comes from the Greek words for "beauty" and "bad"). With the help of several assistants, Goddard traced the history of the family back over six generations to one Martin Kallikak, a Revolutionary War militiaman who, in a moment of weakness, had a fling with a feebleminded tavern maid.

From this liaison came an illegitimate son, a feebleminded wretch nicknamed Old Horror by his contemporaries. Old Horror, in turn, produced offspring, who in turn produced offspring, down through the generations. On this blighted family tree, calculated Goddard, were no fewer than thirty-six bastards, thirty-three prostitutes, and twenty-four alcoholics. Eight ran houses of ill repute.

One-hundred and forty-three of the descendants, he found, were feebleminded. Child molesters, horse-thieves, fornicators, illiterates, arsonists, paupers, and syphilitics abounded. In short, not the kind of folks you would want to lend your lawnmower to.

And what of Martin Kallikak? He rebounded from his one-night stand with the tavern maid and married a respectable Quaker woman. From that line came generations of good citizens, including doctors, lawyers, judges, educators, and landholders.

Goddard pictured the well-kept home of one of these good descendants, "a courteous, scholarly man of the old school," and his charming, attractive wife and children. In contrast, he described the disgusting shack of a descendant of the degenerate branch of the family tree: an imbecilic mother, covered by vermin, holds a "frightful-looking baby" in her arm and another child by the hand, while an older child, a "vulgar, repulsive creature of fifteen," looks on.

(Incidentally, it was long assumed that the Kallikaks inhabited the Pine Barrens. Recent research indicates that they actually lived in Hunterdon County.)

For Goddard, the saga of the Kallikaks proved beyond doubt that heredity was all-important. "No amount of education or good environment" could change their nature, any more than it could change their hair color.

Here Goddard made a distinction between two levels of mental deficiency. At the bottom were "idiots," creatures so mindless that they could not reproduce. "He is indeed loathsome; he is somewhat difficult to take care of; nevertheless, he lives his life and is done," with no offspring to plague society.

But at a higher level were "morons," of whom the Kallikaks were representative. They are self-sufficient enough to produce children, and so threaten to overwhelm society. "There are Kallikak families all about us," warned Goddard. "They are multiplying at twice the rate of the general population."

What to do? Goddard quickly dismissed the idea of euthanasia, what he called "the lethal chamber." "Humanity is steadily tending away from the possibility of that method, and there is no probability that it will ever be practiced." Sterilization had its advantages, but "debauchery and disease" would result from a group of people who could be "free to gratify their instincts without fear of consequences in the form of children."

Instead, he recommended that the feebleminded be segregated from society and placed in institutions like the Vineland Training School. While costly, this solution would eliminate the need for poorhouses and prisons, and by preventing the inhabitants from reproducing, the population of defectives in the United States would fall from 300,000 to 100,000 in a single generation.

To prove his point Goddard described the life of Deborah, a young, feebleminded Kallikak girl who had spent most of her life in the Vineland Training School. She had been taught to cook, to sew, and even to play "The Star-Spangled Banner" on the cornet. But if she were once let loose on society, Goddard warned, she would fall into a life of crime and immorality.

It is possible to poke very large holes in Goddard's account of the Kallikaks. A great part of the story was based on nothing but local gossip and the shaky recollections of old-timers, which casts doubt on the diagnosis of people long dead as either "feeble" or "normal." Only hearsay evidence supported the liaison between the militiaman and the tavern maid, an event that supposedly took place over 130 years before Goddard started his research.

Modern critics of the Kallikak story have also pointed out that mental deficiencies can arise from any number of reasons besides heredity, including a mother's illness during pregnancy, injury at birth, poor nutrition, and environmental disadvantages. These critics have also accused Goddard of deliberately retouching photographs of the Kallikaks to make them look moronic and evil.

It would be nice if we could dismiss the whole lurid story of the Kallikaks as just a wrong turn in the early history of psychology. But there were serious consequences to Goddard's work. His book was a best-seller, and was praised by psychologists.

At the invitation of the United States Public Health Service, Goddard went to Ellis Island in 1912. With the same methods used to diagnose the Kallikaks, he discovered the shocking fact that 83 percent of the Jewish immigrants, 80 percent of the Hungarians, 79 percent of the Italians, and 87 percent of the Russians were—you guessed it—feebleminded. Studies of foreign-born and native-born American soldiers in World War I (using tests that have since been found ridiculously biased) conducted by Goddard's fellow psychologists confirmed the low intelligence of immigrants from Russia, Italy, and Poland, not to mention American-born blacks.

This research went far to justify the Immigration Act of 1924, which established tight quotas to limit the entry of the inferior people of southern and eastern Europe, thus ending the American tradition of open immigration. And the whole line of reasoning about the genetic inferiority of families, ethnic groups, and races culminated a few years later when a group came to power in Germany for whom "the lethal chamber" was not so unthinkable. Not surprisingly, the German translation of Goddard's book was popular with the Nazis.

Of course, Goddard was no Nazi, and it would be unfair to place him in the same category. He was a social scientist, trying to inform the public of what he saw as a major social problem. Unfortunately, his story of the Kallikaks helped to give the veneer of science to racism, and encouraged Americans to regard the mentally handicapped as degenerate monsters. It is fair to say that this was the greatest crime of the Kallikaks.

What is perhaps the most unusual theatrical event in the colorful history of the New York theater occurred on June 13, 1913, when 1,000 New Jersey workers appeared on a stage at Madison Square Garden to present "The Pageant of the Paterson Strike."

The Paterson Pageant grew out of the bitter silk strike that began in January, when 25,000 workers walked out of the mills, dye-houses, and factories of Paterson.

The immediate cause was the owners' plan to introduce multiple

The Paterson

Pageant

looms into the manufacturing process, which would increase the workload of employees. But there were deeper causes: The silk industry in Paterson was notorious for long hours, pitifully low wages, and unhealthy working conditions. The majority of the workers were immigrants—Italians, Poles, Germans, and Jews—with a tradition of radicalism.

The municipal government of Paterson and its police force were firmly against the workers, and there were mass arrests. The press also opposed the strike. The *New York Times,* for example, published an editorial entitled "A Struggle Hopeless and Stupid," which accused the workers of standing in the way of progress.

Supporting the strike was a new, radical labor union—the Industrial Workers of the World. The IWW "Wobblies" rejected the conservative, mainstream unions, which were concerned with earning higher wages for skilled workers and which had in fact opposed the Paterson strike. The IWW instead sought to organize all workers, skilled and unskilled, to fight for a socialist society. Said the IWW constitution, "It is the historic mission of the working class to do away with capitalism."

The possibility of the strike as a turning point in the class struggle attracted the leading radicals of the day to Paterson. William "Big Bill" Haywood, the president of the IWW, shaped the strategy of the strike. The "rebel girl" Elizabeth Gurley Flynn and her lover, the Italian socialist

Carlo Tresca, helped organize the workers. Margaret Sanger, the birth-control pioneer, supervised the evacuation of the strikers' children. The young, Harvard-educated journalist John Reed went to Paterson to cover the strike for the radical magazine *The Masses* and became an active participant—he spent several days locked up in the Passaic County Jail.

A link between the strike and the New York literary scene was provided by the wealthy Mabel Smith Dodge. The Dodge apartment at 23 Fifth Avenue in Greenwich Village was a meeting place for avant-garde artists, writers, and editors. (The apartment downstairs was the home of ninety-three-year-old Dan Sickles, a Civil War general who lost his leg at the battle of Gettysburg. There is something intriguing about this building with the nineteenth century downstairs and the twentieth upstairs.)

Big Bill Haywood was a regular visitor to the Dodge salon. The tall, barrel-chested, stetson-wearing Haywood was a romantic figure to the Greenwich Village crowd. He came from a rough-and-tumble Western background, and claimed to have shot a deputy sheriff in Colorado. Women found him especially attractive, and he returned the favor.

According to Mabel Dodge's memoirs, the idea of the Pageant was born in a conversation between Haywood, Reed, and Dodge at the apartment of a New York City schoolteacher with whom Haywood was having an affair. They were considering the problems faced by the workers: strike funds were running out, morale was slipping, and the press was not reporting the struggle.

Dodge began to speculate about presenting the strike on stage in New York, using the actual workers from Paterson, as a way to regain momentum. Reed responded with instant enthusiasm: "We'll make a pageant of the strike! The first in the world!" (Shades of Mickey Rooney and Judy Garland shouting "Hey, kids, let's put on a show!")

Haywood quickly presented the idea to the strikers, who immediately voted their approval and started rehearsals under the direction of Reed. A group of Greenwich Village artists, designers, and theatrical people volunteered to assist the production. With money raised from New York workers and from Reed's friends, Madison Square Garden was rented for one evening. The show was put on a mere three weeks after Dodge's suggestion.

The Pageant turned out to be a stirring success, at least as a theatrical experience. On the day of the performance thousands of strikers marched up Fifth Avenue to the Garden singing labor songs; some actually walked all the way from Paterson. The strikers rigged up a gigantic light display on the tower of the Garden that spelled out the letters IWW, and festooned the interior with red banners.

Fifteen thousand strikers and their enthusiastic supporters filled the hall, while more than a thousand of their comrades acted out scenes of the strike on the stage. The set was imaginatively designed to look like the street outside the mills.

The show began with the sound of factory whistles as the workers trudged wearily down the aisles, onto the stage, and to the mills to start the work day. Within moments the noise of the machines stopped and the workers, now excited and exuberant, came running out of the mills yelling "Strike! Strike!"

The scenes that followed were drawn from the events of the strike, as pickets surrounded the mills, as the police waded into the crowd swinging clubs, and as arrested strikers were marched off to jail. The actors re-created the death of a Paterson resident, Valentino Modestino, who had been accidentally killed by a police bullet. The funeral of Modestino was reenacted with a band playing the dead march, strikers mourning at the coffin, and Tresca and Haywood eulogizing the martyr to the cause.

The next scene was a meeting of the strikers, with songs in Italian, German, and English, and with passionate speeches. This was followed by a moving depiction of the strikers' children being separated from their parents and sent away from Paterson to the homes of sympathetic IWW members. The production ended with a rousing strike rally, at which the workers pledged to fight on to victory.

It was a stirring evening: a thousand actors marching up and down the block-long stage and into the aisles; bands playing "The Internationale" and "The Marseillaise"; speeches by Haywood, Flynn, Tresca, and company; a wildly supportive audience booing the police and cheering the strikers.

In the long term, the Pageant had important consequences. Scholars like Leslie Fishbein and Martin Green have traced the enormous influence of the Pageant on labor docudramas and on avant-garde theater. And the Pageant did get the press to write about the strike.

But the immediate aftermath of the Pageant was not happy. An accounting disclosed that the Pageant was roughly $2,000 in the red (no pun). Enemies of the IWW spread the rumor (almost certainly false) that someone had dipped into the till.

Big Bill Haywood, whose health was breaking down, departed the scene for a long vacation in New England with one girlfriend and then for Europe with another. John Reed and Mabel Dodge, who had developed an attraction for each other, sailed off to her villa in Italy.

Whatever enthusiasm the Pageant temporarily put back into the strike could not be sustained. The Paterson mill owners began to negotiate on a shop-by-shop basis, and some of the skilled workers agreed on a settlement. With their unity broken, other workers went back to their jobs, and the strike was over by the end of July. The IWW suffered a blow to its prestige from which it never recovered.

Some of the survivors were bitter. Elizabeth Gurley Flynn fumed that the Pageant had actually harmed the strike by raising false hopes, by taking strikers away from Paterson at a critical moment, and by creating jealousy among those not chosen to perform on stage.

It is easy to be cynical; to see the whole episode as the posturing of the intelligentsia at the expense of the workers. There is something of this in the image of John Reed leading the workers in strike songs set to Harvard football cheers. And the Greenwich Village crowd's faith in revolutionary liberation seems naive. Three-quarters of a century after the Russian Revolution, we know that the upheaval created a regime more oppressive than anything the old capitalist mill owners of Paterson could have imagined. (Reed, Haywood, and Flynn, incidentally, all died in the Soviet Union.)

But let us not feel too superior. The Greenwich Village radicals who transformed a New Jersey strike into theater may have been romantic innocents, but at least they acted on their convictions, and took risks to build what they hoped would be a better, more humane society.

These days we are locked in a national debate about whether women should have the right to obtain abortions. Early in the century, the people of New Jersey were arguing a different question: Should women have the right to vote? The debate was every bit as tangled, bitter, and divisive.

On October 19, 1915, the men of New Jersey voted in a referendum on a proposed amendment to the state constitution which would give women the ballot. Passage of the amendment would make New Jersey

Should

Women Vote?

the first eastern, industrial state to permit women's suffrage, so the contest was being watched around the nation.

In the months before the referendum, suffragists campaigned around the state through such organizations as the New Jersey Woman Suffrage Association, the Equal Franchise Society, the Women's Political Union, and the Men's League for Woman Suffrage.

They set up booths at county fairs, they fastened banners to their autos, they marched through the streets, they held mass rallies, and they distributed pamphlets on streetcorners. Through their efforts, prominent New Jersey men like the great inventor Thomas A. Edison and the president of Princeton University, John G. Hibben, publicly supported the amendment. Suffragists persuaded the most prominent New Jerseyan of the day, President Woodrow Wilson, to come out for their cause.

The suffragists used two arguments. First, they said that because women constituted half of the population, simple justice demanded that they have the right to vote. How unfair it was that women were classed with criminals and mental defectives in being denied the ballot.

Second, they predicted that giving women the vote would usher in a better world. The more extreme advocates claimed that women's votes would abolish war, alcoholism, and political corruption. The *Newark Evening News* published a poem from one such suffragist, addressed to men:

> We want our prisons to reform;
>   Our race tracks to suppress;
> The wrongs our sick and helpless poor
>   Now suffer to redress;
> Our cities' politics to cleanse
>   And bid corruption cease;
> Our children in the schools to guard
>   From vice and from disease.
> We want to banish the saloon,
>   And close the haunts of vice,
> That lure our boys from virtue's path,
>   Our girls to sin entice.
> We want to aid you to repeal
>   Laws so pernicious now.
> 'Tis not so much we wish to vote—
>   We want to show you how.

But the men of New Jersey were not so ready to be shown how to vote by the state's women. There was powerful opposition from what was then (and still is) the mightiest force in state politics, the county Democratic and Republican party bosses. Other powerful politicians opposed the amendment, including Governor James Fielder (a Democrat) and former Governor Edward C. Stokes (a Republican). The Democratic and Republican state platforms in 1915 were thunderously silent on the issue of women's voting.

Even Woodrow Wilson hedged his endorsement. He was careful to say that although he was personally in favor of the amendment, he was speaking "not as the leader of my party in the nation, but only upon my private conviction as a citizen of New Jersey."

The intellectual argument against suffrage was presented by William F. Magie, the dean of Princeton College and president of the Men's Anti-Suffrage League of New Jersey. Magie, billed as "a leading student of economics and government," intoned that the building block of civilization was the family. The man was the natural head of the family, and represented it with his vote. The woman's job was to maintain the home. "If we allow women to vote," said the dean, "we consent to the most profound political revolution that any free country has ever experienced. We are changing the basis of representation from the family to the individual." Women's suffrage (an offshoot of the sinister doctrine of feminism, according to Magie) would thus undermine civilization.

On a more practical level, one anti-suffragist wrote a letter to the editor arguing that adding women to the voting rolls would double the expense of elections—to which a pro-suffragist sarcastically replied that there should be an amendment to the constitution "providing for an electorate of one single vote" which would reduce the cost of elections to the lowest possible level.

The suffragists were harmed by their link to the Prohibition crusade. The New Jersey Liquor Dealers Protective Association, at its annual convention in Atlantic City, adopted a resolution condemning women's suffrage, and members gave money to the opposition.

The liquor dealers hit on an ingenious way to scare voters away from women's suffrage. They proposed a bill requiring the state to compensate saloonkeepers in the event Prohibition was adopted. Thus, if women were allowed to vote and if they brought about Prohibition, "it will cost the taxpayers of the state $4,000,000, at the lowest calculation, to make Jersey dry, apart from the enormous loss in license revenue."

Labor unions were angered by the prospect of closed saloons and brewery workers thrown out of their jobs. Anti-suffrage speakers also appealed to working men by pointing out that in Colorado, where women could vote, mineworkers' unions were being violently persecuted. The influential Essex County Trades Council refused to endorse the suffrage amendment, and the state Federation of Labor came out against it.

There was also bad blood between suffrage groups and immigrants. Hostile suffragists complained that a male immigrant fresh off the boat with no knowledge of English could cast a ballot, while a native-born woman could not. Hudson County politicians alleged that women reformers were refusing to endorse Jews or Catholics for the Assembly. The New Jersey Federation of German Catholic Societies passed a resolution against suffrage, and several Catholic bishops and a prominent Newark rabbi publicly opposed the movement.

The suffragists began to realize that the amendment was in trouble. When a group of them invaded the Vailsburgh Velodrome, a bicycle racing track in Newark, to speak to the audience of working men, they were yelled down and pelted with crumpled-up programs and pennies thrown from the stands.

Suffragists tried to be conciliatory. A pamphlet aimed at streetcar workers said: "Conductors! Motormen! Forget your grouch at us. Give us the vote and we will try never to fall off the car backward, never to climb on in front while the car is in motion, never to say, 'Johnny is only three' when he is ten. Vote for the woman suffrage amendment on October 19 and watch us learn."

And now an unpleasant fact: Women themselves formed a powerful force against the suffrage amendment. The prominent Mrs. Garret A.

Hobart of Paterson, widow of a vice president of the United States, served as an officer of the New Jersey Association Opposed to Woman's Suffrage, and warned of the "grave menace to our state" posed by the amendment. The president of the NJAOWS, Mrs. E. Yarde Breese, opined "we women should strive by every means in our power to uphold the men of our country who have so well protected our best interests in state and nation, and not try to wrest from them their well-earned prerogative."

In Morristown, a pro-suffrage banner stretched across Washington Street was reportedly cut down at the request of an outraged woman, Mrs. Frederick R. Babbitt.

A woman who signed herself "X.X." wrote a letter to the *Newark Evening News* that seems to have expressed the anxieties of many of her sisters: "Women, generally speaking, are not prepared for the women's suffrage amendment, neither do they want the vote. Only ten percent of the women of this glorious state are dissatisfied with what the men of our state and country have been doing for us in the past. That ten percent are striving to plunge ninety percent of contented women into the political arena regardless of their efficiency, their preparedness or their desire." X.X. raised the specter of women rubbing shoulders with grubby politicians, and spoke of her own fear of taking on the responsibility of voting. "A Woman Lover of Her Country" wrote that "a good woman and wife will vote as her husband wishes, so why double the vote?"

Mrs. John R. Emery, president of the Morristown branch of the NJAOWS, pointed out that a woman who voted would have to sit on a jury, where she would be forced to deal with cases "of a character as to make it impossible for a mixed jury to discuss them at length, and not only would the woman suffer unspeakably, but the ends of justice would be interfered with."

So divisive was the issue among women that the state Federation of Woman's Clubs refused to bring up the suffrage question at their annual convention.

When election day came, the suffrage amendment was soundly defeated 184,390 to 133,282—a losing margin of 51,108 votes. The measure failed in every county except Ocean. The loss in New Jersey contributed to the defeat of similar referendums the same year in New York, Pennsylvania, and Massachusetts.

Less than a year and a half later, America entered the World War. Women were working in the factories and in hospitals, and the nation was talking about extending democracy around the world. The old anti-suffrage arguments began to sound a bit silly. The New Jersey legislature approved the 19th Amendment in February 1920, the twenty-ninth state to do so, and at last women were allowed to vote in the Garden State.

So in fact, the men of New Jersey never actually did directly vote to give women the ballot. And there may even be one or two churlish males around who are sorry they got it.

A t 2:08 a.m. on the morning of July 30, 1916, New York harbor exploded. This is not a figure of speech; it was not an explosion of fear or an explosion of cheers. What took place was a colossal, ear-splitting, ground-shaking, glass-breaking explosion.

The blast occurred at Black Tom, a depot jutting out from Jersey City into the Hudson River opposite Manhattan. Said the *New York Times*: "A million people, maybe five millions, were awakened by the explosion that shook the houses along the marshy New Jersey shores, rattled the

The Secret War

skyscrapers on the rock foundation of Manhattan, threw people from their beds miles away and sent terror broadcast."

The noise of the explosion was heard as far away as Maryland and Connecticut. Fire alarms and burglar alarms went off; phone lines between New York and New Jersey were severed. On both sides of the Hudson, people in their pajamas rushed out of apartment buildings. Thousands milled around watching the sky turn red from flames as more explosions thundered from the harbor.

In Jersey City, residents swarmed into churches. On Ellis Island, terrified immigrants were evacuated by ferry to the Battery. Shrapnel from the explosion pierced the Statue of Liberty. The Black Tom terminal was completely destroyed.

Property damage was estimated at $20 million. It is not certain how many died, but the fatalities included two workers at Black Tom, as well as a ten-week-old New Jersey infant who was thrown from his crib.

The most common effect of the blast was the smashing of thousands of windows in New Jersey and New York. The joke made the rounds in Jersey City that the broken windows of the local saloons constituted a violation of the Sunday closing law.

Investigators differed over what had caused the blast—perhaps it was spontaneous combustion, or a fire started by workmen to keep away mosquitoes. But whatever the source of the spark, it turned into an explosion because Black Tom was almost literally a powder keg. It consisted of barges and freight cars filled with ammunition awaiting shipment to the armies of Britain and its allies on the Western Front.

Less than six months later the nervous residents of New York City and northern New Jersey experienced another catastrophe, which the *Times* described as "a spectacle more magnificent than the munitions fire at Black Tom Island." At 4:30 p.m. on January 11, 1917, a factory in Kingsland, Bergen County, exploded. The factory, owned by a Canadian company, had been manufacturing artillery shells for the Russian army.

For four hours artillery shells roared aloft and came cascading down. Some landed as far away as Long Island. The hardest hit area was a nearby Italian immigrant shantytown, known as Guinea Hill in the crude language of the day, where houses were destroyed by shells. Roads throughout the region were jammed when people fleeing from the explosion collided with others heading toward it to try to find their families. A man who tried to escape the area by leaping onto a moving train was killed.

The *Newark Evening News* described the scene: "Mothers lost their children in the fear-maddened rush; little chaps and tiny little girls, shrieking with fright, and alone, struggled to keep up in the race for safety." At a local insane asylum, the staff hastily threw together a party with ice cream and candy for the inmates to reassure them that the world was not coming to an end.

Once again, investigators searched for an answer. Speculation ranged from careless workers to a spark from a defective light bulb. "No Hint of a Plot" said the *New York Times* headline next day.

But in fact, there was a plot. What really happened has been unearthed by Jules Witcover in his 1989 book *Sabotage at Black Tom*. It is an amazing story.

To understand Black Tom, imagine you are Count Johan von Bernstorff, the aristocratic German ambassador to the United States at the start of the First World War. You have a ticklish problem. The hated British navy has blockaded Germany. The Allies can thus buy guns and supplies from neutral America, but you cannot. Germany can stop this trade by using submarines to destroy Atlantic shipping, but every time an American life is lost at sea, the United States is pushed closer to joining the Allies.

So, count, how do you prevent arms from getting to the Allies while still keeping America from declaring war on Germany?

The answer that occurred to von Bernstorff and his superiors in Berlin was sabotage. Early in the war, von Bernstorff was given $150 million to establish a sabotage network in America. And he organized a pretty efficient one, consisting of an assortment of embassy staff members, German nationals, British-hating Irish, and other malcontents, drifters, and soldiers of fortune. Today we would call them terrorists.

The headquarters of the ring was a brownstone at 123 West 15th Street in Manhattan. Besides being a spy nest and rendezvous for German sympathizers on the East Coast, it was a house of prostitution, presided over by a cheery former opera singer.

At secret locations near the harbor, the saboteurs constructed clever bombs consisting of chemicals that could be set to burst into flames at a specified time. (They were not always reliable, however; one went off in a saboteur's pants.) These gizmos were placed on ships, on the docks, in factories, on trains—whereever war materiel was being made or shipped to the Allies. The gang also encouraged dockyard strikes and injected horses being shipped overseas with crippling diseases.

New Jersey was a strategic spot, and many of the saboteurs' activities were aimed at the state. Indeed, the first act of sabotage was an explosion at the Roebling wire and cable plant in Trenton on January 1, 1915. Bombs were planted at factories at Wallington, Carneys Point, and Pompton Lakes; on a munitions train in Metuchen; and in a railroad grain elevator in Weehawken.

What probably happened at Black Tom, according to Witcover, was that von Bernstorff's agents sneaked into the depot after dark where they started fires and set incendiary devices. Security was tighter at Kingsland, and there it was necessary to infiltrate two men as workers into the plant, where they surreptitiously set fires.

There was some speculation in America that pro-German saboteurs were at work, and in fact two German embassy officials were expelled. But the vast scope of von Bernstorff's sabotage network remained undetected. Indeed, when the United States finally entered the war in April 1917, it was over international issues like submarine warfare and German intrigue in Mexico, not domestic sabotage.

After the war, the owners of Black Tom and Kingsland sued Germany for damages before a German-American commission established to decide claims arising out of the conflict. For years the Germans denied responsibility, throwing the old "spontaneous combustion" findings back at the Americans. Finally, in 1940, as another war had begun in Europe, the commission concluded that Germany had been guilty of sabotage.

So ends the story of Black Tom. You might say that this was the first time since the American Revolution that our state was under attack, and we didn't even know it was happening. The site of Black Tom is today Liberty State Park, which is visited by thousands of tourists on their way to Ellis Island and the Statue of Liberty. How many realize that they are visiting the battlefield of a secret war?

The armistice ending World War I was signed at five o'clock on the morning of November 11, 1918, and took effect at 11 a.m.

For generations, the "11th hour of the 11th day of the 11th month" has been regarded as a solemn moment, for it marked the end of a war that had cost the lives of 13 million soldiers and 5 million civilians. November 11 is a national day of remembrance in Canada, the United States, Britain, Belgium, and France.

But the armistice marked only the cessation of fighting. The Treaty of

The War to End

War Ended

in Somerset County

Versailles, which formally established the peace, was not signed until June 28, 1919. And in the case of the United States, formal peace did not come for another two years: July 2, 1921.

The place the war ended was in rural Somerset County.

Although the other Allies accepted the Treaty of Versailles, a vicious partisan battle over its adoption erupted in the United States.

On one side was President Woodrow Wilson, who had played a major role in drafting the treaty and who refused to allow its provision for a League of Nations to be watered down. On the other side was a small group of Republican United States senators, the Irreconcilibles, who saw the League as an infringement on American autonomy.

In one of the great and tragic failures of common sense, efforts to reach a compromise were unsuccessful, and the treaty was defeated in the Senate in November 1919. Technically, the United States remained at war with Germany.

In the presidential election the following year, the Democratic candidate, James M. Cox, supported the treaty. The Republican, Warren G. Harding, neatly fudged the issue.

The Republicans won by a sweeping majority, and President Harding, in one of his first acts, called on Congress to adopt a resolution ending the war. By the end of June, the Senate and House had hammered out a joint resolution "terminating the state of war between the imperial German Government and the United States of America and between the imperial and royal Austro-Hungarian Government and the United States of America."

The resolution contained some of the provisions of the Treaty of Versailles, but not membership in the League of Nations.

As the debate in Congress was ending, President Harding left to spend a relaxing Fourth of July weekend at the picturesque country home of his friend Senator Joseph S. Frelinghuysen in Raritan Borough.

The president was accompanied by his wife and a group of cronies from the Senate and the House. The presidential party arrived on Friday evening, July 1, after taking the Baltimore & Ohio Railroad from Washington to Bound Brook.

The following day, a White House courier arrived with the resolution that had just been adopted by Congress, and reporters described the ensuing events with the sort of colorful journalistic detail that characterized newspaper reporting in those days.

President Harding, who had been playing golf at the Somerset Hills Country Club, returned to the Frelinghuysen home in an automobile. He was wearing "a Palm Beach suit, white shoes, white socks with black clocks, a white shirt buttoned by removable gold studs and a green and red bow tie."

He met the White House courier on the front porch, where he read through the documents. The president then entered through the front door and sat at a table.

About thirty people crowded into the room, including reporters, photographers, Secret Service agents, Washington dignitaries, the Frelinghuysen children, the acting governor of New Jersey, butlers, maids, chauffeurs, and gardeners.

A reporter asked Senator Frelinghuysen what he called the room.

"Oh, I don't know," he said, "library, living room, parlor—anything you please."

A group of Somerset County officials, including Sheriff Bogart Conkling, had brought along a feathery quill pen for the president to use, but he instead took a "new steel pen in an ordinary wooden holder" from Senator Frelinghuysen.

In silence, except for the clicking of cameras, the president signed the resolution. "That's all," he said, in what must be one of the most unmemorable lines ever uttered in a historic moment.

At that point, a large drop of ink fell from the pen to the page, obscuring part of Mr. Harding's signature. An aide applied a blotter, and the document was placed in a leather pouch to be returned to Washington.

After a few moments of conversation, the president and his party departed for some more golf, this time at the Raritan Valley Country Club.

On any normal day, the president's action would have dominated the news. But this day it was dwarfed by the Dempsey-Carpentier prizefight that was going on fifty miles away in Jersey City. News about the boxing match filled the newspapers; the signing ceremony was pushed to a corner.

The *New York Times* observed nevertheless that "the modest Frelinghuysen ancestral home will have a place in history long after an international heavyweight championship is forgot."

In fact, the Dempsey-Carpentier fight lives on in public memory; the signing of the resolution is all but forgotten. President Harding died two years later, and the chief debate among historians is whether he was the second- or third-worst president in U.S. history.

The "war to end all wars" wasn't. It is sometimes argued that the World War that began two decades later might have been averted if the United States had joined the League of Nations.

The Frelinghuysen home never did achieve a place in history. It was torn down some time later, and what is left are two stone pillars covered by shrubbery alongside the Route 28 traffic circle, not far from Toys R Us.

10   *The War to End War Ended in Somerset County.* After the end of the First World War, the United States failed to ratify the Treaty of Versailles. The official end of American involvement in the war came in July 1921, when President Warren G. Harding signed a joint congressional resolution. Harding was on a golfing vacation in New Jersey when the resolution was sent to him from Washington. He was driven from the links to the home of Senator Joseph Frelinghuysen, where he signed the document. (New Jersey Historical Society, Newark)

What was the greatest day in the history of the metropolis of Jersey City? Without question it was July 2, 1921, when 90,000 fight fans came to see the American Jack Dempsey battle the Frenchman Georges Carpentier for the heavyweight championship of the world.

Americans are used to celebrities and celebrity events. Elvis Presley, Madonna, Lady Di, Cher, Mike Tyson: we've seen them up close and personal on trashy television shows and in supermarket celebrity maga-

Jersey City

Tastes Glory

zines. We have watched alimony battles, fights of the century, royal weddings, and the like, and we are probably a bit bored by it all.

But back in 1921, this sort of celebrity worship was still quite new. The Dempsey-Carpentier fight, one of the first masterpieces of hype and promotion, stirred up the nation as it had never been stirred before.

The artist who created this masterpiece was the fight promoter Tex Rickard, an ex-cowboy, ex-bartender, and ex-gold prospector. In November 1920, Rickard signed the two fighters to a match, promising $300,000 to Dempsey and $200,000 to Carpentier, plus equal shares of the film revenue to both men. This was a breathtakingly large purse: newspapers of the time noted in astonishment that Dempsey would make more for one fight than the president made in his entire term.

Rickard realized that to make the fight appeal to an audience beyond the usual crowd of sweaty boxing fans, he had to create an air of glamour and excitement. He promoted the event not as a mere boxing match, but as the clash of two personalities, one evil and one good. In this respect, the contest was the granddaddy of today's TV wrestling industry.

In the words of boxing historian Randy Roberts, the publicity ground out in advance of the fight depicted Carpentier as a "rosy-cheeked, clear-complexioned Lancelot to cheer," and Dempsey as "a thick-bearded, scowling Simon Legree to boo and jeer."

Dempsey fit the part of the scowling villain. The Manassa Mauler had begun his career as a barroom brawler, traveling as a hobo from town to town in the West to beat any man in the house. He fought his way into professional boxing, where he became heavyweight champion in 1919 by knocking out "the Great White Hope," Jess Willard. (It should not be assumed that this made Dempsey some sort of racial liberal; like most boxers of his day, he refused to enter the ring against a black opponent.)

Along the way, Dempsey had married a dance hall entertainer from Salt Lake City, Maxine Cates. After their marriage broke up and he became a celebrity, Maxine publicly charged him with avoiding military service during World War I. Although a San Francisco jury acquitted Dempsey of the charge in 1920, the taint of draft dodger continued to haunt him. One widely circulated photo showed him posing as a riveter in a shipyard during the war—while wearing shiny patent-leather dress shoes under his overalls. Maxine, who admitted she had worked as a prostitute, also accused Dempsey of beating her while they were married.

To go with his unsavory reputation of draft dodger and wife beater, Dempsey had the bashed-in, scarred face of a bruiser.

The hero, Georges Carpentier, was a lithe, suave, and handsome Frenchman. As a pilot in his country's air corps during the First World War, he had been wounded in combat and had received the Croix de Guerre.

After the war, he had stunned Europe by effortlessly knocking out the heavyweight champion of Britain, Joe Beckett, in a bout in London attended by high society and royalty. Carpentier had a great following among intellectuals in Europe and the United States who saw him as the embodiment of gallantry and grace.

The governor of New York considered prizefights to be immoral, and Rickard's request to hold the bout in New York City was turned down. The governor of New Jersey, Edward I. Edwards, invited Rickard to his state, and the promoter selected a marshy field known as Boyle's 30 Acres on the outskirts of Jersey City. The match was scheduled for July 2.

A pinewood arena was hastily erected. It was first planned for 50,000, but when it became clear that the match was going to be well attended, it was enlarged to a capacity of 91,613. Prices went from $5 for seats on the periphery to $50 for ringside.

The city, under Mayor Frank Hague, a boxing enthusiast, was absolutely enraptured at being the center of national—nay world—attention. For once, it would not live in the shadow of New York City.

The city's main newspaper, the *Jersey Journal,* threw aside all pretense at journalistic objectivity to crow about what was happening. A typical front- page story began:

> Jersey City is today in the world's limelight and beginning to trot out some jazz. From all points of the compass world's celebrities are traveling to this city—by rail, by automobile, by steamship and by yacht. When Referee Harry Ertle calls time on July 2 afternoon, Jersey City will witness the greatest gathering of notables of modern times. Bankers and railroad builders, diplomats and doctors, artists and authors and actors, clergymen and captains-of-industry, they'll all be there to see whether Dempsey or Carp will put it over.

Perlmutters, a women's apparel shop on Monticello Avenue, echoed this enthusiasm in an advertisement: "The whole world today is thinking about and talking about the big event that next Saturday is to happen in Jersey City. . . . If this don't give you a thrill, go and see your physician to change your white corpuscles for red ones."

A moment of melodrama was provided by a band of reformers, the Clergyman's Community Club of Jersey City, which opposed the fight and tried to get it banned. The ministers argued that the two fighters were planning to knock each other out, thus conspiring to change the event from an innocent boxing match to an illegal prizefight. City residents railed at these "ridiculous fanatics," and rejoiced when the Hudson County Grand Jury turned the reformers down flat.

On the night before the fight, the city was filled with excitement. Said the *Journal*: "Mothers down in Wayne Street and up in Hudson City were confronted with the unique problem of how to get their boys home before midnight. Most of the lads were staging a miniature Dempsey-Carpentier boxing contest for the championship of the back alley nearest home."

On the glorious, never-to-be-forgotten day of the fight, two thousand city police and firemen were in and around the arena to keep order. Six hundred ushers squinted at tickets to prevent counterfeits. Special trains were run from Manhattan to bring in fight fans.

It turned out to be everything Rickard had hoped. It was the largest crowd ever to witness a sporting event, the first ever to be broadcast on radio, and the first to gross over a million dollars ($1,789,238, to be precise). At ringside were celebrities like John D. Rockefeller, Jr., Al Jolson, Tom Mix, and Henry Ford. Aspiring champions pounded each other in preliminary bouts, while planes swooped overhead.

An unusually large number of women, about two thousand, attended. The press treated them like representatives from some alien tribe, which, in the male world of boxing, they were. One New York City newspaper said, "Practically all the women went with male escorts, although there were several groups of twenty or thirty each with only a man or two among them."

At three o'clock, the champion Dempsey and the contender Carpentier climbed into the ring. The crowd could see that the American was the larger and more powerful of the two. Just before the bell rang to start the fight, Mayor Hague and Governor Edwards shook hands with the two opponents.

When it was all over the news of the fight made headlines around the world. The *Jersey Journal* boasted that it had scooped its rivals by getting an extra on the street sixteen minutes after the end of the match. The editorial page gloated: "Today, Jersey City shows that it is 'there.' Today, Jersey City tastes international glory."

Who won, by the way? Dempsey clobbered Carpentier eleven minutes into the fight. What did you expect?

There are still a few deluded souls in New Jersey who call them-selves Klansmen. Every once in a while a handful of them show up in white bedsheets for a rally, where they are usually outnum-bered by police and protesters.

It was not always so. In the 1920s, when the Ku Klux Klan was at the height of its power in the United States, the Jersey Klan had an estimated sixty thousand members, making it the tenth largest in the nation. There were crosses burned in places like Hoboken, Metuchen, Jersey City, Perth

The Klan

Amboy, and the Watchung Mountains. On Independence Day 1922, a cross burned on a mountain overlooking Paterson was visible to the entire city. On Labor Day in 1924, an estimated one thousand cars filled with Klansmen and Klanswomen drove through Trenton. That evening, 25,000 Klan supporters joined together for a rally in the park at which a fifty-foot cross was burned, 500 new members were signed up, 2 mar-riages performed, and 50 people baptized.

The modern Ku Klux Klan was founded on a mountaintop in Georgia on Thanksgiving eve, 1915. The new Klan was a revival of the original hooded order, which had appeared briefly in the South right after the Civil War.

The new Klan was the brainchild of William J. Simmons, whose previ-ous line of work had been selling memberships in fraternal organizations like the Masons. It is thought that he was inspired by the movie *Birth of a Nation.*

Simmons established the organization as sort of a franchise: each recruit's $10 initiation fee was sliced up among the local recruiter (the Kleagle), the state leader (the Grand Dragon), the regional sales manager (the Grand Goblin), and the national office (headed by the Imperial Wiz-ard Simmonds) in Atlanta.

The order was successful, spreading over the nation in a few years. The Klan first appeared in New Jersey in 1921 with the establishment of the Leif Ericsson chapter in Paterson. Before long the Klan could be found in all parts of the state; in cities like Newark, Trenton, Camden, in suburban towns like Montclair and Bloomfield, and in rural counties like

11   *The Klan.* In the 1920s, New Jersey had an estimated sixty thousand members of the Ku Klux Klan, the tenth largest Klan membership in the nation. This photo shows a Klan induction ceremony in New Brunswick. (New Jersey Historical Society, Newark)

Somerset. The order was particularly strong in the industrial northern part of the state and in the Monmouth County shore resorts like Long Branch, Asbury Park, and Ocean Grove.

The members of the Klan in New Jersey, as in the rest of the nation, were native-born, white Anglo-Saxon Protestants. Although the order drew members from all of the Protestant denominations in New Jersey, it found a particularly warm welcome in the Methodist Church and in the Pillar of Fire sect in Zarephath. Jersey Klansmen also tended to vote Republican, especially after the Democrats ran a Catholic, Al Smith, for president.

The historical evidence suggests that most Klansmen were poorly educated men drawn from the working classes: the factory worker, the linesman, the mailman, the iceman. But there was an occasional professional, like the state's Grand Dragon, attorney Arthur Bell of Bloomfield.

What were tens of thousands of New Jerseyans so afraid of that they took the Klan oath and donned robes and hoods? If you were a native-born white Protestant in New Jersey in the 1920s, you would have a lot to worry you. Immigration, urbanization, and industrialization were changing the world you had grown up in. In those years Protestants were becoming a minority of the state's inhabitants, and one out of every five whites was foreign-born.

But the problem was more than demographics. The 1920s were a disturbing time: a decade when your daughter wore short skirts and lipstick, danced to jazz music, drank bootleg gin in speakeasies, and necked at night in a Model T with some boy whose parents you didn't know.

Your anxiety focused on the Catholics: you saw them as aliens who owed allegiance to the pope and who were dominating the growing cities. You also saw the Jews as a threat. After all, you were told that they controlled the banks and were bringing Russian Bolshevism to America. "Do you know that the white slave traffic of America is controlled by Jews to which 100,000 girls each year enter houses of prostitution to take the places of those that have died?" asked an ungrammatical Klan leader at a Somerset County rally.

And then there were the Negroes. Although they made up only 5 percent of the New Jersey population in the 1920s, you believed the stories of their lust for white women. Grand Dragon Bell warned that there were 87,000 cases of white girls living with non-whites.

The Klan devoted its efforts to restoring an imagined golden age of white Protestant morality. Through the efforts of the KKK and other groups, the Bloomfield Board of Education pulled a set of the *Catholic Encyclopedia* out of the high school. The Klan was strong enough along the Monmouth County shore that for a time Catholics and Jews stayed away from the resort towns.

The Jersey Klan's specialty was making threats, mostly to fellow white men who were suspected of some sort of hanky-panky. An Atlantic City hotelkeeper received a letter that said "Please stop bootlegging and run a decent place. First and last notice. K.K.K." A Hackensack man who was suspected of having an affair with a married woman was told to leave town.

Klan leaflets in Cape May warned: "Wife beaters and wrong-doers watch your step." In Asbury Park, the Klan charged that the mayor had attended an orgy. ("The charge that a nude woman sat in my lap is a damnable lie," retorted the mayor.) In Plainfield, the Klan took out an advertisement to warn against showing movies on Sunday. Blacks, too, received threats, including an Atlantic City attorney who received a warning letter for opposing the segregation of the city's public schools.

The Klan invaded a black church in Belmar to lecture the congregation on white supremacy.

In its public relations, the Klan in New Jersey tried to portray itself as a charitable and patriotic organization, which gave money to churches, crippled children, and orphans, and which paraded on national holidays. The Klan even tried to softpedal its racism. In March 1923, forty robed Klansmen suddenly appeared at a Sunday evening service of a white Methodist church in Newark. Their leader read a speech from the pulpit defending the Klan: "This is a white man's organization for exalting the Caucasian race and teaching the doctrine of white supremacy. This does not mean, as some would have you believe, that we are enemies of the colored and mongrel races, but does mean that we are organized to maintain the solidarity of the white race."

Elsewhere in the nation, the Klan was linked to lynching, kidnapping, and murder. Klan violence was a frequent event in such states as Georgia, Alabama, Texas, Florida, Louisiana, and California. But the Garden State was different. One modern student of the Jersey Klan has been unable to find any evidence of Klan violence in the state. Although an occasional brawl was attributed to the order, it usually turned out to have been a family squabble. In one case, two masked men thought to be Klansmen attacked a man said to be a wife beater. But the attackers were the son and son-in-law of the wife.

Indeed, New Jersey was one of the few states where there was more violence committed against the Klan than by it. In May 1923, 1,000 people attacked a Klan rally in Bound Brook. Three months later, a mob of 6,000 angry Perth Amboy residents attacked 250 Klansmen attending a meeting at the Odd Fellows Hall. The state police had to be called to protect the terrified Klansmen. In the midst of the riot Policeman Lester Seaman found a crowd of men trying to throw an unconscious Klansman down a manhole into a sewer. "My God," shouted Seaman, "don't do that! That's murder." The policeman had to use his nightstick to rescue the defender of white Protestantism.

In other states, the Klan held awesome political power, and was able to control local and state elections. In New Jersey, the Klan was denounced by mayors, governors, police chiefs, and church officials. "Newark is a pretty well governed city, and can take care of itself in maintaining law and order without the assistance of the Ku Klux Klan," sniffed the mayor of the state's largest city. The mayor of Atlantic City put it more bluntly when he directed his policemen to "break your clubs over their heads."

The greatest problem the Jersey Klan faced was the embarrassing state of the national Klan. One high Klan official in Atlanta was caught in an extramarital affair; the leader of the Midwest Klan was convicted of abducting a woman who later committed suicide. The national Klan split apart when Imperial Wizard Simmons was ousted by a rival.

The divisiveness spread to New Jersey. In Hoboken, King Kleagle George B. Apgar and 135 of his followers withdrew from the national Klan. In fact, the Klan was only one of many racist, crackpot organizations that existed in New Jersey in the 1920s, and the KKK had to compete for members with splinter groups and rivals like the Junior Order of United American Mechanics, the Patriotic Sons of America, the Loyal Sons of America, and the Royal Riders of the Red Robe.

The split in the ranks, coupled with bully-boy violence, sickened the public and alienated members. Across the nation in the late 1920s the order shriveled away.

The Klan was (and is) a hateful organization; a native version of the Nazi party. But we ought to know when to laugh at our enemies. Perhaps it is a tribute to the vitality of New Jersey, but here the Klan was a bit less sinister, a bit more confused.

Consider the moment in 1925 when 1,500 members of the Ku Klux Klan marched in a parade of Protestant churchmen in Jersey City. "A queer anomaly of the parade," wrote a reporter for the *Jersey Journal*, "was the fact that Klansmen and colored people marched almost side by side along the Boulevard."

Only in New Jersey.

T he yuppie baby boomers who are now gentrifying Jersey City in areas like Hamilton Park and Van Vorst Park know "the Boss" as the Jersey rock star Bruce Springsteen.

But in other parts of the city—in taverns and benches around the county courthouse and city hall—there are men and women from older generations for whom the Boss is someone quite different. They remember the Boss as Frank Hague, who was born in Jersey City January 17, 1876, and who died in New York on January 1, 1956.

"I Am the Law"

For most of the first half of the century, Boss Hague was the most powerful political figure in the state; a man who controlled the careers of governors, judges, senators, congressmen, and state legislators, and whose influence extended to the White House.

The Jersey City Hague grew up in is a sort of archetypical immigrant, industrial town—a city one can picture in the mind, like Charles Dickens's London and Wyatt Earp's Dodge City. In Jersey City, Irish, Italian, and Slavic immigrants crowded in neighborhoods by the waterfront, each community with its saloon and church, looked after by Democratic ward bosses. Further west, in "the Heights," were the homes of the middle class and the mansions of the Protestant Republican factory owners and bankers.

Hague was born in a tenement in the heart of the Irish district. He left school—some say he was expelled—at age fourteen and went to work running errands for the Democratic machine. He had a talent for organization, a hot temper, and a reputation for using his fists.

As a young man he rose through the ranks, as constable, city hall custodian, and a street and water commissioner, at each point building circles of supporters. He had a knack for switching allegiance from one faction of the party to another at the right time.

In 1913, Hague cannily exploited the progressive sentiment inspired in New Jersey by Woodrow Wilson by running for a seat on the city's governing commission as a reform candidate. As commissioner, he headed the Department of Public Safety, which enabled him to build a power base in the police department. In 1917 he became mayor, a position he held for the next thirty years.

THE CLUTCHING HAND

12   *"I Am the Law."* From his base in Jersey City, "Boss" Frank Hague exercised enormous influence in state politics. This Republican cartoon from the 1940 gubernatorial election shows Hague capturing the State House. (Special Collections and Archives, Rutgers University Libraries)

Hague liked to claim that the reason he won election after election was that he provided efficient, moral government to the city, government that reflected the values of family and church. Things seemed to work in Jersey City, and there were some major achievements, notably the free health care provided by the Jersey City Medical Center.

Hague's famous remark, "I am the law," came when he brushed aside the regulations of the court system in order to establish a rehabilitation program for juvenile delinquents. He tolerated "clean" crime such as gambling and speakeasies, while keeping out prostitution and narcotics.

But for all his claims of good government, Hague's power rested, at bottom, on the vote-getting machine that he conquered and perfected. Hague lieutenants operated in every ward and neighborhood to turn out the vote. The organization actually kept written records on city families, noting who voted faithfully and who did not. On election day the machine worked furiously and thoroughly to get every registered Democrat (and some who were not registered) to the polls.

Using the city and county payroll, Hague rewarded the faithful with jobs and promotions. In return, employees were expected to pay 3 percent of their salaries to the Democratic organization. Businesses that got contracts with the city were also expected to return a share.

Occasionally the machine could use force on its opponents. One unfortunate rebel who dared to run against Hague in a primary found himself arrested and jailed for vote fraud. When the mayor of Bayonne stepped out of line, the county vice squad raided his town. Other opponents would suddenly find their tax assessments increased.

Hague had special scorn for "Reds," and he used the law against disorderly persons to run labor organizers out of town—until the U.S. Supreme Court ruled the practice unconstitutional.

The power of the machine to turn out tens of thousands of Democratic votes in Hudson County enabled the Boss to extend his influence over New Jersey. At the time Hague became mayor, Hudson County was a densely populated urban center in a largely rural state. Any Democrat running for governor or senator could not win without the votes of Hudson.

In 1925, for example, Hague's candidate for governor beat his Republican opponent by 38,000 votes statewide, but by 103,000 votes in Hudson County. The Boss thus largely decided who got to run for statewide office on the Democratic ticket.

Once in office, governors had to clear appointments to state agencies and judgeships with Hague. Even Republicans in office found that political life was much easier if Hague's wishes were considered.

The most striking example of Hague's power came in 1944, when a proposed new state constitution was defeated at the last minute because Hague found it objectionable.

This same power extended to the national level. To win New Jersey's electoral votes, Franklin D. Roosevelt had to maintain good relations with Hague, a man he found personally repellent. Federal relief jobs in New Jersey during the Depression had to be cleared with the Boss.

Life in Jersey City under Hague had elements of ritual. Every New Year's Day came the reception at city hall, where the loyal party workers and office-seekers came to pay their respects to their leader. At every election there were rallies in Journal Square and a predictable round of endorsements from well-disciplined civic organizations and ethnic clubs.

Hague himself was remarkable for being astonishingly colorless. His ordinary features were difficult for cartoonists to caricature, and except for a certain taste for fine suits, horse racing, and boxing matches, there were no idiosyncrasies or quirks that marked him out. He did not smoke, drink, or womanize. Not a single joke or witticism has ever been attributed to Hague. As one of Hague's enemies put it, the Boss was "humorless, vindictive, and unimaginative."

Hague was never convicted of corruption, but there is little doubt that a large portion of the money going each month to the machine from salary and contract kickbacks made its way into his pockets. According to the writer Thomas Fleming, whose father was a ward leader for Hague, a city employee was given the job of delivering a suitcase from the Boss to some bankers and brokers in New York. After doing this for some time, the flunky asked the Boss what was in the suitcase. "Money, you stupid bastard," Hague replied.

In the end, after three decades in office, Hague lost touch with Jersey City. He spent more and more time at his homes in Miami and at the Jersey shore, giving day-to-day power to Johnny Malone, his loyal aide. The town itself was changing. Jersey City was no longer the robust immigrant town of Hague's youth. After the Second World War it went into the same decline faced by other New Jersey cities as jobs and middle-class families moved to the suburbs.

In 1947, Hague announced that he was resigning as mayor and he named his nephew, Frank Hague Eggers, as his successor. Hague made it clear, however, that he would remain the real power in town as chairman of the county and state Democratic party and as city commissioner.

John V. Kenny, a former ward leader for Hague, saw an opportunity, and ran in the mayoral election of 1949 on the "Freedom Ticket" against Hague and Eggers. Kenny hammered away at such evidence of misrule as the Boss's vacation homes and his fondness for $25 silk underwear and $75 shirts. Kenny won, and after a losing attempt to regain power, Hague resigned from his Democratic party offices and went into bitter but well-heeled exile in Manhattan.

What is the final verdict on Hague? He was certainly not the "Hudson

County Hitler" that his enemies called him. Like other political bosses, he brought into power immigrant groups. He also brought a measure of effective government to Jersey City: the streets were kept clean and the garbage was collected on time.

In these days in Jersey City, when factions bitterly fight for political power, when the decrepit and corrupt public school system has been taken over by the state, when new immigrant groups are the victims of gang violence, and when poorer residents are being forced out by gentrification, perhaps we can excuse the nostalgia that some old-timers feel for the days when the Boss kept things under control.

But in the last analysis, the hint of force behind the clean streets, the control of judges and schools, the kickbacks and shady deals all constituted a sort of government that ought not to be tolerated by free Americans.

If you think your line of work is tough, consider Ira L. Reeves, whose job it was to keep New Jerseyans sober. Sisyphus, move over.

The Eighteenth Amendment banning the sale, consumption, and production of alcohol in the United States officially went into effect in 1920. To enforce the law, the Prohibition Bureau established local enforcement offices throughout the country. In 1926, the bureau placed the fifty-four-year-old Reeves in charge of the New Jersey district, with headquarters in Newark.

Keeping
New Jersey
Sober

It would not be easy. Support for Prohibition was strongest in the rural, fundamentalist Protestant states of the South and Midwest. New Jersey was an eastern, urban, industrialized state, with a vast European immigrant population that had little patience with what was regarded as a ridiculous amendment preventing a person from having an honest drink. Most of the state's political leaders and big-city newspapers were firmly against Prohibition. Edward I. Edwards, a Jersey politician who had been elected governor and U.S. senator on anti-Prohibition platforms, proudly announced that he was "as wet as the Atlantic Ocean."

But Reeves was confident. He thought of himself as the "Prohibition St. Patrick of New Jersey" who would drive the bootleggers out of the state. And Reeves did have qualifications for the job. He was a twice-wounded army veteran who had a citation for bravery and who had risen to the rank of colonel in World War I. He was a teetotaler and a churchgoer, and he had once been president of a military college.

He made a stout try. He and his armed agents made raids all over the state: Ocean City, Lambertville, Newark, New Brunswick, Princeton, the Oranges, Palisades Park, Jersey City, Trenton, and Hoboken. They closed speakeasies, roadhouses, cutting plants, stills, breweries, bottling plants, denaturing plants, and needling plants. They confiscated alcohol shipped into the state by boat, rail, and truck.

Reeves had some adventures along the way. He was shot at by gunmen, faced down threats from bootleggers, and endured the hostility of angry city mobs that would gather whenever he closed an illegal establishment.

There were also some laughs. At a raid at a large distillery known as the Bone Yard, because it was combined with a rendering plant to hide the odor of alcohol, Reeves encountered the owner who told him that there had been some mistake, that the fix was in with Reeves.

"Would you recognize him if you saw him?" asked Reeves.

"Sure," the owner replied.

"Well here I am, why don't you recognize me?" said Reeves, as he made the arrest.

At a dinner party given by a friend, Reeves was taunted by guests drinking what they thought was genuine imported Canadian Black Horse Ale. Not long after, Reeves raided a brewery located on an isolated Jersey farm. In an old cow barn he found a stack of counterfeit Black Horse Ale labels. He also found a large dead rat floating in a beer vat in the hayloft. Reeves sent both the rat and the labels to his friend.

In order to gather evidence, Reeves sometimes used undercover agents. One of the most effective was a young woman he described as "an innocent-looking baby-faced flapper." She would visit roadhouses with a male agent who was disguised as a "rounder," and would obtain evidence by pouring drinks into a container in her purse. Her undercover work led to the arrest of a Jersey City druggist who was dispensing bootleg liquor and shaking down speakeasies.

Despite his successes, Reeves was soon disillusioned. He was flabbergasted by the fact that everyone around him drank with abandon, from high school students to state legislators. He once had to promise that he would not raid the state legislature's annual dinner in Atlantic City. He was dismayed that he even discovered a still in Princeton, "one of the cleanest towns, morally, in the United States."

Worse than the drinking was the pervasive corruption. He found that bootleggers were everywhere protected by the law enforcement authorities. The police chief of Trenton threatened to arrest Reeves's agents for carrying concealed guns. In Essex County, a squad of police showed up to protect a still. Reeves accused the coast guard of obstructing his efforts to nab rumrunners.

His own office was a center of corruption. Agents who made no more than $3,000 per year were offered bribes of thousands of dollars a week.

Reeves was convinced that papers were being stolen from his desk, his phone was tapped, and his mail read. He believed that his agents were tipping off bootleggers of impending raids and blackmailing small-time operators. He came to realize that the anonymous tips he received were often from rival bootleggers trying to get rid of the competition.

Reeves even had to dismiss his undercover flapper because he suspected her of taking bribes.

He was dismayed by the Prohibition Bureau in Washington, which seemed to cave in to pressure from New Jersey politicians to ease up. He complained that he got nothing but interference from reform groups like the Anti-Saloon League.

Reeves became convinced that the flow of liquor could never be dried up, thanks to the ingenuity of bootleggers. One way for agents to identify a case of bottles was simply by shaking it to hear the liquid slosh around. Bootleggers would place small sponges in the bottles to prevent the sloshing, or place a package of broken glass or nails in the case to cover up the sound.

Shipments of booze in trucks and boxcars would be hidden under loads of bananas, inside bales of hay, or under lumber. In cars, the liquor was hidden under seats occupied by innocent-looking women and children. Chemists were employed to turn industrial alcohol into gin, scotch, bourbon, or anything else the public fancied.

He concluded that his work had been a failure; that all he had managed to do after countless raids and arrests was to raise the price and lower the quality of alcohol in the state.

It might be added that Reeves was something of a martinet. His enthusiasm for army-style uniforms and training for his agents earned sarcastic remarks from the press about the "militarization of the New Jersey Prohibition enforcers." Reeves also seems to have had a great deal of contempt for liquor-loving foreigners, especially those "of the fiery Latin temperament," although he did say that his best agent was an Italian.

After eight months on the job, Reeves quit. He became convinced that Prohibition was unworkable and that it was turning America into a nation of lawbreakers. He became active in The Crusaders, an anti-Prohibition organization in Chicago, and wrote articles and speeches advocating repeal. In 1931 he published a book about his experiences in New Jersey entitled *Ol' Rum River.* (It just keeps rollin' along.)

In his book he sounded a sad complaint. He was never, not even once, thanked for his efforts to keep New Jersey sober: "I never participated in a raid, nor have I known anyone else who has, where the raiders received a single word of commendation, or a single act of assistance from any member of the reform agencies, or from any citizen in the ever-present crowd of onlookers."

It may be the better part of a century too late, but let us raise our voices, although perhaps not our glasses: Thank you, Colonel Reeves, for a nice try in an impossible job.

This is the story the Pig Woman told the jury: On the night of September 14, 1922, she had ridden her mule down the road from her hardscrabble Somerset County farm, looking for thieves who had been stealing her crops. Hoping to catch the robbers in the act, she tied her mule to a tree, and crept through the woods. She heard loud voices coming from a clearing. Peering in, she saw two men grappling in the dust while a woman screamed.

A shot was fired and a man fell dead. As the terrified Pig Woman

What the Pig Woman Saw

raced back to her mule, she heard three more shots, and the screaming suddenly stopped.

What the Pig Woman witnessed, or claimed to have witnessed on that night was the murder of the Reverend Edward Wheeler Hall, forty-one, the minister of the Episcopal church of St. John the Evangelist in New Brunswick, and his lover Mrs. Eleanor Rinehardt Mills, thirty-four, a soprano in the church choir. The murder was one of those strange, violent events of the years between the world wars that caught enormous public interest—like the Leopold and Loeb murders and the Saint Valentine's Day massacre.

The facts in the case are these. On September 16, 1922, the bodies of the Reverend Hall and Mrs. Mills were found side by side under a crab apple tree in a lovers' lane in Franklin, just outside New Brunswick. Both victims had been shot in the head; in addition, Mrs. Mills's throat had been cut.

Passionate love letters from Mrs. Mills to the minister were scattered at their feet; neatly propped up against the minister's foot was his calling card. The couple had been carefully laid out, with the minister's arm gently cradling the choir singer.

Newspapers picked up the story immediately. Law enforcement authorities from Middlesex County, where the victims had resided, and from Somerset County, where the bodies were found, began a search for

13   *What the Pig Woman Saw.* Two detectives demonstrate the position of the bodies of the Reverend Hall and Mrs. Mills. Note that the crab apple tree, *center,* has already been partially stripped by souvenir hunters. (From *The Hall-Mills Murder Case: The Minister and the Choir Singer* by William M. Kunstler. Photo courtesy of the author and Rutgers University Press)

the killers (and also began a fight among themselves about who had jurisdiction).

Suspicion quickly fell on the minister's widow, Mrs. Frances Stevens Hall, forty-eight, a respected New Brunswick society matron. The lawmen theorized that Mrs. Hall, aided by three male relatives, had followed the clergyman to a rendezvous with his lover, confronted the adulterous pair, and killed them.

A grand jury that heard the evidence two months after the murder refused to return an indictment. But interest in the case remained high, and under pressure from the newspapers, especially Hearst's tabloid *New York Mirror,* the governor reopened the case in 1926 by appointing a special prosecutor, State Senator Alexander Simpson.

This time the grand jury acted, charging Mrs. Hall, her two brothers, Willie and Henry Stevens, and her cousin Henry Carpender with the murder. The trial began in the county courthouse in Somerville on November 3, 1926.

The center of the prosecution's case was Mrs. Jane Gibson, nicknamed the "Pig Woman" by reporters because she raised swine on her farm. Mrs. Gibson was in the hospital at the time of the trial, so she was brought to Somerville in an ambulance and testified in the middle of the courtroom on a hospital bed. In a voice so weak that the court stenographer had to repeat her words, Mrs. Gibson told of her mule ride, and identified Mrs. Hall and her relatives as the murderers.

The defense team, led by the prominent lawyer Robert McCarter, attacked the Pig Woman's story. Testimony was obtained from the Pig Woman's neighbors to the effect that she was a habitual liar.

The defense was able to counter other incriminating evidence. Expert witnesses refuted the State's claim that Willie Stevens's fingerprint was on the calling card. Eyewitnesses refuted the State's claim that Mrs. Hall had a scar on her face in the days after the murder.

A key part of the State's case was the telephone call from the choir singer to the minister on the evening of the murder. The prosecution claimed that Mrs. Hall had eavesdropped on the call, and learned that her husband was planning to meet Mrs. Mills in lovers' lane that night. But the maid testified that Mrs. Hall had hung up the phone once her husband picked up the upstairs extension.

Perhaps the most effective witness was Mrs. Hall herself, who lived up to the defense's picture of her as a devoted wife who never suspected her husband of infidelity, and who on the night of the murder had been home worrying about her missing spouse.

After five weeks of testimony, the jury found the defendants not guilty.

Whodunit? Mrs. Hall remains the suspect with the strongest motive, but in view of the scanty evidence the jury seems to have been quite correct in acquitting her. The husband of the choir singer, James Mills, has been suspected, but his alibi for the night of the murder was reasonably sound.

Could it have been a random murder-robbery? Perhaps, but why the elaborate arrangement of the bodies, the love letters, and the calling card?

In the best study of the case, the 1964 book *The Minister and the Choir Singer,* the attorney William Kunstler suggested that the murder was committed by the Ku Klux Klan, which had punished immoral ministers in other parts of the country. But Kunstler admits that there is no direct evidence, and judging by what we know of the Jersey Klan, that sort of violence was quite unlikely. Others have suggested that thugs hired by Mrs. Hall committed the crime.

Two-thirds of a century later, there is little chance that the case will ever be solved.

But there is more to the puzzle than just the identity of the murderer. The other question is why the murder proved so fascinating to Americans in the 1920s, easily outdrawing such news as the rise of fascism in Italy. To understand why this case aroused intense and lasting public attention while other unsolved murders faded out of sight tells us something about the fantasies and the anxieties of people in the 1920s.

First, there was the sheer creepy horror of a double murder in sleepy central New Jersey in the '20s. The picture of the bodies, murdered so brutally and arranged so lovingly by the crab apple tree, stays in the mind.

Then there were the trappings of the classic murder mystery, as exemplified in Agatha Christie novels and Hollywood movies. A juicy cast of characters was involved, including the icy Widow Hall, the attractive Mrs. Mills, the bizarre Pig Woman, and a supporting cast of nosy neighbors, baffled police, and feisty reporters.

One of the most colorful characters in the story was Mrs. Hall's slightly deranged brother, Willie Stevens, a childlike eccentric with a fondness for chasing fire engines.

It was also dramatically appealing that the murder took place among the upper crust: Mrs. Hall and her husband lived in one of the finer homes in New Brunswick, with maids and a chauffeur. Neither the press nor the public was much interested in the drab Mr. Mills, who worked as a janitor and lived in a shabby apartment.

Then there was the sex. The 1920s, even more than our era, was a time of changing morality. Newly mass-produced automobiles were "bedrooms on wheels." Movies and popular songs focused on the fact that birds do it and bees do it. To be a flapper was to rebel against the values of the older generation.

The fact that a minister, the upholder of official morality, was having a sexual liaison struck the public imagination, and the newspapers trumpeted this aspect of the case. (The *New York Times* on the day the news broke noted in its front-page headline that the minister and the choir singer "had long been friendly.")

Small items turned up in the course of the investigation provide hints about the morality of a New Jersey town in the 1920s. It was discovered that on the night of the murder, at least two couples were parked on lovers' lane—one was a married man and his girlfriend. The bodies of the murder victims were found on a Saturday morning by a local boy and girl off for a tryst. The Pig Woman herself evidently had a live-in male friend.

We should not feel too superior to Jerseyans of the 1920s in their enthusiasm for the Hall-Mills murder. Our own smirking interest in the sexual transgressions of television evangelists and in the crimes of the rich and famous are not much different, except possibly that we are more jaded.

It is fair to say that the Hall-Mills case was the first sex and scandal murder of the age of mass media, and so continues to fascinate us. The very fact, dear reader, that you have read this far suggests that you share something with the crowds of reporters and townspeople who came to gawk at the clearing in the woods around the crab apple tree that long-ago September.

I n the early 1920s, young women in Essex County began showing up in the offices of doctors and dentists with assorted problems such as aching bones, ulcers of the gum, tooth loss, anemia, pneumonia, and angina. The most common condition was "jaw rot," the painful decay of bone and tissue in the mouth.

One fact seemed to unite all these cases: the women had worked at one time or another at the United States Radium Corporation in Orange, New Jersey, where their job was to brush watch dials with a glow-in-the-

The Radium

Girls

dark paint containing radium. They would routinely put the paint-coated brushes to their lips to get a sharp point so that they could apply the paint neatly. By 1924, fifty women who had worked at the plant were ill and a dozen had died.

Now, reader, since you and I are living in the post-Hiroshima age, we know that those radium-soaked brushes were as deadly as rattlesnakes. But in the early 1920s, radium was mostly regarded as a harmless novelty item—a gimmick that enabled you to read your watch dial at night.

The authorities floundered around trying to find why the dial painters were dying. An investigation of the radium factory by the New Jersey Department of Labor failed to find any known industrial hazard.

The company itself refused to accept blame, maintaining that the workers' ills were due to poor dental habits, or in the words of the company president, "a hysterical condition brought about by coincidence." An industrial hygiene expert from Columbia University hired by the company gave the opinion that the women were suffering from syphilis, which he said they had contracted by sitting together in the crowded factory.

But others, including a team of doctors from Harvard and a statistician from the Prudential Insurance Company, suspected that radium had something to do with the workers' deaths.

Now enters into the story Dr. Harrison S. Martland, the medical examiner of Essex County. The plain-talking Martland, a pathologist at Newark City Hospital, enjoyed solving medical mysteries. He would conduct minutely detailed autopsies, so wrapped up in his work that he absentmindedly dropped ashes from the cigarette in his mouth onto the cadaver he was working on.

In the spring of 1925, Martland was called in to investigate the case of a thirty-six-year-old man who had died of anemia. What made the case interesting was that the dead man had been a chemist at the United States Radium Corporation. When he did an autopsy, Martland was puzzled. Death had occurred much too swiftly for a normal case of anemia. (Feminists should note that it was the death of a man, not of the women who died before, that nudged science toward a solution.)

Martland turned for help to an expert on radiation, Dr. Sabin A. von Sochocky. The Austrian-born von Sochocky was a founder and the technical director of the United States Radium Corporation. It was he who had invented the radium paint used by the workers. Von Sochocky agreed to help Martland, but because of his concern for his company's legal liability, he kept his involvement in the investigation quiet.

With von Sochocky's help, tissue and bone from the dead chemist were analyzed at the radium factory laboratory. The results showed that the corpse was saturated with radioactivity.

Martland, von Sochocky, and two local doctors recruited by them rigged up a crude sort of Geiger counter to find out if other people who had worked at the factory were contaminated. They took the device to the bedside of one of the women who was dying at St. Mary's Hospital. When she laboriously breathed into the contraption, it indicated that she was highly radioactive. She died a few days later. During the autopsy Martland removed a splinter of bone from her body. He found that the bone was hot enough to produce an image on photographic film.

The Geiger counter device was tried on other dial painters: whether they were healthy or sick their breaths showed radioactivity. Just for fun, von Sochocky himself exhaled into the machine. He discovered to his horror that his breath contained more radiation than anyone they had tested so far. His death came three years later of painful symptoms that included jaw rot. "He died a horrible death," Martland recalled.

Martland hurriedly wrote up his findings, which appeared in the December 5, 1925, issue of the *Journal of the American Medical Association*. This pioneering work established for the first time the deadly effects of radiation, and how the act of licking their brushes had doomed the dial painters.

The scene now shifts from the pathology lab to the courtroom. With the encouragement of a reform group, the New Jersey Consumers' League, five surviving workers of the United States Radium Corporation sued the company for damages.

The company refused to pay because, under New Jersey law, a worker who claimed to have been harmed by a hazardous substance had to bring legal action within two years of exposure to that substance. But the dial painters' maladies had taken many years to develop, and it had taken still more years to prove that radium was to blame.

The press loved the story of "The Five Women Doomed to Die." There were melodramatic accounts of how the innocent dial painters were faced with crushing debt and crippling disease, and how they actually glowed in the dark. One of the "radium girls," as they were called, Albina Larice, had suffered two stillbirths and could no longer walk. Grace Fryer had undergone twenty operations on her jaw.

When a settlement was delayed for more than a year through legal maneuvering, newspapers expressed outrage that the radium girls were dying while lawyers and judges dragged the case on. "This is one of the most damnable travesties on justice that has ever come to our attention," thundered the *New York World*.

Faced with this public pressure, the radium company finally agreed in June 1928 to provide each of the five women with a payment of $10,000 and a yearly pension of $600. The company continued to deny any liability and fought lawsuits brought against it by other workers. The corporation finally went out of business in the 1930s.

The radium girls continued to die. The one we know most about is Katherine Schaub, one of the plaintiffs in the suit against the company. She had gone to work painting dials at age fifteen, along with her cousin. Schaub would instruct newcomers to the factory, showing them how to get a good point on their brushes.

Her cousin developed jaw rot and anemia, and died a painful death. Then Schaub herself began to show the same symptoms. She was one of the workers whose breath was found by Martland to be radioactive, and she knew she was doomed to die. "I was not as frightened as I thought I would be," she wrote later. Katherine Schaub died in 1933 at the age of thirty-one.

For the rest of his life, Harrison Martland followed the fate of the radium girls. He compiled a list of those women who had licked the deadly brushes, and each time one died he would carefully mark a red "D" after her name. By 1951, forty-one were dead.

This grim tale has a Dracula-like sequel. Scientists from the Federal

Environmental Protection Agency and the State Department of Environmental Protection have found soil with dangerously high levels of radioactivity underneath houses in Montclair, Glen Ridge, and West Orange, as well as at the former site of the Radium Corporation in Orange. These scientists are convinced that the radiation comes from uranium-contaminated waste that was produced at the plant and dumped in rural parts of Essex County back in the 1920s.

The experts say this waste will be a threat to human health for another 1,600 years.

Throughout the story of Robert E. Burns involves brutality, escape, betrayal, and a Hollywood movie. It pits the sovereign states of Georgia and New Jersey against each other, and ends in a dramatic confrontation under the dome of the State House in Trenton. Not bad for 1,100 words.

Burns was a Brooklyn-born World War I veteran who become a drifter after the war. Flat broke in Atlanta in 1922, he fell in with bad company and participated in the armed robbery of a grocery store that netted

Georgia

on His Mind

$5.80. He was quickly captured by the police and sentenced to six to ten years on a chain gang.

According to Burns, life on the chain gang was hell. Prisoners carried around twenty-pound leg chains to prevent them from escaping. They toiled at backbreaking labor from sunrise to sunset. They were fed rancid scraps of food and chained together at night in filthy barracks. Men who glanced disrespectfully at the guards were whipped on their buttocks till the blood ran down their legs.

After four months he managed to slip out of his chains and run away. He eluded guards, bloodhounds, sheriffs, and police to catch a northbound train.

Burns made his way to Chicago. After a year or so of working at menial jobs, he began to make some money renovating and renting apartments. He had some talent as a writer, and with profits from his apartments he started a real estate publication, *The Greater Chicago Magazine*. He became known in the Chicago business community, and he married a divorcé. His past was a secret from everyone except his wife.

Seven years after he had escaped, two detectives arrested him in his magazine office. It seems that his wife, outraged that he had left her for another woman, informed on him to the Georgia authorities.

Burns was brought back to Georgia and found himself once more on a chain gang. Once again he was shuffling in chains and breaking rocks, surrounded by sadistic guards and brutalized prisoners. Once again he made a daring escape. This time, however, he went to New Jersey to be near his brother, a Unitarian minister in Palisades, who had campaigned for Burns's release.

While he worked at odd jobs under an assumed name in Newark, Burns used his talent as a writer to write a best-selling 1932 book, *I Am a Fugitive from a Georgia Chain Gang*. Warner Brothers bought the story, and the movie version, starring Paul Muni, was released in November 1932.

Burns enjoyed the publicity created by the book and the movie. He daringly allowed himself to be interviewed by reporters, he lectured to audiences, and he visited Paul Muni at a Broadway theater. Thanks to all this publicity, it was easy for the police to locate Burns. He was arrested under Georgia warrants and placed in a Newark jail.

But it was not going to be easy to extradite the fugitive. The book and movie had made Burns a national figure. Americans across the country had read his melodramatic account of the horrors of the chain gang and had watched Paul Muni as Burns, struggling through the Georgia swamp pursued by baying hounds.

The governor of New Jersey, A. Harry Moore, was flooded with protests from supporters of Burns, including the American Civil Liberties Union and veterans groups. Governor Moore announced that he had secretly met Burns long before the arrest, and had pledged to give him a fair hearing if he was ever captured.

So it was that on December 21, 1932, Robert E. Burns was brought to the State House Assembly Chamber in Trenton for an extradition hearing before Governor Moore.

Burns sat in a front-row chair, handcuffed to a deputy sheriff. A reporter described the fugitive as "a nervous little man with shell-rimmed glasses." (You would be nervous too, under the circumstances.) The gallery was packed with 500 supporters who cheered and applauded for Burns throughout the proceedings.

Burns was defended by two Newark attorneys and by a nationally-known civil liberties lawyer from New York, Arthur Garfield Hays. An expert from the National Society of Penal Information testified that the prison system of Georgia was the worst in the nation. Other experts corroborated Burns's story of whipping and torture on the chain gang. A letter supporting Burns from the famous lawyer Clarence Darrow was produced.

Burns's gray-haired mother was called to testify about what a wonderful child he had been, and how his war service had affected him. Burns's brother, the minister, testified how a Georgia prosecutor had yelled at him, "I want to tell you that any damned Yankee that comes down here to steal is going to get all that's coming to him."

The most dramatic moment came when Burns's lawyers produced one Samuel Bernstein, now of Queens, who ten years before had been the Atlanta grocer robbed by Burns. Did he think Burns should go back to a chain gang? Bernstein was asked. "Your honor, I do not," he replied.

With that the defense rested.

The crowd in the balcony booed loudly as the case against Burns was presented by the assistant attorney general of Georgia, John I. Kelly, and by Merrit Lane, a Newark lawyer retained by Georgia. Kelly and Lane argued that Burns's story of the hardships of the chain gang was over-drawn, and that New Jersey had an obligation to return the escaped felon. "Do you want New Jersey to become a haven for every escaped criminal?" asked Lane.

After four hours of testimony, Governor Moore announced his decision: Burns would not be extradited.

Troopers escorted the happy Burns through a mob of supporters. He embraced his mother, and then shook hands with the governor, who said, "As long as you live the life of a decent citizen in New Jersey, I'll not sign a warrant for your return to Georgia. The best way you can express your thanks to me is by living as a decent citizen. Never mind the publicity stuff."

As it happened, Burns did mind the publicity stuff, and before long he was rehearsing a vaudeville show, complete with black men in chains singing prison songs.

Governor Richard Russell of Georgia issued a statement accusing New Jersey of coddling criminals. "The Governor of New Jersey is either desirous of basking in the light of some cheap publicity or else is completely taken in by statements and writings of Burns, which have been proven false and are a slander on the State of Georgia and its institutions."

Over the next few years, Georgia repeatedly tried to get its hands on Burns, and New Jersey officials repeatedly said no. Finally, in 1945, a reform governor of Georgia invited the fugitive to Atlanta, where amidst great publicity the charges against him were dismissed.

The only person he never managed to win over was his long-abandoned wife in Chicago, who described him to *Time* magazine as "a four-flusher and a big mouth."

The date is February 13, 1935, and you, reader, are a member of the jury in the trial of Bruno Richard Hauptmann for the kidnap-murder of Charles A. Lindbergh, Jr.

For the past six weeks you and your eleven fellow jurors have spent your days in the courtroom in Flemington, New Jersey, listening to the evidence in what the press calls the trial of the century. You are the focus of attention of hundreds of reporters and spectators from around the world, including celebrities like Walter Winchell, Damon Runyon,

Was Hauptmann

Guilty?

Jack Benny, Edna Ferber, and Jack Dempsey. You have seen the great hero aviator, Col. Charles Lindbergh, at close hand, along with quite another sort of celebrity, the accused kidnapper Hauptmann.

Your evenings and weekends are spent sequestered in the Union Hotel, across the street from the courthouse. You are being paid $3.00 a day for jury service.

The case against Hauptmann has been presented by the young attorney general of New Jersey, David Wilentz. The defense team (paid by the Hearst press in exchange for the right to exclusive interviews) has been led by the florid Edward Reilly, a well-known Brooklyn criminal lawyer.

Now the thirty-odd days of testimony are over, and Judge Trenchard has sent you to the jury room to arrive at a verdict.

The facts in the case are by now quite familiar to you: at 10 p.m. on the night of March 1, 1932, the nursemaid at the Lindbergh estate on Amwell Road in Hopewell found that twenty-month-old Charles Jr. was missing from his crib. A kidnapper's note demanding a ransom of $50,000 was found in the nursery.

Colonel Lindbergh paid the ransom one month after the kidnapping, but the baby was not returned. The body of the child was later found in the woods four and a half miles from the Lindbergh home; Charles Jr. had apparently been killed on the night of the crime and dumped there.

Two and a half years after the kidnapping, the police arrested a German-born Bronx carpenter, Hauptmann, who had been caught passing bills from the ransom money. He was charged with murder and brought to Flemington for trial.

Now consider the main points of evidence.

The Ransom Money

After Hauptmann's arrest, the police found $13,760 of the ransom money hidden behind the wall of his garage. Hauptmann's story was that a shady business partner, Isidore Fisch, had given him a shoebox for safe-keeping just before Fisch sailed to Germany. Fisch died overseas, and when Hauptmann later opened the box he discovered the money. Because Fisch owed him a debt, and in complete ignorance that it was connected with a crime, Hauptmann spent it. The prosecution ridiculed the Fisch story, and brought forward a movie theater cashier who claimed that she had received a $5 bill (part of the ransom money) from Hauptmann on a November evening more than half a year before he claimed he opened the shoebox.

Placing Hauptmann at the Scene of the Crime

Hauptmann claimed that on the evening of the kidnapping he had been in the Bronx, picking up his wife, Anna, from her job at a bakery. The defense presented witnesses who corroborated this story.

The prosecution counterattacked with its own witnesses. For example, one of the defense witnesses who placed Hauptmann at the bakery was a man named Carlstrom. But the prosecution brought forth one Larsen, who said that he and Carlstrom had been in Dunellen that evening. In the same way, the defense attacked the witnesses who said they had seen Hauptmann in the vicinity of the Lindbergh estate. One of these prosecution witnesses, the defense charged, was nearsighted and the other was a well-known neighborhood liar.

The Cemetery Meetings

A key witness in the case was a retired Bronx school principal, Dr. John F. Condon. Shortly after the kidnapping, Condon wrote a letter to a local paper offering to serve as go-between. He was contacted by a man calling himself "John" who said he was a member of the kidnap gang. Condon met this person on two occasions at night in Bronx cemeteries;

WANTED

INFORMATION AS TO THE WHEREABOUTS OF

CHAS. A. LINDBERGH, JR.

OF HOPEWELL, N. J.

SON OF COL. CHAS. A. LINDBERGH

World-Famous Aviator

This child was kidnaped from his home in Hopewell, N. J., between 8 and 10 p. m. on Tuesday, March 1, 1932.

DESCRIPTION:

Age, 20 months   Hair, blond, curly
Weight, 27 to 30 lbs.   Eyes, dark blue
Height, 29 inches   Complexion, light
Deep dimple in center of chin
Dressed in one-piece coverall night suit

ADDRESS ALL COMMUNICATIONS TO
COL. H. N. SCHWARZKOPF, TRENTON, N. J., or
COL. CHAS. A. LINDBERGH, HOPEWELL, N. J.

ALL COMMUNICATIONS WILL BE TREATED IN CONFIDENCE

COL. H. NORMAN SCHWARZKOPF
March 11, 1932   Supt. New Jersey State Police, Trenton, N. J.

at their last meeting, April 2, Condon handed over the ransom while Colonel Lindbergh waited in a nearby car. At the trial, Condon identified Hauptmann as John. But Condon was a blustering, melodramatic character (he gave himself the code name "Jafsie," from his initials) who in the early stages of the investigation had been unsure in his identification of Hauptmann.

Lindbergh testified that it was Hauptmann's voice he had heard calling to Condon on the night the ransom was paid. Another link was provided by a taxi driver, who identified Hauptmann as the man who had paid him a dollar one night in March to deliver a note to Condon. The defense, on the other hand, claimed that on the evening of the ransom payment Hauptmann had again gone to pick up Anna at the bakery and had spent the rest of the evening at home with Anna and a friend.

The Ladder

At the time of the kidnapping the police discovered a crudely made ladder not far from the house; it had most likely been used to take the Lindbergh baby from the second-floor nursery. The prosecution brought forward an expert from the U.S. Department of Agriculture who claimed that wood used in the ladder had come from floor boards in Hauptmann's attic. The defense argued that this evidence had been planted by the police, and brought forth two woodworkers who said that the planks did not match.

(Incidentally, at the time of the crime Col. Lindbergh heard a loud noise of cracking wood. The fact that one of the ladder rungs was broken suggests that the baby might have been killed accidentally while being carried down the ladder.)

The Handwriting

The prosecution presented eight handwriting experts who identified Hauptmann as the man who wrote the ransom notes. The defense, claiming it could not afford any more, presented one expert who said

14   *Was Hauptmann Guilty?* In 1932, the infant son of hero aviator Charles A. Lindbergh was kidnapped from his crib at the family's home in Hopewell. By the time this poster was issued by the New Jersey State Police, the infant was dead. Bruno Richard Hauptmann, a German immigrant carpenter living in the Bronx, was later convicted of murder. (Special Collections and Archives, Rutgers University Libraries)

that the handwriting on the notes was absolutely not Hauptmann's. Another significant piece of writing was Dr. Condon's phone number, which had been written behind the door of a closet in Hauptmann's home. The defense asserted that the closet writing had been planted by the police.

Hauptmann's Finances

Hauptmann had quit his job as a carpenter right after the $50,000 ransom was paid, and did not seek a regular job again. Although he was without work in the height of the Depression, he seemed to have lived fairly comfortably, with a vacation to Florida, a trip for his wife to Germany, and expensive purchases. Hauptmann claimed that all of this was possible because of shrewd investments on the stock market. The prosecution brought forward a Treasury Department accountant who calculated that Hauptmann's family budget was based on a large influx of cash—roughly $50,000.

The Character of Hauptmann

The defense pictured Hauptmann as an innocent man and a loving father and husband, who was linked to the crime only through Fisch's money. He was a victim, said the defense, of the State's need to find a culprit for the crime of the century. The prosecution pointed out that this supposedly harmless man had once served time in a German prison for burglary and armed robbery.

So, ladies and gentlemen of the jury, how do you find the defendant?

In 1935, after eleven hours of deliberation, the real jurors found Hauptmann guilty of first-degree murder, and he was sentenced to death. After his appeals were denied, he was executed in Trenton State Prison on April 3, 1936.

In the years since, there have been doubts about Hauptmann's guilt. Nobody, after all, saw him commit the crime. It has also never been explained how a Bronx carpenter could have known so much about the layout and routine of the Lindbergh estate.

Finally, there is the nagging fact that Hauptmann never swerved from declaring his innocence—even when he could have changed his death sentence to life imprisonment by confessing. Among those who have continued to believe in Hauptmann is his widow, Anna, who in 1981 launched a suit to clear his name. In 1986, the suit reached the United States Supreme Court, which dismissed it without comment. Mrs. Hauptmann is still pursuing the case.

But if Hauptmann was not guilty then he must have been the victim of a complex chain of coincidence, and of a complicated frame-up by police and government officials in New York and New Jersey. The ladder, the handwriting, the telephone number behind the closet door, the fact that he quit his job right after the ransom was paid, the identification by Condon, the theater cashier, and the taxi driver—all of these suggest that there was no frame-up and no coincidences; that Hauptmann was clearly involved in the crime.

And yet, juror, would you have been confident enough in this evidence to send him to the electric chair?

On October 23, 1935, Dutch Schultz and three members of his mob were gunned down in the back room of a restaurant. It was one of the bloodiest rubouts in gangster history, second in body count only to the Saint Valentine's Day massacre in Al Capone's Chicago. (The statistics on this sort of thing are a bit obscure, and it may be that drug smugglers have since set a new record.)

In TV shows and movies, the Schultz hit is often depicted as happening in New York City. But in real life, or rather real death, it took place in

The Chop

House Rubout

the Palace Chop House on East Park Street in downtown Newark, New Jersey. It is time to reclaim this lost bit of the Garden State's heritage.

Dutch Schultz, whose real name was Arthur Flegenheimer, was one of a generation of Jewish gangsters from immigrant New York. He grew up in the Bronx, where his reputation for toughness earned him the nickname Dutch Schultz after a legendary neighborhood gang leader.

Schultz combined a head for business with a stomach for violence that enabled him to make a great deal of money in the underworld. By the age of thirty he was raking in hundreds of thousands of dollars from bootlegging. He expanded into the Harlem policy racket, pushing aside the local blacks who had run the game. One of those was the proud Stephanie St. Claire, known as "Madam Queen of Policy." (Explanatory note for young readers: "policy" was an illegal and wicked form of betting on numbers, which has since been replaced by the socially beneficial Pick-6.) Schultz also did well at labor racketeering, and he controlled corrupt unions for waiters and window washers.

In 1934, Schultz was brought to court by the federal government for income tax evasion. His team of expensive lawyers got him acquitted after two trials, but New York was planning to indict him on other charges. Thus it was that he shifted his base of operations across the Hudson River to Newark. While his lawyers (including an ex-governor of New Jersey) fought off indictments, Schultz worked to rebuild and defend the rackets he had neglected during his trials. He used the Palace Chop House as his headquarters, which brings us to the night of October 23.

It was a little after 10:00 p.m. at the Palace. The only customers in the place were Schultz and three henchmen: Bernard (Lulu) Rosenkranz, Otto (Abbadabba) Berman, and Abe (he didn't have a nickname) Landau. They had spent the evening at a table in the back room going over the receipts from their assorted enterprises.

In the front room of the restaurant, the bartender saw a tough-looking hood come through the front door and pull out a pistol. A second man followed with a sawed-off shotgun. The bartender slid under the bar as the gunmen made their way into the back room.

What the bartender heard next reminded him of his World War I experience in the trenches. The gunmen let loose a fusillade at Schultz's men. Rosenkranz, Landau, and Berman went down before they could shoot back. But where was Schultz? The gunman with the pistol strode to the door of the men's room at the far end and kicked it open, where he found Schultz at the urinal. The gunman fired a round into Schultz's stomach and made for the exit.

Landau, although badly wounded, was able to pull himself to his feet and follow the last gunman out the door, shooting at him with his .45. Landau made it as far as the sidewalk, where he dropped his gun and collapsed onto a trashcan.

Ambulances and police arrived a few minutes later. Astonishingly, the four wounded gangsters were still alive. They were taken to the Newark City Hospital, where they began to die, one by one. Dutch's life ended at 8:35 p.m. the next evening. As he lay dying, a telegram arrived at the hospital from Stephanie St. Claire. "As ye sow, so shall ye reap," it said.

Why was Schultz murdered? In his 1971 book *Kill the Dutchman!*, Paul Sann argues that Schultz was becoming an embarrassment to the leaders of organized crime. He was too flamboyant and unpredictable, too much a loose cannon in the increasingly corporate environment of the mob. His worst offense had been to threaten to kill Thomas E. Dewey, the New York State prosecutor who was investigating organized crime. The mob leaders felt that murdering a well-known lawman like Dewey (who later became governor of New York and Republican candidate for president) would bring a crackdown on their business.

Two hitmen were hired to shut up Schultz: Mendy Weiss, the one with the shotgun, and Charlie "the Bug" Workman, the one who pulled the trigger on Schultz. A kid known as "Piggy" was the driver.

It may have been better for the mobsters to have let Schultz kill Dewey, since the prosecutor eventually cracked the syndicate leadership and sent many to prison and the electric chair. In the course of one investigation five years after the Chop House shooting, a mobster in custody squealed to police about several unsolved crimes, including who had done the Schultz hit.

Charlie the Bug was brought to trial in Newark in 1941 and sentenced to life in prison; he got out after twenty-three years in New Jersey jails. Mendy Weiss died in the electric chair for other crimes.

The rubout of Dutch Schultz has a curious place in literature. On his deathbed in the Newark hospital, Schultz slipped into a 106-degree fever and delirium. He began to babble in strange, disjointed sentences, and the police put a stenographer by his bed in case he said anything of interest.

The result was page after page of dreamlike prose. Some examples: "Oh, oh, dog biscuit, and when he is happy he doesn't get snappy . . . the glove will fit what I say . . . thinks he is grandpa again and he is jumping around . . . get up your onions and we will throw up the truce flag . . . he eats like a little sausage baloney maker . . . the sidewalk was in trouble and the bears were in trouble . . . no payrolls, no walls, no coupons . . . a boy has never wept nor dashed a thousand kim . . . Sam, you are a boiled man . . . French Canadian bean soup."

This stream-of-consciousness prose appealed to the avant-garde. The writer William S. Burroughs did an experimental work entitled *The Last Words of Dutch Schultz* based on the stenographer's transcript.

Schultz has appeared in other literary works. He is a central character in Francis Ford Coppola's 1984 film *The Cotton Club* where he seems to represent the Jew as eternal outsider. In E. L. Doctorow's 1989 novel *Billy Bathgate,* and the movie based on it, Schultz initiates the hero of the story, Billy, into the adult world of sex and violence.

One suspects that Schultz would have enjoyed this attention. He loved to give interviews to reporters and pose for news photos—which was one of the reasons he was gunned down.

One figure who never received much attention is the mysterious Piggy, the wheelman in the Schultz rubout. He is described only as a kid who worked for a Jersey City gang, a kid who got so scared that night in Newark that he took off in the car with Mendy Weiss before Charlie Workman got out of the restaurant, which forced the Bug to escape on foot.

Piggy was never apprehended and his real name is unknown. It is quite possible that Piggy is still alive. Maybe he still lives in Jersey City. Or maybe with a married daughter in the suburbs. Maybe in a South Jersey retirement community. Maybe he is reading this right now.

On May 6, 1937, the airship *Hindenburg* exploded while coming in for a landing at Lakehurst. Thirty-six lives were lost in the disaster, which, when you think about it, is not a big deal in this day of airplane crashes that take hundreds of lives at once. What makes the story of the *Hindenburg* so engrossing is the drama and mystery of its last flight.

The *Hindenburg* was a remarkable human artifact. To use the standard American unit of measurement, it was about almost three football

The *Hindenburg*

fields long—roughly the size of an ocean liner.

The aircraft was kept aloft by 7 million cubic feet of hydrogen, and moved forward at a top speed of eighty-four miles an hour by four Mercedes-Benz diesel engines. It had the capacity to transport over one hundred human beings across the Atlantic, with the amenities of a dining salon, bar, staterooms, lounge, and baggage areas.

In 1936, the *Hindenburg* went into regular passenger service between Germany and New York, at a time when there was no airline service from Europe to North America. Hitler's government used the giant airship to trumpet the technological superiority of the Third Reich.

Imagine this colossal piece of Nazi Germany, with giant swastikas painted on the tail fins, floating effortlessly in the air overhead. When it appeared over American cities and towns, traffic would stop and people would stare as it passed majestically by.

On May 3, 1937, the *Hindenburg* took off from Frankfurt to inaugurate its second year of service. On board were sixty-one crew members and thirty-six passengers. On May 6, the ship reached the East Coast of North America, making its stately way over Boston and New York City. At Ebbets Field, a baseball game between the Dodgers and the Pirates stopped while fans and players gawked at the giant ship 600 feet above them.

The *Hindenburg's* destination was the U.S. navy air station at Lakehurst. After a delay of several hours because of thunderstorms, the *Hindenburg* approached the mooring mast at Lakehurst and began its descent shortly after 7 p.m.

15   *The* Hindenburg. The German zeppelin *Hindenburg* explodes above Lakehurst on May 6, 1937. Thirty-six people died in this disaster. The offical verdict was that the explosion was an accident, but over the years it has been alleged that the craft was destroyed by a bomb hidden on board. (New Jersey Historical Society, Newark)

Gathered below were newsreel photographers, friends and relatives of the passengers, customs agents, and a 230-man ground crew. A Chicago radio announcer, Herbert Morrison, was there to describe the event. As the ship descended, lines were dropped from the bow and stern to the handlers on the ground.

At 7:25 p.m., observers on the ground noticed a tongue of flame appear near the stern. The flame spread rapidly; within a few seconds the zeppelin exploded in a huge ball of fire that consumed the rear half. The ship fell tail first with flames shooting out the nose. It crashed into the ground thirty-two seconds after the flame was first spotted.

Announcer Herbert Morrison shouted into his microphone:

It's burst into flames—Get out of the way, please, oh my, this is terrible, oh my, get out of the way, please! It is burning, bursting into flames and is falling on the mooring mast and all the folks we ... this is one of the worst catastrophes in the world!—It's a terrific sight—Oh, the humanity and all the passengers!"

When the ship tilted, passengers who had gathered in the dining salon to watch the landing were thrown on top of one another. Some were able to untangle themselves and jump to the ground through open windows. The ground crew was able to rescue others from the flames once the ship hit the ground.

In the cavernous interior of the ship, twelve crewman who had been stationed at the bow desperately clung to handholds as the craft tilted. One by one, eleven of them fell into the fire that boiled beneath them.

Twenty-two crew members died, thirteen passengers, and one member of the Lakehurst ground crew. One of the victims was Captain Ernst Lehmann. He was led away from the crash muttering "Das versteh ich nicht" (I don't understand). He died the next day.

What caused the death of the *Hindenburg*? It is evident that a spark ignited the dangerously explosive hydrogen gas. But how did the spark meet the hydrogen? The German Zeppelin Company (Deutsche Zeppelin-Reederei) that operated the *Hindenburg* took great precautions to prevent such an accident. The hydrogen gas was kept secure in sixteen enormous rubberized fabric bags, called cells, in the interior of the ship. Crew members wore special metal-free coveralls and shoes to prevent accidental sparks. Passengers were kept away from the interior, and smoking was permitted only in a special, sealed-off lounge.

The most dramatic theory about the demise of the *Hindenburg*, popularized in books and movies, is sabotage. Conspiracy buffs argue that the swastika-bedecked Hindenburg was an attractive target for those who wanted to discredit Hitler. Indeed, the Germans did suspect that the *Hindenburg* might be attacked, and before it took off from Frankfurt, security men searched the ship and the passengers' baggage.

If it was sabotage, the most likely instrument was a bomb hidden in one of the gas cells. Who placed it there? The most likely suspect is an obscure twenty-seven-year-old crew member named Eric Spehl, who died in the explosion. Spehl was a rigger; his job was to maintain the ship's fabric, and he would frequently be near the gas cells. Spehl was said to have been an amateur photographer, so he might have had the knowledge to put together a device consisting of a timer, a battery, and a flashbulb. He was not known to be an opponent of the Nazi regime, but it is said he had a girlfriend who may have had radical, anti-fascist connections.

It is at least equally possible, although a bit less exciting, to conclude the *Hindenburg* was destroyed by natural causes. That was, in fact, the conclusion of investigations by the U.S. Department of Commerce and by the German government at the time.

The U.S. investigation suggested that when the airship turned to land at Lakehurst, an internal cable might have snapped, rupturing a gas cell. Witnesses did in fact see a rippling on the surface of the ship at the same spot where the fire began seconds later. This rippling could have been caused by escaping gas.

In the opinion of experts, the lightning-charged atmosphere over Lakehurst that evening and the drenching of the *Hindenburg's* outer skin by rain, along with the wet landing lines dropped from the ship to the ground below, could have set up conditions for a spark to be generated.

Such a spark could have jumped from the skin of the ship to the metal framework underneath where, by an unhappy coincidence, the ruptured cell was leaking hydrogen gas.

So was it the furtive Spehl or a random act of God that caused the *Hindenburg* to explode? Both explanations rely on maybes and perhapses. Like Captain Lehmann, we still don't understand the cause of the fiery tragedy that took away thirty-six lives that night in Lakehurst.

Oh, the humanity.

F or a brief moment in the late 1930s, a flame from the evil of Nazism burned in the cities and countryside of New Jersey.

The German-American Bund was an American version of the Nazi party. Bundists, most of whom were German-born immigrants, dressed in Nazi-style uniforms and gave the fascist salute. The organization contained an elite unit modeled on the SS and a branch for children modeled on the Hitler Youth.

The Bund circulated such Nazi propaganda as *Mein Kampf* and *The*

Swastikas

in Sussex County

Protocols of the Elders of Zion and encouraged members to patronize only "Aryan" merchants.

The leader of the Bund during the height of its influence, 1936–1939, was Fritz Kuhn. Bundesleiter Kuhn, a Munich-born former chemist, wore high black boots, a belted uniform, and slicked-back hair. He would pose in Hitler fashion, hands on his hips and legs apart, and he demanded absolute obedience from his followers.

The headquarters of the Bund was in the Yorkville section of Manhattan, with chapters in those cities and states across the nation that had a high proportion of German-Americans. New Jersey was one of these states: in the 1930s Germans in the Garden State constituted the largest foreign-born population after the Italians. Bund chapters existed in Union City, Passaic, Clifton, North Bergen, Hackensack, Fairfield, and Newark.

New Jersey also furnished leaders to the Bund. The director of publicity, Gerhard Wilhelm Kunze of Union City, played Goebbels to Kuhn's Hitler, and succeeded him as Bundesleiter in 1939. The leader of the Bund in New Jersey, August Klapprott, was a member of the inner circle.

But perhaps the most significant contribution made by New Jersey to the Bund movement was as the home of Camp Nordland, a sort of tin-pot version of Nuremberg, which served as the site of the Bund's rallies, ceremonies, and holidays.

Camp Nordland consisted of 205 acres of wooded campground on a picturesque lake, just outside the small (population 479) town of Andover in rural Sussex County. Here the Bundists established their own world, with signs in German like "zu dem Jungendlager" (to the children's camp). At the center of the Nordland was a recreation hall with a clock tower; on the main wall inside was a large picture of Hitler. Behind the hall was a parade ground for marches and ceremonies. Four hundred children attended summer camp at Nordland, and families could buy bungalows there.

The Bund operated other camps in New Jersey at Griggstown and Bloomingdale, as well as in Wisconsin, Pennsylvania, California, New York State, and Michigan. But because of its proximity to New York City, Nordland was the one used most frequently by the Bund and was of special importance to Bundesleiter Kuhn.

"Our camp," he declared in an exquisite example of the Bund's turgid, bloated prose, "is designed principally to be a place which breathes the spirit of the New Germany." It was where young people "shall be strengthened and confirmed in National Socialism so that they will be conscious of the role which has been assigned to them as the future carriers of German racial ideals to America."

On summer weekends, Bund members and their families would travel to Camp Nordland for what strikes us as a chilling mix of innocent fun and seething hate. A newspaper reporter described how 4,000 Bundists celebrated May Day 1938 at Nordland: "Picnicking, beer drinking, marching by the uniformed camp police and boys and girls of the Youth Organization, dancing and oratorical attacks on Jews and Communists were the principal activities."

Anti-Semitism wrapped in American patriotism was the standard theme at Nordland. At one summer rally, Kuhn led several thousand followers in a pledge to the "Constitution, the flag, and the ideals of the founders of the nation." He then called for a "Gentile-ruled United States," where Jews would be barred from "all positions of importance in government, national defense, and educational institutions," and where there would be a "cleaning of the Hollywood film industries of all alien, subversive doctrines." At another rally, Kunze urged Bundists to make the United States "a white man's Christian country again."

Nordland was the scene of Bund efforts to ally with other hate groups. Representatives of the Ku Klux Klan meet at Nordland with Bundists on several occasions, and in August 1940 members of the two organizations burned a forty-foot cross while Nazi marching songs were played

16   *Swastikas in Sussex County.* Camp Nordland was a center of the German-American Bund in the period before Pearl Harbor. In this photo August Klapprott, a Bund official from New Jersey, addresses a group of Bundists outside the camp's main hall in June 1940. (New Jersey Historical Society, Newark)

over loudspeakers. Other visitors to Nordland included New Jersey Blackshirt supporters of Mussolini.

But for all its oratory, uniforms, and alliances, the Bund did little to spread fascism in the United States. In retrospect, it is clear that the main contribution of the Bund was to help turn public opinion against Hitler. Events in Germany after 1930—the military expansion, the suppression of democratic institutions, and the persecution of the Jews—were disturbing to Americans. (One example of the lunacy unleashed in the Fatherland was the claim by a prominent Nazi that the Lindbergh kidnapping was a ritual murder conducted by Jews, who had framed the German immigrant Hauptmann.) The posturing of Kuhn and his followers seemed to reflect this overseas madness.

Opposition arose quite early and quite vigorously in New Jersey. In 1935, the state became one of the first to pass a law aimed at the Bund, making it illegal to promote "hatred, abuse, violence or hostility" against any group because of race, color, or religion. State probes of the Bund lead to a 1939 law prohibiting quasi-military uniforms and the Hitler salute. The Bundists defiantly kept their uniforms and their salute.

Organizations like the Non-Sectarian Anti-Nazi League of Newark, the German-American League for Culture, the Jewish-American War Veterans, the American Legion, and a group called the Minute Men heckled at Bund rallies in New Jersey. Five men were arrested and fifteen were beaten when two thousand protesters attacked Bundists at a meeting in Newark.

"No Nazis will be allowed in our parade," declared a spokesman for Governor A. Harry Moore when the Bund threatened to march in a Jersey City civic celebration. The *Star Ledger* wrote in an editorial: "We will do our utmost to prove that the German-American Bund is a menace to Germans, to Americans, and to simple decency."

Most New Jerseyans of German descent regarded the Bund as an embarrassment. Of the state's 112,000 German-born residents, only a few hundred were members. Among the protestors at Bund rallies were Germans with signs reading "Hitler ist nicht Deutschland" (Hitler is not Germany).

Perhaps the most active enemies of the Bund were the Jerseyans who lived in the vicinity of Nordland. Local authorities harassed the camp by revoking its liquor license and recording the license plates of cars parked there. On at least one occasion, Bundists at Nordland called the police to protect them from local residents who were throwing rocks.

In 1941, Kunze, Klapprott, and seven other Bund members were arrested in a raid at Nordland and indicted by the Sussex County grand jury for violating the 1935 law prohibiting the promotion of hatred based on race or religion. Camp Nordland was closed by the county as a public nuisance. (It was sold after the war to a boys' camp.)

The New Jersey Supreme Court overturned the conviction of Kunze and Klapprott on the grounds that the 1935 law violated the New Jersey constitution—a decision that the Nazis probably regarded as proof of the weakness of American democracy, but which we should take as a sign of its strength.

The court's decision, announced two days before Pearl Harbor, came too late to help the Bund. By that time Kuhn was serving a sentence in Sing Sing for larceny and forgery, Kunze was in hiding, and the organization was bankrupt.

Half a century later, one wonders what happened to the Bundists who picnicked at Nordland in the summer and went to Christmas parties at the Bund House in Union City. Where are those blond children in uniform (boys in the Jüngenschaft and girls in the Mädchenschaft) who smile at us out of the old photographs? Are they remorseful? Ashamed?

Or do they echo Kuhn who, as a minor war criminal in and out of custody in devastated postwar Germany, was asked why he had followed Hitler. "Who would have known it would end like this?" he shrugged.

Sunday, December 7, 1941, was a clear and crisp late fall day in New Jersey. The weather turned cloudy and colder in the following days, with temperatures in the 20s and the threat of snow by the end of the week. Winter was coming.

On Sunday afternoon, many New Jerseyans were listening to the Giants football game on WHN when the news of the Japanese attack on Pearl Harbor interrupted the broadcast. In Orange, twenty-four-year-old Rocco Cappeto translated the bulletins into Italian for his anxious

The

First Week

of the War

mother. In East Orange, Peggy Brinley, fifteen, was in the kitchen, listening to music on the radio and baking a cake when she heard the news. Thinking about what might happen to her brothers now that the war had begun, she cried into the batter.

One elderly New Jerseyan refused to believe the news. He called the radio station to say "Ha! You got me on that Martian stunt; I had a hunch you'd try it again."

William H. Jaqui, the New Brunswick coroner, told a reporter that "nobody can lick us, and with the element of surprise removed, sooner or later, we'll finish them." A customer at a diner warned "the Japs started this war and we'll give them plenty." Governor Charles Edison was equally confident: "Our navy will give a good account of itself in the Pacific."

The news caused people to rush to their phones: New Jersey Bell Telephone reported that requests for long distance connections on Sunday had increased by 27 percent over normal.

There was a quick surge of enlistees. By Monday evening, 222 volunteers had signed up for the army in the North Jersey region, more than for the entire month of November. Recruiting stations announced that they would stay open twenty-four hours a day to handle the crush.

Voluntary activities were quickly organized. The Red Cross scheduled a blood drive for downtown Newark. The students at the New Jersey College for Women began knitting for the army.

But for all the optimistic statements and purposeful activity, the news that New Jerseyans read in their papers and heard on the radio in the days after Pearl Harbor was grim. On Monday came the U.S. declaration of war on Japan; Tuesday the first casualty lists were published; Wednesday brought news of the sinking of two British warships and the Japanese invasion of Luzon; Thursday the declaration of war against Germany and Italy; Friday the Japanese attack on Guam and Midway.

The first New Jerseyans to receive a telegram telling them of their son's death were the parents of George Schmersahl, twenty-two, of Bloomfield, who has been any army sergeant at Pearl Harbor. As more and more deaths were announced, the War Department stopped releasing casualty lists.

There was a pervasive belief that New Jersey might be attacked from the air, just as had happened in Hawaii. Housewives were urged to buy supplies for blackouts, like black fabric, black paint, fire buckets, and candles. Crowbars and hatchets were recommended "to dig oneself out should a blast cave in the house."

Among the instructions distributed to the public was the following disquieting advice: "If incendiary bombs fall, spray water on them. Never use splash or stream of water, as the bomb will explode. Bomb will burn fifteen minutes if left alone, only two minutes if sprayed."

Guards and roadblocks were set up at the Johnson & Johnson plant in New Brunswick, the Federal Building in Newark, the Picatinny Arsenal near Dover, the R.C.A. plant in Camden, the Standard Oil refinery in Bayonne, and other important sites. Mines were laid in the ocean off Sandy Hook.

New Jersey cities and towns hastily came up with plans to cope with air raids. In New Brunswick, the local Defense Council announced a plan to evacuate residents by bus and truck "immediately upon enemy aircraft attacking the Raritan River bridges."

The chairman of the Monmouth Beach city council warned that fifth columnists might start fires along the Jersey shore that would guide enemy airplanes to the East Coast.

Each community worked out its own signals of sirens and whistles to warn of enemy planes approaching. In Englishtown, it was "one long continuous blow of two minutes"; in Freehold, "a series of long blasts"; in Keyport "five long blasts of the fire alarm on the boro hall"; in the Cliffwood section of Matawan, "six blasts on the fire alarms." The police chief of Spring Lake offered the opinion that all of these different signals might cause confusion for persons traveling between towns.

During that first week there were countless false alarms and unannounced air raid tests. Newspapers and radios reported that hostile planes had been spotted over the area. On Wednesday, the rumor spread through Newark that an attacking force of airplanes was on the way. Police headquarters received 3,000 calls from panicked residents trying to find out where to find air raid shelters.

A *Newark Evening News* reader angrily complained in a letter to the editor that false alarms "are absolutely out of place at time like this when we are continually being warned by the various authorities in charge of civilian safety to be calm, careful not to spread rumors and avoid panic."

New Jersey had 190,000 Italian nationals and 112,000 German nationals living within the state, as well as numbers of Japanese businessmen, domestics, and factory workers. The FBI and the police, using registration forms filled out before Pearl Harbor, rounded up thirty enemy aliens in the first two days. Suspicious-looking foreigners were also nabbed: patrolmen picked up a Japanese man spotted near a Newark train station holding a map of Brooklyn.

Newark city commissioner Ralph Villani defended the loyalty of Italian-Americans: "We are 100 per cent Americans who resent wholeheartedly the unwarranted attack of Japan on our country and now the unpardonable declaration of war by Germany and Italy." In Paterson, the Italian National Circle, a civic club, hastily changed its name to the Panthers of Paterson, Inc.

Otto Stiefel, an officer of the German-American Federation in Newark, said German-Americans will "do their duty with a heavy heart, but do it they will, as the last war proved."

One jubilant group of foreigners were the Chinese, whose country had been under Japanese attack for years. Henry Li Sooey, a leader from Newark's Chinatown district, predicted the war would be won in less than six months.

At the Hatfield Wire and Cable Company in Hillside, employees refused to work with two of their fellow employees who, as Jehovah's Witnesses, balked at reciting the Pledge of Allegiance. The two were fired. The Hudson County chapter of America First canceled an antiwar rally scheduled for Jersey City on December 10. The Kearny chapter announced that it was disbanding.

Despite the outbreak of war, life continued much as it always had in New Jersey. The fashion pages announced that "Big Handbags Have a Big Place on Women's Christmas Want List." New Jersey college teams played basketball, a motorcyclist was killed in an accident, a bank messenger was robbed, and department stores ran holiday advertisements. Mothers doing their Christmas shopping brought their children to see Santa Claus.

But the world had changed forever, and 13,172 New Jerseyans who were alive on the morning of December 7 would die in the war.

Sometime early in the morning of February 26, 1959, Abner Zwillman committed suicide in his mansion at 50 Beverly Road, West Orange, New Jersey.

He had hanged himself with a plastic cord tied to the rafters in the basement. He had tranquilizers in the pocket of his bathrobe, and a half-empty bottle of bourbon whiskey nearby. His body was discovered at 10:10 a.m. when his wife, who thought he had gone to his office that day, went down to the basement to look for a box of tissues.

Longie

Zwillman was a fifty-four-year-old businessman who had run into a string of legal and health problems. But this was not just a routine suicide by a middle-aged man for whom life had turned sour. His death made banner headlines in Newark's newspapers, and his obituary made the front page of the *New York Times*. A crowd of 1,500 people packed the sidewalk outside the funeral home. Abner Zwillman, better known as Longie, was a major American hood, ranking with Dutch Schultz, Lucky Luciano, and other notables from the golden age of gangsterdom. He was New Jersey's version of the Godfather.

Longie was born to an immigrant Jewish family in Newark in 1904. His home was the ghetto neighborhood of the Third Ward, where he spent his childhood roaming the streets with a gang of kids, peddling fruits and vegetables, and running errands for local politicians. He grew to be a tall, good-looking 6 feet 2 inches (hence the Longie nickname) with brains and daring.

He was a teenager when Prohibition began, and it offered him the same opportunity to amass wealth that the 1980s Wall Street bull market offered to young junk bond traders. He entered the business as a delivery boy, taking illegal liquor from the Newark docks to warehouses and speakeasies. Eventually he became a partner with a major Newark boot-legger, Joe Reinfeld.

Longie flourished in the world of corrupt policemen, judges, and politicians, and he surrounded himself with henchmen like James (Niggy) Rutkin, Gerardo (Jerry) Catena, Sam (Big Sue) Katz, and Joseph (Doc) Stacher. He came to know mobsters from other parts of the country, including Al Capone of Chicago.

By the time Prohibition ended, Longie was an extraordinarily wealthy young man. He was able to maintain that wealth after repeal by a combination of legal and illegal activities. The legal side was the Public Service Tobacco Company, which placed cigarette vending machines in bars. He also invested more or less legally in liquor distributorships, nightclubs, racetracks, truck franchises, coin-operated laundry machines, steel, and railroads. He backed real estate deals in Las Vegas, New York, and Miami, and movie deals in Hollywood.

The illegal side of his operations also consisted of a mixed portfolio of investments and businesses: loansharking, gambling casinos, and bookmaking. He controlled crooked unions for liquor salesmen, movie projectionists, operating engineers, window cleaners, retail clerks, and truckers.

Longie was a powerful force in New Jersey politics. Not by chance was he able to win a truck leasing contract with the city of Newark, even though he was not the low bidder. In 1932 he went to the national Democratic convention to help Franklin Roosevelt win the nomination. In 1949 he helped unseat Boss Hague of Jersey City.

Zwillman was reported to be part of an inner circle of New York area gangsters that controlled mob activity, a "Big Six" that consisted of Meyer Lansky, Lucky Luciano, Frank Costello, Joe Adonis, and Bugsy Siegel.

It required occasional violence, or at least the threat of violence, to keep this empire going. During Prohibition, Longie is reputed to have shot a rival in the testicles. He was arrested on several assault charges. He had a shadowy connection to gangland killings, like the rubouts of Dutch Schultz in 1935 and Bugsy Siegel in 1947. But the only jail term Longie ever served was a six-month stretch for the 1928 beating of Preston Buzzard, a black numbers runner who had tried to double-cross him.

Despite the violence, and despite the fact that he dropped out of school in the eighth grade, Zwillman did not have the air of a thug. He was a courtly, intelligent man; it was said that he liked books and classical music and that he hired a tutor to polish his pronunciation of English. He gave money to charity, including a Catholic soup kitchen in Newark, and he dutifully found jobs for his family and his in-laws.

When one of his gang members smashed a *Newark Evening News* photographer's camera, Zwillman quickly sent an apology and $350 for a new camera. He had a sense of humor—in 1951 a Senate committee member asked him whether he knew the girlfriend of a murdered mobster. "From seeing her on the television," he replied sarcastically, "she didn't look too hard to know."

And in fact, Longie seems to have known a lot of women in his younger days. It is said he had an affair with the glamorous movie star Jean Harlow. In 1939, Longie married a socially prominent divorced woman, and settled down to life in a mansion in suburban Essex County with two children (one a stepchild from his wife's first marriage).

And so Longie spent his middle years. He hung out at Duke's restaurant in Cliffside Park, at Toots Shor's in New York, and at his tobacco company office in Hillside.

But then came his time of troubles. In March 1951 he was called to Washington to testify, on television, before the Senate committee investigating organized crime. He took the Fifth Amendment forty-one times, repeating "I decline to answer on the grounds it will incriminate me." In the same year, *Collier's* magazine published an article on "The Man to See in New Jersey," identifying Longie as the source of corruption in the Garden State.

After the Senate hearings, the Internal Revenue Service began to investigate Longie's financial empire. Following years of legal maneuvering by his expensive team of lawyers, he went on trial in Newark in 1956 for income tax evasion. The government said he had underreported his income by approximately $100,000.

The defense admitted that Longie had been a bootlegger during Prohibition and had accumulated great wealth in those years. But the statute of limitations had expired on that money, his lawyers said; today he was an honest businessman who paid taxes on every penny he made. The defense rested on this claim without calling a single witness.

The jury reported that it was deadlocked and could not reach a verdict. Longie was free.

But his troubles were not over. The United States Senate announced its intention to investigate the vending machine industry, and Zwillman was mentioned as a target.

Then, in January 1959, came worse news: the Federal Bureau of Investigation arrested two of his henchmen, charging them with bribing a juror in Longie's tax evasion trial. It was obvious that the chain of indictments would soon lead to Zwillman.

He began having periodic depression and suffered from high blood pressure. He complained about chest pains and started seeing a doctor.

A month after the jury tampering news broke, Longie made his fatal trip to the basement.

Was it really suicide? There has been a lingering suspicion that Zwillman was actually murdered in his home that night. Lucky Luciano, in exile in Italy, later claimed that the mob killed Longie to prevent him from squealing. "So they beat him up and trussed him up like a pig and hung him in his own cellar," Luciano said.

But it seems unlikely. In the end, he was a sad old mobster with the government closing in and with his power and influence ebbing.

So the great Godfather died. One wonders if in those last moments down in the basement, through the fog of bourbon and pills, he somehow felt remorse for his life of bribery, corruption, and violence.

Probably not.

During the McCarthy era of the early 1950s, New Jersey, like the rest of the nation, was obsessed with fears of Communist subversion. It was a time of loyalty oaths, committee investigations, and background checks.

Consider four episodes from that time: a prominent black educator was denied permission to speak, army engineers were suspended on suspicion of being spies, college professors lost their jobs for taking the

Fighting
Communism in the
Garden State

Fifth Amendment, and a candidate for the United States Senate was accused of harboring a Communist in his family.

Free Speech in Englewood

The wealthy suburban town of Englewood was bitterly divided in the early 1950s. An ultra-conservative group, the Englewood Anti-Communist League, attacked the public school system as a center of left-wing sentiment, and broke up a meeting of United Nations supporters.

In 1952, Dr. Mary McLeod Bethune was invited by the Women's Auxiliary of American Legion Post 58 to speak at the Englewood Junior High School. The seventy-six-year-old Bethune, a former college president and New Deal official, was perhaps the most distinguished black woman in America.

The Anti-Communist League protested to Mayor Leslie Denning that Bethune was a member of twenty Communist-front organizations and that she should be forbidden from poisoning the minds of the people of Englewood. Based on the league's charges, the invitation was withdrawn until she explained herself.

Supporters of Bethune condemned Englewood's actions. The president of the National Council of Negro Women declared that the town "should bow its head in shame." Local sympathizers arranged for Bethune to speak at a black church on the night she was supposed to have spoken at the junior high.

The authorities in Englewood, echoing the sentiments of the time, claimed that they were not crude enemies of free speech, but were simply conducting an investigation of the charges raised by the Anti-Communist League.

Bethune wrote two letters to the town stating that although she had once belonged to subversive organizations, she had withdrawn from them when she learned their true nature. The town authorities treated these letters as a sort of confession and repentance by Bethune, and loftily declared that they would now permit her to speak. She dutifully did so.

The Rutgers Professors

About the same time as the Bethune episode, two Rutgers faculty members, historian Moses I. Finley and mathematician Simon Heimlich, were called before a Senate Committee investigating Communist fronts. Both men took the Fifth Amendment rather than answer questions that might place them in legal jeopardy.

The news hit Rutgers hard. The governor of the state and major newspapers called for the two men to be fired. President Lewis Webster Jones appointed a special faculty committee to determine the guilt or innocence of the pair. The committee concluded that Finley and Heimlich had acted within their constitutional rights.

The matter was thereupon turned over to the trustees of the university, who, by unanimous vote, rejected the conclusion of the faculty committee and fired the two professors.

There were heated protests by the faculty over the procedure used by the trustees in the case, but by a vote of 520 to 52, the faculty endorsed the policy that Communists should not be allowed to teach at Rutgers. In the end, Finley and Heimlich stayed fired.

The Subversives of Fort Monmouth

In 1953, Joseph McCarthy's Senate Subcommittee on Investigations alleged that Communists had infiltrated the United States Army Signal Corps base at Fort Monmouth. Public hearings were held by McCarthy's subcommittee, and the FBI and the Pentagon investigated the charges. When it was all over not a single spy was uncovered, but forty-two civilian engineering employees were suspended.

There was a streak of anti-Semitism running through this episode. A large number of engineers on the base were New York-area Jews who had trained at the City University of New York, and who had found jobs in the army when they were turned down by private industry. Jewish workers constituted only one-fourth of the civilian employees at Fort Monmouth, but of the forty-two who were suspended, thirty-nine were Jewish. (Of the three others, one had a Jewish wife and one was black.)

The case against the engineers was flimsy. The major charge against one, a thirty-three-year-old World War II veteran, was that his brother had once attended a rally in Yankee Stadium at which Paul Robeson had been one of the speakers.

Most of the engineers were ultimately reinstated, although some had to wait five years for a federal court to exonerate them. Years later one of the engineers complained to the historian David Oshinsky that the army never bothered to apologize: "Nobody even said, 'I'm sorry. We made a mistake.' And that hurts most of all."

The Candidate's Sister

In the election of 1954, Congressman Clifford Case was running as the Republican candidate for the United States Senate. But the party was not united behind the candidate. His outspoken hostility to McCarthyism split the party so badly that President Dwight Eisenhower himself worked to rally Jersey Republicans behind Case.

From Washington, Senator Joe McCarthy announced that he supported every Republican candidate in the nation except for Case, and he hinted darkly that damaging information about the candidate would soon be made public.

Then, two weeks before the election, a front-page article in the pro-McCarthy *Newark Star Ledger* alleged that Case's sister Adelaide had been the member of Communist-front organizations in New York in the 1940s.

Case halted the campaign while he and his aides worked on how he could counter these charges. Three days later, a grim-faced Case appeared on television. His sister had never been a Communist, he said, and had not been in New York at the time of her alleged Red activity. But then he confessed a painful family secret. While suffering from mental illness, he said, Adelaide had made a "confused and disconnected" confession that she had been involved with a left-wing group. "Wicked and unscrupulous persons" were exploiting his sister's disability.

"I have one thing to say to these character murderers," he concluded, "Adelaide Case is not running for the Senate of the United States. Clifford Case is the candidate. Smear me if you can. Leave my sister alone."

In the November election, Case won by the razor-thin margin of 3,369 votes out of 1.7 million cast.

It is worth noting that the victims of the McCarthy era in New Jersey were not treated as harshly as, say, dissidents in the Soviet Union. There were no executions and no labor camps. Bethune did get to speak, Finley and Heimlich did find other jobs, the engineers were reinstated, and Case won the election. But for a state whose constitution pledges that "every person may freely speak, write and publish his sentiments on all subjects," it was a shameful time.

Not counting the incumbent, forty-eight white males have served as governor since New Jersey became a state in 1776.

This column fearlessly names the three best and the three worst among our governors. We begin with the three best, starting at the top of the list.

Woodrow Wilson (Democrat) did not spend much time in the governor's chair. He took office in mid-January 1911, and was elected president of the United States less than two years later. But what a two

The Best

and the Worst

Governors

years that was! By cajoling, pushing, and shoving, he got the New Jersey legislature (a body not known for blinding speed) to pass bills reforming the election process, workers' compensation, corrupt practices, public utilities, city government, public education, and labor unions. He defied the political bosses, and broke with tradition by going directly to the legislature.

It is possible to poke holes in this record; to complain that he dashed off to the White House on a wave of popular acclaim, leaving his successors to face failed reforms and broken promises. But without question, Wilson was the most dynamic and energetic governor in the history of our state; a man who accomplished more in a briefer period of time than just about any governor of any state anywhere, anytime. The professor transformed sleepy, backwater New Jersey into the center of national attention.

William Livingston (Federalist) was the first elected governor of the state, and the one who faced the worst crisis in its history—the Revolutionary War. Livingston was a wealthy New York lawyer who had come to New Jersey for a pleasant retirement. But his plans were interrupted by the outbreak of the Revolution. Because New Jersey was the corridor

17   *The Best and the Worst Governors.* Woodrow Wilson had served as governor of New Jersey for less than two years when he was elected president of the United States. In that brief time he proved to be the state's most dynamic and energetic chief executive ever. (New Jersey Historical Society, Newark)

18   *The Best and the Worst Governors.* William Livingston was elected governor in the tumultuous year 1776. During the Revolution he kept the patriot cause alive in New Jersey, sometimes while on the run from the British. (New Jersey Historical Society, Newark)

19   *The Best and the Worst Governors.* Alfred E. Driscoll pushed New Jersey to adopt a new constitution that is still one of the best in the nation. (New Jersey Historical Society, Newark)

between New York and Philadelphia, the state was devastated by British and American armies fighting back and forth. Livingston, who took office under the hastily put-together constitution of 1776, often had to direct the affairs of government on the run from the British.

Although that constitution gave the governor very limited powers, Livingston effectively kept the Rebel cause alive. As commander of the often reluctant militia, he provided badly needed support to Washington's army. As president of the Council of Safety, he kept civil order and suppressed the Tories. And as if this were not enough, he penned dozens of newspaper essays and letters to encourage the patriot cause.

Livingston was elected to fourteen annual terms by the legislature (direct election of governors did not come until the Constitution of 1844), and came to symbolize the Revolutionary struggle to his fellow citizens. He was an amazing leader in an amazing generation of Americans.

Alfred E. Driscoll (Republican) was a brilliant, hard-driving governor. A graduate of Harvard Law School, he routinely put in sixteen-hour days. Among his accomplishments in his two terms (1947–1954) were the reorganization of state agencies, strong civil rights legislation, low-cost housing, and the New Jersey Turnpike. But his most significant achievement, and the one that puts him on this list, was his masterly effort to provide New Jersey with a new constitution. The old constitution, adopted in 1844, was a model of weakness and inefficiency, but previous efforts to write a new one had bogged down in politics. Driscoll laid the groundwork for a constitutional convention, and guided the convention into producing and the voters into adopting a document that is still among the best in the nation.

Now let us turn from the best governors to the other end of the scale, the turkeys, starting with the worst.

Harold G. Hoffman (Republican) takes the prize (not the only thing he took, as we shall see). Hoffman's term in office (1935-1938) at first seemed quite promising. As a young Republican governor in the Democratic New Deal, he was mentioned as a possible contender for the

20   *The Best and the Worst Governors.* Harold G. Hoffman was one of New Jersey's worst governors. At the time of his death it was revealed that he had been on the take throughout his political career. Among other crimes, he had embezzled $300,000 from a South Amboy bank. (New Jersey Historical Society, Newark)

21   *The Best and the Worst Governors.* Rodman M. Price was accused by the navy of stealing $88,000. As governor, he supported the slave-holding South. In old age he spent time in the Hackensack jail as a result of real estate speculations. (New Jersey Historical Society, Newark)

presidency. But he soon demonstrated a lack of leadership. He became embroiled in a battle with his own party that put him into the hands of the notorious Democratic boss, Frank Hague of Jersey City. Hoffman then wandered off on a bizarre tangent by blundering into the Lindbergh kidnapping case; he claimed that the convicted kidnapper Hauptmann had been framed.

All of this does not qualify him for the title of worst governor. What does is the fact, which came out at the time of his death in 1954, that he had been on the take throughout his political career. Among other things, he had embezzled $300,000 from a South Amboy bank, and had been blackmailed for $150,000.

Rodman M. Price (Democrat) represents the nadir of the pre–Civil War governors. As a young man he had used his political connections to obtain a commission in the navy; while stationed on the West Coast he devoted most of his talents to making California real estate deals. The navy accused him of channeling funds into his own pocket, and sued him for $88,000 in missing government funds.

Despite his legal problems, he was elected congressman from Essex County. His most notable contribution in the House was to argue in favor of flogging as a method of discipline in the navy.

As governor (1854–1857), he was firmly in the grip of the powerful railroad interests. On the national scene, he supported the slave South. As an ex-governor at the start of the Civil War he advocated that New Jersey join the Confederacy. In old age his real estate speculations got the better of him, and he spent time in the Hackensack jail.

George T. Werts (Democrat) took office in difficult times. Economically, the state was crippled by the Depression of 1893. Politically, divisions between Protestants and new Catholic immigrants had broken out over such issues as legalized racetrack gambling and state aid to parochial schools. A strong leader might have faced the issue head on; a conciliatory leader might have tried to restore unity.

Werts's approach was to dash for cover, prevaricating and avoiding the issues. His worst failure came with a debacle in the Senate. The election of 1893 brought in a Republican majority; the defeated Senate Democrats claimed that the election was invalid, and carried on as a rump Senate. Werts caved in to party pressure and lamely recognized the Democratic rebels, leaving state government crippled until the State Supreme Court ruled against the rump Senate. Werts's dismal record during his single term (1893–1896) helped to end his party's long hold on the governorship; another Democrat was not elected until Woodrow Wilson, fifteen years later.

22   *The Best and the Worst Governors.* George T. Werts was a loyal party man who refused to admit that the opposition Republicans had captured the State Senate. Thanks to his weak-kneed response to the state's economic and political problems, another Democrat was not elected governor for fifteen years. (New Jersey Historical Society, Newark)

Overall, New Jersey has been reasonably fortunate in its governors. The good ones have been very good indeed, and the bad ones, by and large, more inept than venal. Indeed, it would be easy to extend the list of good governors with men like Leon Abbett, Peter D. Vroom, Walter E. Edge, Joel Parker, Brendan Byrne, Richard Hughes, William Paterson, Joseph Bloomfield, and Thomas Kean. It is much harder to find other really bad governors to add to the bottom of the list.

Suggestions for Further Reading

The Walam Olum

Two thorough works on the Delaware (or Lenape) Indians discuss the Walam Olum and the evidence for and against its authenticity: C. A. Weslager, *The Delaware Indians: A History* (New Brunswick, N.J.: Rutgers University Press, 1972) and Herbert C. Kraft, *The Lenape: Archaeology, History, Ethnography* (Newark, N.J., New Jersey Historical Society, 1988). A modern translation of the document, with articles that argue that it is a genuine creation myth dating from the pre-contact period, is *The Walam Olum* (Indianapolis: Indiana Historical Society, 1954).

Trenton Man

Abbott described his theories on the Indians of New Jersey in several different works. The most complete is his *Primitive Industry*, (Salem Mass.: George A. Bates, 1881). The debate over those theories is discussed in Lucy Aiello, "Charles Conrad Abbott, M.D., Discoverer of Ancient Man in the Delaware Valley," *Bulletin of the New Jersey Academy of Science* 12 (Fall 1967): 3–6.

The Man Who Discovered New Jersey

Samuel Eliot Morison retraces Verrazano's voyage in his *The European Discovery of America: The Northern Voyages, A.D. 500–1600* (New York: Oxford University Press, 1971). A well-reasoned analysis of the evidence is Lawrence C. Wroth, *The Voyages of Giovanni da Verrazano, 1524–1528* (New Haven: Yale University Press, 1970).

Conquered by New York

The history of the proprietary governments is examined in two books by John E. Pomfret: *The Province of West New Jersey, 1609–1702: A History of the Origins of an American Colony* (Princeton: Princeton University Press, 1956); and *The Province of East New Jersey, 1609–1702: The Rebellious Proprietary* (Princeton: Princeton University Press, 1962).

The First Bribe

Accounts of the shady career of Lord Cornbury can be found in many histories of colonial New Jersey, including Donald L. Kemmerer, *Path to Freedom: The Struggle for Self-Government in Colonial New Jersey* (Princeton: Princeton University Press, 1940) and John E. Pomfret, *Colonial New Jersey: A History* (New York: Charles Scribner's Sons, 1973). Patricia Bonomi of New York University promises to rehabilitate Cornbury's reputation in a forthcoming book.

The Witches of Burlington County

Herbert Leventhal, *In the Shadow of the Enlightenment: Occultism and Renaissance Science in Eighteenth-Century America* (New York: New York University Press, 1976) mentions the Franklin article and its history. Benjamin Franklin's hostility to superstition and his enjoyment of satire have been treated by many biographers, for example, Esmond Wright, *Franklin of Philadelphia* (Cambridge, Mass.: Harvard University Press, 1986).

The Burglary of the Treasury

The best work on the treasury robbery is Larry R. Gerlach, "Politics and Prerogatives: The Aftermath of the Robbery of the East Jersey Treasury in 1768," *New Jersey History* 90 (Autumn 1972): 133–168.

Tories

The literature on the Tories is vast. One collection of primary sources that includes material on the Loyalists is Larry R. Gerlach, ed., *New Jersey in the American Revolution, 1763–1783* (Trenton: New Jersey Historical Commission, 1975). A fine pamphlet on the subject is Dennis Patrick Ryan, *New Jersey's Loyalists* (Trenton: New Jersey Historical Commission, 1976).

Lee at Monmouth

The famous encounter between Washington and Lee on the Monmouth battlefield has often been described. One good analysis, which is favorable to Lee, is Theodore Thayer, *The Making of a Scapegoat: Washington and Lee at Monmouth* (Port Washington, N.Y.: Kennikat Press, 1976). A collection of viewpoints is Mary R. Murrin, ed., *Conflict at Monmouth Court House* (Trenton: New Jersey Historical Commission, 1983). An interesting sidelight is Theodore B. Lewis, "Was Washington Profane at Monmouth?" *New Jersey History* 89 (Fall 1971): 149–162.

The Hanging of Captain Huddy

Curiously, only one book has examined the Huddy-Asgill business, and this book is unabashedly pro-British: Katherine Mayo, *General Washington's Dilemma* (New York: Harcourt, Brace and Company, 1938). A good analysis of one aspect of the case is Larry Bowman, "The Court-Martial of Captain Richard Lippencot," *New Jersey History* 89 (Spring 1971): 23–36.

Trenton, N.J., Was Almost Washington, D.C.

The debate over making Trenton the capital of the new nation is mentioned in Richard P. McCormick, *Experiment in Independence: New Jersey in the Critical Period, 1781–1789* (New Brunswick, N.J.: Rutgers University Press, 1950).

Free White Males Only

The definitive analysis is Richard P. McCormick, *The History of Voting in New Jersey: A Study of the Development of Election Machinery, 1664–1911* (New Brunswick, N.J.: Rutgers University Press, 1953). More specialized works have been done on blacks and women: Marion Thompson Wright, "Negro Suffrage in New Jersey, 1776-1875," *Journal of Negro History* 33 (1948): 168-224 and Mary Philbrook, "Woman's Suffrage in New Jersey," *Proceedings of the New Jersey Historical Society* 57 (April 1939): 87–98.

She Never Lost Her Scars

The biography of Sylvia Dubois was originally published by C. W. Larison in 1883. For more on Larison, see pages 98–102 of the present book. A modern edition of Larison's book, edited by Jared C. Lobdell, is *Silvia Dubois: A Biografy of the Slav who Whipt her Mistres and Gand her Fredom*, The Schomberg Library of Nineteenth-Century Black Women Writers (New York: Oxford University Press, 1988). Lobdell has done much research on Dubois, and he believes that she was born in 1788–89, and not in 1768. For information on the abolition of slavery in New Jersey see Arthur Zilversmit, "Liberty and Property: New Jersey and the Abolition of Slavery," *New Jersey History* 88 (Autumn 1970): 215–226.

The Buried Treasure Hoax

The case of Ransford Rogers is mentioned briefly in Herbert Leventhal, *In the Shadow of the Enlightenment: Occultism and Renaissance Science in Eighteenth-Century America* (New York: New York University Press, 1976). An article by James J. Flynn and Charles A. Huguenin, "The Hoax of the Pedagogues," *Proceedings of the New Jersey Historical Society* 76 (October 1958): 239–264, provides some information on the story, but is mostly written to lampoon the gullible residents of Morristown. Original copies and reprints of the Morristown Ghost pamphlet are rare, but can be found in the Newark Public Library and the Rutgers University Libraries Special Collections.

Aunt Polly among the Indians

The leading historian of the Mary Kinnan story is Oscar M. Vorhees: "'Aunt Polly' Kinnan: An Indian Tragedy of the Eighteenth Century," *Somerset County Historical Quarterly* 1 (1912): 179–190 and "A New Jersey Woman's Captivity among Indians, May 1791 to August 1793," *Proceedings of the New Jersey Historical Society* 13 (January 1928): 152–165. A book that reprints the original pamphlet and provides more background is Jack D. Filipiak, ed. *The Indian Captivity of Mary Kinnan, 1791–1794: A Long-Forgotten Frontier Tragedy* (Boulder, Colo.: Pruett Press, 1967).

Alexander Hamilton in the Emergency Room

An intriguing book on the death of Hamilton is Harold Syrett, ed., *Interview in Weehawken: The Burr-Hamilton Duel, as Told in the Original Documents* (Middletown, Conn.: Wesleyan University Press, 1960).

Jumping to the Wrong Conclusion

Richard M. Dorson has written repeatedly about Sam Patch and his significance in American folklore. For example, "The Wonderful Leaps of Sam Patch," *American Heritage,* December 1966, 12–19. Another survey of Patch's life, death, and legends is Kathleen M. Kavanagh, "The Limited Fame of Sam Patch," *New York Folklore Quarterly* 28 (1972): 118–134.

The Beautiful Cigar Girl

A splendid account of the case, and a fine example of literary detection in its own right, is John E. Walsh, *Poe the Detective: The Curious Circumstances Behind the Mystery of Marie Roget* (New Brunswick, N.J.: Rutgers University Press, 1967).

Dorothea Dix Visits the Lunatics

The best analysis of Dix's work in New Jersey is Frederick M. Herrmann, *Dorothea L. Dix and the Politics of Institutional Reform* (Trenton: New Jersey Historical Commission, n.d).

Getting Wrong with Lincoln

The standard work on the subject is Charles Mirriam Knapp, *New Jersey Politics During the Period of the Civil War and Reconstruction* (Geneva, N.Y.: W. F. Humphrey, 1924). Additional material can be found in Earl Schenck Miers, *New Jersey and the Civil War* (Princeton, D. Van Nostrand, 1964) and in Maurice Tandler, "The Political Front in Civil War New Jersey," *Proceedings of the New Jersey Historical Society* 83 (1965): 223–233. Professor William Gillette of Rutgers is writing a new book that promises to be a major reinterpretation of New Jersey's role in the Civil War.

Jeff Davis and the Jersey Doctor

Edward K. Eckert, ed., *"Fiction Distorting Fact": The Prison Life, Annotated by Jefferson Davis* (Macon, Ga.: Mercer University Press, 1987) is a fascinating book that reprints Craven's book with Davis's marginal notes, and provides a critical analysis of the controversy. Eckert concludes that the book is mostly a work of fiction.

The Treasurer and the Bandits

This classic story of political corruption cries out for a longer study, but so far the only source is a chapter in William E. Sackett, *Modern Battles of Trenton, Being a History of New Jersey's Politics and Legislation from the Year 1868 to the Year 1894* (Trenton: John L. Murphy, 1895).

Poor Mary Pomeroy

The only published source, apart from contemporary newspaper accounts, is the sensational pamphlet *Poor Mary Pomeroy!* (Philadelphia: Old Franklin Publishing House, 1874). This publication has been attributed to Charles Wesley Alexander.

A President Dies in Jersey

Articles on the Garfield assassination from a medical perspective can be found in A. Scott Earle, M.D., ed., *Surgery in America,* 2nd ed. (New York: Praeger, 1983).

The Great Eccentric

The definitive (and completely deadpan) biography of the celebrated Dr. Larison is Harry B. Weiss, *Country Doctor: Cornelius Wilson Larison of Ringoes, Hunterdon County, New Jersey, 1837–1910* (Trenton: New Jersey Agricultural Society, 1953).

Blasphemy on Trial

Colonel Ingersoll's courtroom speech was published as a separate pamphlet shortly after the Reynolds trial, and is also included in *The Works of Robert Ingersoll,* 12 vols. (New York: Dresden Publishing Co., 1907). For a useful biography of Ingersoll, see David D. Anderson, *Robert Ingersoll,* (New York: Twayne, 1972).

"To Sherlock Holmes, She Is Always *the* Woman"

Anyone interested in Conan Doyle's original stories of the great detective and in the pseudo-scholarship that has grown up around them should read William S. Baring Gould, ed., *The Annotated Sherlock Holmes,* 2 vols. (New York: Clarkson N. Potter, 1967).

President Hobart? It Might Have Been

There are no modern biographies of Hobart (and not too many old ones, for that matter). The standard, worshipful work is David Magie, *Life of Garret Augustus Hobart, Twenty-fourth Vice President of the United States* (New York: G. P. Putnam's Sons, 1910).

Paterson Man Kills King

Although Bresci is mentioned in several works dealing with larger themes, such as the Sacco and Vanzetti case and the history of anarchism, there is no single published work dealing him and his crime. There is, however, an outstanding unpublished paper in the Rutgers University Special Collections department, George W. Carey, "The Vessel, the Deed, and the Idea: Anarchists in Paterson, 1895–1908."

The Clifton Avenue Horror

The accusations about the trial are contained in a progressive tract, Hester Eloise Hosford, *The Forerunners of Woodrow Wilson* (East Orange, N.J.: East Orange Record, 1914).

The Traitor State

Steffens's "Traitor State" article appeared in the April and May 1905 issues of *McClure's Magazine.* The story about the article and its aftermath can be found in Lincoln Steffens, *The Autobiography of Lincoln Steffens* (San Diego: Harcourt Brace Jovanovich, 1958) and in Justin Kaplan, *Lincoln Steffens: A Biography* (New York: Simon and Schuster, 1974). For details of New Jersey and the trusts, see Christopher Grandy, "New Jersey Corporate Chartermongering 1875–1929," *Journal of Economic History* 49 (September 1989): 677–692.

A Minor Murder

The only published accounts of this murder can be found in contemporary newspapers, notably the *New Brunswick Home News* and the *New York Times.*

The Professor and the Boss

The classic book on Woodrow Wilson's career in New Jersey is Arthur S. Link, *Woodrow Wilson: The Road to the White House* (Princeton: Princeton University Press, 1947). A collection of documents, including Wilson's Jersey City speech, are in David W. Hirst, ed., *Woodrow Wilson: Reform Governor* (Princeton: D. Van Nostrand, 1965). Wilson's youngest daughter wrote an interesting memoir that touches on the Smith episode: Eleanor Wilson McAdoo, *The Woodrow Wilsons* (New York: Macmillan, 1937).

Mrs. Minerva Miller Goes to the Movies

The only published account, apart from contemporary newspapers, is a brief article: Michael H. Ebner, "Mrs. Miller and the 'Paterson Show': A 1911 Defeat for Racial Discrimination," *New Jersey History* 86 (Summer 1968): 88–91.

The Crime of the Kallikaks

A fine, critical account of the work of Goddard and its impact is David J. Smith, *Minds Made Feeble* (Rockville, Md.: Aspen Systems Corp, 1985). A broader study of the whole issue of intelligence is Stephen Jay Gould, *The Mismeasure of Man* (New York: Norton, 1981).

The Paterson Pageant

An excellent recent study of the Paterson strike is Steve Golin, *A Fragile Bridge: Paterson Silk Strike, 1913* (Philadelphia: Temple University Press, 1988). Specialized studies of the Pageant can be found in Martin Green, *New York 1913: The Armory Show and the Paterson Pageant* (New York: Charles Scribner's Sons, 1988) and Leslie Fishbein, "The Paterson Pageant (1913): The Birth of Docudrama as a Weapon in the Class Struggle," *Journal of Regional Cultures* 4 (Fall/Winter 1984): 95–129.

Should Women Vote?

Felice D. Gordon, *After Winning: The Legacy of the New Jersey Suffragists, 1920–1947* (New Brunswick, N.J.: Rutgers University Press, 1986) contains an account of the failed 1915 effort to win the vote. The election is studied in greater detail in Joseph F. Mahoney, "Woman Suffrage and the Urban Masses," *New Jersey History* 87 (Autumn 1969): 151–172.

The Secret War

The definitive book is Jules Witcover, *Sabotage at Black Tom: Imperial Germany's Secret War in America, 1914–1917* (Chapel Hill, N.C.: Algonquin Books, 1989).

The War to End War Ended in Somerset County

For an entertaining biolgraphy of Harding, see Francis Russell, *The Shadow of Blooming Grove: Warren G. Harding in His Times* (New York: McGraw-Hill, 1968).

Jersey City Tastes Glory

A biography of Dempsey that includes a chapter on his fight with Carpentier is Randy Roberts, *Jack Dempsey: The Manassa Mauler* (Baton Rouge: Louisiana State University Press, 1979).

The Klan

A standard work on the Klan, with a chapter on New Jersey, is David M. Chalmers, *Hooded Americanism*, 3d ed. (Durham, N.C.: Duke University Press, 1987). A look at the hostility of the Klan to the state's immigrant population is contained in Rudolph Vecoli, *The People of New Jersey* (Princeton: D. Van Nostrand, 1965).

"I Am the Law"

An analysis of how Hague achieved and held on to political power is Richard J. Connors, *A Cycle of Power: The Career of Jersey City Mayor Frank Hague* (Metuchen, N.J.: Scarecrow Press, 1971). Another interesting study is George C. Rapport, *The Statesman and the Boss, a Study of American Political Leadership Exemplified by Woodrow Wilson and Frank Hague* (New York: Vantage, 1961).

Keeping New Jersey Sober

Ira L. Reeves's book is *Ol' Rum River: Revelations of a Prohibition Administrator* (Chicago: Thomas S. Rockwell, 1931). The problem of enforcement in the Prohibition era is treated in many books, for example John Kobler, *Ardent Spirits: The Rise and Fall of Prohibition* (New York: Putnam, 1973). A good study of the influence of Prohibition on state politics is Warren E. Stickle III, "The Applejack Campaign of 1919: 'As Wet as the Atlantic Ocean,'" *New Jersey History* 89 (Spring 1971): 5–22.

What the Pig Woman Saw

By far the best account of this celebrated trial is William M. Kunstler, *The Hall-Mills Murder Case* (Original title: *The Minister and the Choir Singer*) (New Brunswick, N.J.: Rutgers University Press, 1980).

The Radium Girls

A biography of Martland by a friend has a chapter on the radium case: Samuel Berg, *Harrison Stanford Martland, M.D.: The Story of a Physician, a Hospital, an Era* (New York: Vantage Press, 1978). Among the useful articles are William Sharpe, "Radium Ostetis with Osteogenic Sarcoma: The Chronology and Natural History of a Fatal Case," *Bulletin of the New York Academy of Medicine* 47 (September 1971): 1059–1079; and Claudia Clark, "Physicians, Reformers and Occupational Disease: The Discovery of Radium Poisoning," *Women & Health* 12 (1987): 147–167.

Georgia on His Mind

Burns's book is *I Am a Fugitive from a Georgia Chain Gang* (New York: Grosset and Dunlap, 1932). A study of the movie made from the book, which includes the script and biographical information about Burns, is John E. O'Connor, ed., *I Am a Fugitive from a Georgia Chain Gang* (Madison: University of Wisconsin Press, 1981).

Was Hauptmann Guilty?

The debate over the guilt or innocence of Bruno Richard Hauptmann has been carried on in many books. One that takes the position that Hauptmann was innocent is Ludovic Kennedy, *The Airman and the Carpenter: The Lindbergh Kidnapping and the Framing of Richard Hauptmann* (New York: Viking, 1985). A strong case for Hauptmann's guilt is in Jim Fisher, *The Lindbergh Case* (New Brunswick, N.J.: Rutgers University Press, 1987).

The Chop House Rubout

A hugely entertaining book about the life and death of Flegenheimer is Paul Sann, *Kill the Dutchman! The Story of Dutch Schultz* (New Rochelle, N.Y.: Arlington House, 1971).

The *Hindenburg*

Two popular books that allege sabotage are Michael Macdonald Mooney, *The Hindenburg* (New York: Dodd, Mead, 1972) and Adolph A. Hoehling, *Who Destroyed the Hindenburg?* (Boston: Little, Brown, 1962). A contrary view which provides a scientific explanation is J. Gordon Vaeth, "What Happened to the Hindenburg," *Weatherwise* 43 (December 1990): 315–322.

Swastikas in Sussex County

Sander A. Diamond, *The Nazi Movement in the United States, 1924–1941* (Ithaca, N.Y.: Cornell University Press, 1974) traces the evolution of the Bund across the nation; an account of what happened in our state is Martha Glaser, "The German-American Bund in New Jersey," *New Jersey History* 92 (Spring 1974): 33–49.

The First Week of the War

There are no published articles about the immediate aftermath of Pearl Harbor on the New Jersey homefront. Two books on America during the war are John M. Blum, *V Was for Victory: Politics and American Culture During World War II* (New York: Harcourt Brace Jovanovich, 1976) and Richard R. Lingeman, *Don't You Know There's a War On?* (New York: G. P. Putnam's Sons, 1970). See also James E. Jandrowitz, "'This is Not a Drill': An Oral History of Four New Jersey Pearl Harbor Survivors," *New Jersey History* 106 (Spring/Summer 1988): 41–59.

Longie

The only book devoted to Zwillman is flawed by invented dialogue. It does, however, have some useful facts about the gangster: Mark A. Stuart, *Gangster #2— Longy Swillman, the Man Who Invented Organized Crime* (Secaucus, N.J.: Lyle Stuart, 1985). The expose on Zwillman is Lester Velie, "The Man to See in New Jersey," *Collier's,* 25 August 1951, 16ff., and 1 September 1951, 28ff.

Fighting Communism in the Garden State

A portrait of McCarthy and his era is provided in David Oshinsky, *A Conspiracy So Immense: The World of Joe McCarthy* (New York: Free Press, 1983). Information on aspects of McCarthyism in New Jersey are in David Oshinsky, "Fort Monmouth and McCarthy: The Victims Remember," *New Jersey History* 100 (1982): 1–13; and Ellen Schrecker, *No Ivory Tower: McCarthyism and the Universities* (New York: Oxford University Press, 1986).

The Best and the Worst Governors

The indispensable source on the subject is Paul A. Stellhorn and Michael J. Birkner, eds., *The Govenors of New Jersey, 1664–1974: Bibliographical Essays* (Trenton: New Jersey Historical Commission, 1982).

Index